A League of Our Own

The Cymru Premier Story 1992-93 to 2022-23

A League of Our Own

The Cymru Premier Story
1992-93 to 2022-23

Mark Langshaw

ST DAVID'S PRESS

Cardiff

Published in Wales by St. David's Press, an imprint of

Ashley Drake Publishing Ltd
PO Box 733
Cardiff
CF14 7ZY

www.st-davids-press.wales

First Impression – 2023

ISBN
Paperback: 978-1-904609-10-0
eBook: 978-1-904609-11-7

British Library Cataloguing-in-Publication Data.
A CIP catalogue for this book is available from the British Library.

Typeset by Prepress Plus, www.prepressplus.in
Cover design by Welsh Books Council, Aberystwyth, Wales

Contents

For my parents, whose love of football I gratefully inherited

Acknowledgements

I had always envisaged that writing a book would be a solitary project, with long hours in self-imposed isolation, but the reality of authoring *A League of Our Own – The Cymru Premier Story 1992-2023* was the totally opposite experience, and could not have happened without the help of a small village's worth of people, before finding its way to the publisher.

To start off, I'd like to thank the following for sharing their first-hand experiences in Welsh football: Trefor Lloyd Hughes, John Deakin, Norman Parselle, Nigel Adkins, Marc Lloyd Williams, Darren Ryan, Mike Harris, Jamie Moralee, Neville Southall, Dave Jones, Rhys Griffiths, Greg Strong, Craig Garside, Craig Harrison, Gavin Chesterfield, Chris O'Neal, Dave Rapson, Jamie Insall, Nicky John, Gwyn Derfel and Alex Ramsay. Your unique voices, exclusive to this book and all presented as italicised quotes, really brought each chapter to life.

All of the league tables were provided by *The Welsh Football Data Archive* (WFDA) and published with their permission. I'd also like to thank Ian Garland of the WFDA for taking the time to read through sample chapters and provide invaluable feedback.

I must extend my appreciation to Clint Jones of *The 94th Minute* blog for casting an expert eye over a few chapters, as well as Jordan Jones of *Y Clwb Pêl-Droed* whose insight was invaluable. I'd also like to tip my hat to my friend, colleague and fellow sports writer Mike Whitehead for encouraging me to take this project seriously and see it through to completion.

Furthermore, I'm grateful to Ashley Drake of St. David's Press for agreeing to take a look at my completed manuscript and providing essential advice that helped shape this book.

For providing photographs, I must thank Andy J Havelot, Owain Hughes, Flint Town United FC, Clint Jones, Cwmbrân Town AFC, Steven Humphreys, Rod Davies, Phil Blagg, Brian Jones, Norman Parselle, Luke Tugwell, Richard Birch, Olly Allen and the Football Association of Wales, John Smith, Bala Town FC, Jeff McInery, Nik

Mesney, Andre Pepper, David Collins of *Welsh Football Magazine*, Terry Lewis, Phil Blagg, Lewis Mitchell, Phil Crocker, Tomos Lewis, Christopher Williams, Huw Pritchard and Rhyl 1879 chairman Tom Jamieson.

On a personal note, a big thank you goes out to Phillip Anderson, Barry Zeisz and Adam Heron for allowing me to drag them on a ground-hopping adventure to Connah's Quay in the middle of winter. That trip to Deeside is where this book began and I'm glad they could join me.

Finally, I would like to thank my immediate family, Laura, Harriet, Bea and Bella, as well as my mother and father, my two sisters Claire and Amy, and my grandmother, Joan. Without your ongoing love and support, I'd never have been in a position to research and write this book.

Introduction

People often ask me why an Englishman, who grew up watching Everton in the Premier League and spent his early career reporting on football at this level, decided to write a book about the Cymru Premier. This was a passion project for me and I'd like a moment to explain why.

Presumably you picked up this book to read about the history of Welsh domestic football, and not me personally, so I'll keep this brief. And, let's face it, most people skip these intros anyway.

I spent over a decade dabbling in football journalism, writing for publications including *Four Four Two*, *Sports Mole* and the *Red Bull* website. I've always enjoyed football at all levels, whether that's the simple thrills of a grassroots kickabout or the bright lights of the Champions League.

As a football writer, I was drawn to the untold stories, the obscure facts and the unsung heroes. There wasn't always a lot of opportunity to cover this kind of thing, since the English Premier League and the other top leagues in Europe are what drives readership and online clicks.

I left journalism behind in 2018 to take a job as a copyeditor in financial services. It was a good move from a career perspective, but it wasn't long before there was a niggling itch I had to scratch. I missed writing about the beautiful game, so I started planning a side project, one that would immerse me back into my favourite sport and let me tell stories from within it once again.

That project was this book, an exploration of the competition that began life as The League of Wales in 1992, became the Welsh Premier League after that, and is now the Cymru Premier.

Why the Cymru Premier? Well, aside from my love of all things obscure and niche within the footballing world, it struck me that there was no definitive book about the Welsh top flight. Sure, there are books about Welsh football - very good ones, in fact - but the majority are dedicated to the Welsh national team, Cardiff City, Swansea City, Newport and Wrexham, a club we'll probably be hearing plenty about in the coming years now Hollywood millions have come their way.

My interest in Welsh football began a year or two before I started work on the book. I've always been hungry to learn as much as possible about every football club in the UK, and the world, for that matter. For me, it's a real shame that so many people's footballing universe extends no further than the boundaries of the English Premier League or the EFL Championship.

There are so many teams with storied histories and time-tested traditions outside of the mainstream, whether that's the English non-league or the Welsh system. It was the desire to learn more about such clubs that took me to Connah's Quay on a cold March evening in 2019.

I dragged three friends along to watch Connah's Quay Nomads take on The New Saints in what was then the Welsh Premier League. We had to take two trains and a bus to get to what the lads must have felt was the football tourism equivalent of a wet weekend at Butlins.

After arriving in the Flintshire town, we piled onto said bus and asked the driver if he would be passing the football ground. "We've got a football ground in Connah's Quay?" came his bemused response. Little more than a year later, this Nomads side would be champions of Wales and Champions League debutantes, yet some of the locals were unaware they existed.

This opened my eyes to just how little publicity and fanfare the Welsh top flight has received over the years. A local football team is something to be treasured, so it saddened me to think that there are people in Wales, and further beyond, who are unaware they even have one.

The match we took in that Saturday evening was an eventful 2-0 win to TNS. We got to experience two goals and a red card as well as mild cases of hypothermia at Deeside Stadium, but it was worth it because what we witnessed was football boiled down to its essence.

At this level, there are no overpaid *prima donnas* on the pitch, glory supporters on the terraces, or VAR delays tempering the goal celebrations. This was the sport we live for, unfiltered.

That journey to Connah's Quay was one of many trips across the border to take in matches across the Welsh pyramid. I watched games play out under the shadow of great mountains, surrounded by dense thickets of trees, and a stone's throw from picturesque lakes.

Granted, these matches were a world away from the Everton games I grew up watching, but they compelled me to find out more about the local clubs in this corner of the world. I took a deep dive into Welsh football and was taken aback by the amount of history there is here.

When I began researching this book, I didn't know the story about how the League of Wales was originally founded three decades ago and the controversy it flared up, but I quickly realised that it was a saga in its own right. This alone is a tale that could fill its own hefty tome, but the stories from Welsh domestic football that have really captivated me are the ones about fan power. Although relatively small in number, the fans of these clubs are their lifeblood and they have achieved great things when rallying together behind their local teams.

Barry Town's achievements at the height of their dominance were phenomenal, but they were nothing compared to the feat their supporters pulled off when they brought the team back from the brink following a catastrophic financial decline. There are similar tales behind the rise and fall of Rhyl and Bangor City, and the emergence of the phoenix clubs that rose from their ashes.

Hearing these stories first-hand from people who were at the heart of them mesmerised me, and I was equally fascinated to learn of the British and world records that have toppled in Welsh football, set by the likes of The New Saints and Bangor on their greatest winning streaks.

These are just a few of the highlights you'll find in this book, but the reason I'm citing them now is because they're undeniable proof that the Cymru Premier deserves a bigger spotlight.

Despite the humble facilities these clubs have and the modest crowds their matches attract, they have proud histories, legacies that will never die and traditions that have stood the test of time.

I wrote this book because this unique league deserves one covering and chronicling the first 30 years of its life, but above all, to celebrate the clubs that have made the Welsh top flight what it is today, help raise their profile and encourage people to support their local teams.

I hope reading it brings you as much joy as my Welsh football odyssey has brought me.

Mark Langshaw
May 2023

1

How the Land Lay

All books have to begin somewhere, and this one starts with a question: Why are there Welsh football clubs playing in the English leagues?

Only by addressing this matter can we begin to comprehend the challenges the domestic game has always faced in Wales, and understand why the country's first national football championship took the form it did when it launched in the early 1990s.

To find the answer, we have to flip the pages of the calendar back to the 1920s. In those days, the biggest clubs in Wales, Cardiff City and Swansea City, were seeking a league to join, but their only options on home soil were low-key regional divisions that didn't match their ambitions.

Cardiff, who turned fully professional in 1910, successfully applied for English Football League membership 10 years later, securing a place in the Second Division for the 1920-21 season. They were also the opponents, in 1912, for Swansea's first match as a full-time club, a 1-1 draw at the Vetch Field that marked the beginning of a new era for one of football's greatest rivalries. The Swans were one of several Welsh teams to flock to England's Southern League system, and were founder members of the Football League's Third Division in 1920.

Swansea and Cardiff are, of course, just two of several Welsh teams who ply their trade across the border. Wrexham entered the English system from regional Welsh football, via the Birmingham and District League in 1905-06, before landing a spot in the Third Division in 1921.

There are similar stories behind the cross-border migration of Newport County, Merthyr Town, Bangor City, Barry Town, Caernarfon Town, Colwyn Bay, Newtown and Rhyl - all of whom were competing in England when talk of a Welsh national championship began many decades later.

The lack of a professional league in Wales, or any kind of national structure, meant that the country lost its biggest and best-supported clubs to the Football League, and this put Welsh football at a serious disadvantage when its main domestic leagues were being assembled.

Imagine the difficulties the Scottish Premiership might face if Rangers and Celtic hopped the fence to England. Attendances and television revenue would certainly take a hit. Now consider what impact it could have had on the English Premier League if the top teams in the country - today's so-called 'Big Six' - had declined to join the division when it launched in 1992. Would Sky TV have been so willing to invest £304 million into the competition without them?

Without Swansea, Cardiff and Wrexham, the early football leagues in Wales struggled to gain much traction, and the poor transport links between the north and south of the nation prior to World War II made the prospect of a Welsh top flight nigh on impossible.

One man who knows the full extent of these challenges all too well is Trefor Lloyd Hughes. He has had a lifelong connection to Welsh football and served on the Football Association of Wales (FAW) council from 1989. When serious talk of a national league began to gather pace, he was privy to these conversations as a key figure in domestic football. Hughes, who went on to become the president of the FAW, provides a fascinating insight on what Welsh football was like before the League of Wales:

> *I would say it was a big challenge trying to put any kind of significant league together without the main Anglo-Welsh teams. They were off pursuing professional football in England and the league we were planning would not have full-time status.*
>
> *Not having the biggest teams in the country on side made things difficult, but it wasn't the only hurdle we faced. Even today, the transport links are far from perfect and this makes cross-country travel tough, plus we had to convince the whole of Welsh domestic football to support sweeping changes. People don't like change, but a national championship had to happen at some point and I think the launch of one has been good for Wales as a country and a footballing nation.*

Despite these challenges, Wales did have football leagues before 1992, albeit regionalised ones that were overshadowed by the exploits of the Welsh clubs competing across the border.

In the south, the Welsh Football League was a footballing pyramid of three levels. Founded in 1904, with Aberdare winning the inaugural Division One title, its top flight was the highest level of league competition for southern clubs until the League of Wales began the best part of a century later.

Between 1904 and 1992, there were 22 different winners of the Welsh Football League's first division. The league allowed the teams playing in the English pyramid to field reserve teams

Trefor Lloyd Hughes (© FAW)

and they claimed many titles between them, with Swansea's reserves winning it 12 times, Cardiff City's reserves six times, and Newport County's on five occasions. Other winners of the Welsh Football League title include future League of Wales members Llanelli (six titles), Ton Pentre (six titles), Abergavenny Thursdays (four titles) and Haverfordwest County (three titles).

According to Hughes, the standard of football in the upper reaches of the Welsh Football League wasn't radically different to the League of Wales that would come later:

> You have to remember how many people reside along the south Wales corridor, all the way up to Welshpool and Newtown. There's a lot of people living there, so their choice of football teams to support has always been much greater than those in the north.
>
> In my opinion, I don't think there was much difference in the standards between the top flight of the Welsh Football League and the early days of the League of Wales. It took a while to see any significant change, but I honestly believe it was difficult to separate them in terms of quality.
>
> The challenges that Welsh domestic clubs faced when all of the leagues were regionalised were very much the same as they have been in the Premier League era - the financial situation. This was a big problem for teams in the Welsh Football League back then.

Football in north and mid Wales was more fragmented and attempts to form an equivalent to the Welsh Football League fell by the wayside until 1990, when firm plans came together at a meeting on 12 February – held in Flint – between the Football Association of Wales, regional football representatives and interested clubs.

The then-FAW secretary general Alun Evans believed that a unified league covering north and mid Wales was necessary to improve the standards and interest in football, but he was anticipating opposition from clubs who were happy with the *status quo*. "There *will* be a north Wales equivalent to the Welsh Football League in the south next season," said Evans in a statement issued back in 1990. "Some leagues will be ruffled by what is going to happen but soccer in this region has been stagnating for too long. It is a bold step forward which is being imposed on those who could not previously agree."

Of the 18 clubs present, 16 expressed an interest in founding the new league, the Cymru Alliance, a competition comprising feeder teams from the Welsh Alliance League, Central Wales League and the Welsh National League (Wrexham Area). Although it did not feature any teams from the south, the Cymru Alliance was a precursor to the League of Wales that would arrive hot on its heels. Serious talk of a national championship was well underway at this stage, so all of the clubs who applied to the new regional division - 22 in total - were asked to pledge their support to a fully-unified Welsh league.

Trefor Lloyd Hughes, the Welsh Alliance secretary at the time, was "wholeheartedly behind" the discussions for the new league:

> I think all of the clubs knew there was going to be a national league before this point. When the Cymru Alliance launched, the plans weren't finalised at that stage, and from a financial standpoint, I think the member clubs were concerned.

The FAW eventually whittled down the shortlist of member clubs for the Cymru Alliance to 16: Caersws FC, Carno FC, CPD Penrhyncoch, Llanidloes Town and Welshpool AFC from the Central Wales League; Bethesda Athletic, Connah's Quay Nomads, Conwy United, CPD Porthmadog, Flint Town United, Holywell Town and Nantlle Vale FC of the Welsh Alliance; while Brymbo Steelworks, Gresford Athletic and Mold Alexandra were earmarked to join from the Welsh National League.

However, it was ultimately 13 out of these 16 clubs who became founding members as Bethesda Athletic, Nantlle Vale and Brymbo Steelworks did not join up at its launch. Mostyn, meanwhile, were a late addition to the plans, joining from the Clwyd League to take the total number of Cymru Alliance clubs to 14 for its debut season. Other clubs threatened to drop out before the plans were set in stone.

4

Flint Town United, for example, made it clear that their preference was to apply for membership to the English North West Counties League, but made a U-turn when their application was rejected.

Although the FAW had no experience running a national league, the governing body had overseen the Welsh Cup for more than a century by the time the League of Wales began. Established in 1877, the Welsh Cup is the third-oldest association football competition in the world and has always been the country's most prestigious domestic cup. Until 1995, when a host of teams including Cardiff and Swansea were expelled from the competition, it gave clubs the chance to secure glamour ties against the Welsh giants playing in the English football pyramid.

In addition to the Welsh participants, football clubs from the lower reaches of the English system - usually those based around, or close to, the Welsh border - were often invited to make guest appearances in the national knockout competition. Notable participants over the years included Shrewsbury Town, Tranmere Rovers, Hereford United, Chester City and Bristol City, with English slides lifting the trophy on no fewer than 21 occasions. Shrewsbury hold the record with six titles and Hereford have the honour of being the last non-Welsh side to win it, in 1990.

For the most part, the Welsh teams competing in England were totally dominant in the Welsh Cup, with Wrexham winning it 23 times, Cardiff 22 and Swansea 10. There was a period where interest in the cup began to wane among these clubs, but this quickly changed in the 1960s when the FAW secured a place in the European Cup Winners' Cup for the victors.

English sides have never been able to enter Europe via this Welsh backdoor route, and whenever a guest participant won it, the Cup Winners' Cup spot went to the best-placed Welsh club. Prior to 1994, it was almost exclusively Welsh clubs in the English pyramid who reached Europe via the Welsh Cup, and those teams have enjoyed some of the best nights in their history as a result.

Cardiff can claim an impressive record in the Cup Winners' Cup, having reached the semi-finals in 1967-68, where they narrowly lost 4-3 on aggregate to Hamburger SV of Germany. The Bluebirds have also made it to the quarters on two occasions, most memorably in 1970-71 when they were drawn against Real Madrid. More than 47,000 reportedly showed up for the first leg under the lights at Ninian Park, where they were treated to a giant killing for the ages.

Cardiff, who were then in the old Division Two, defeated *Los Blancos* by a goal to nil, courtesy of a bullet header from Brian Clark. Cardiff lost the away leg 2-0 in Spain, but bowed out with their pride fully intact and went on to represent Wales in the Cup Winners' Cup another eight times between then and 1994.

Swansea and Wrexham have similar tales of big European outings to tell, but somewhat surprisingly, so do the likes of Bangor City and Newport County. Despite playing in Division Three at the time, Newport enjoyed a remarkable run to the quarter-finals of the 1980-81 Cup Winners' Cup, where they narrowly lost over two legs to German outfit FC Carl Zeiss Jena.

Bangor, meanwhile, have a proud record of European participation that predates their League of Wales membership. Citizens fans from a certain generation can regale you with stories of their exploits against European behemoths like Napoli and Atlético Madrid, and their European outings continued long after this path to the continent was blocked for the English pyramid clubs.

Hughes firmly believes that their non-participation in the Welsh Cup is a great loss to the teams playing in the English system, not least because winning it provided a ticket to Europe and the financial rewards that come with it:

> *I would imagine that financially, the Welsh Cup has been greatly missed by the likes of Cardiff, Swansea and Wrexham because the European revenue would have been a big boost to them. It wasn't our decision to exile them from the cup. It was down to UEFA and FIFA. You never know what could happen with teams like Wrexham in the future, but for now the door to Europe appears to be closed for them and the likes of Newport County.*

That was the lay of the land in Welsh football as the 1990s, a decade of sweeping change for the 'beautiful game', approached: the Welsh Cup was dominated by English-pyramid teams; the south had its own league system; while the north and mid Wales regions were merging their disparate divisions. The 1991-92 season was pivotal as it would be the last in which the Welsh football pyramid used this format.

The highest level of the Welsh Football League, known as the National Division between 1983 and 1992, saw Abergavenny Thursdays starting the campaign as champions after winning their first league title since 1960 the season before. Meanwhile, the Cymru Alliance, which was sponsored by Manweb, had only been running for one season and its inaugural winners were Flint Town United, ironic champions given their reluctance to sign up for the league when it was being established.

Flint and Abergavenny then faced off in a battle of title winners to decide who would be crowned 'Welsh Non-League' champions. This final, the only one of its kind ever played, saw The Silkmen triumph by two goals to one to cap off an excellent season with another piece of silverware.

Wales' representatives in Europe for the 1991-92 season would be Swansea City, who had defeated Wrexham 2-0 in the

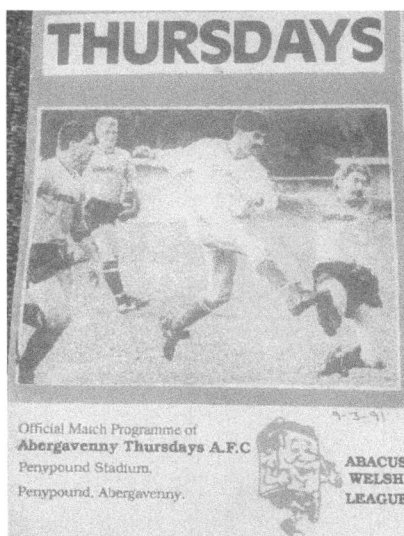

An official matchday programme from a Welsh Football League contest between Abergavenny Thursdays and Cwmbrân Town. (© Andy J Havelot)

previous year's Welsh Cup final. It was their seventh Cup Winners' Cup campaign, and it was ultimately a short European tour. In the first round Terry Yorath's Swans were drawn against a Monaco side managed by Arsène Wenger, and competed well in the first leg at the Vetch Field, narrowly losing 2-1 to the French league leaders, who had George Weah and Rui Barros among their ranks.

Future Wales international Andy Legg netted a late consolation for the hosts, who simply refused to be swept aside. After the game, during a televised interview, Wenger hailed Swansea's performance, describing them as playing a "great game" and having a "big heart". The cricket score everyone feared did, however, come in the second leg when Monaco were relentless on their home turf and steamrollered the Swans 8-0, with Weah and Barros both amongst the goals, along with an up-and-coming Youri Djorkaeff.

Back on the domestic front, Abergavenny Thursdays continued to enjoy one of the most successful periods in their history as the League of Wales dawned. They retained their crown by winning the National Division with 74 points - four more than Briton Ferry Athletic in second place - losing only twice all season, and conceding just 24 goals in 30 league matches.

Elsewhere, the second season of the Cymru Alliance was seriously competitive. Defending champions Flint Town could only manage a fourth-placed finish but there were only four points between them and eventual winners Caersws. Runners-up Llansantffraid - a newly-promoted village side from the Mid Wales Football League - were only two points behind, and third-placed Porthmadog a further point behind.

Reflecting on the Cymru Alliance's campaigns as a regional top flight competition, Hughes commented:

> *I think those two seasons were a success. It helped prepare the teams for the new national league that was just around the corner and we made it clear to them what the requirements would be for it. I think the standard of football in the Cymru Alliance was pretty much on par with the highest level of the Welsh Football League during those two seasons. The clubs in the Cymru Alliance always had a disadvantage because I think the press were far more keen to push the south Wales teams, and that didn't help the situation.*

In the Welsh Cup, several clubs from the Welsh leagues had a good run in the competition and by the quarter-final stage, there were

The Flint Town United side that won the 1990-91 Cymru Alliance title.
(© Flint Town United FC)

still three teams from the Welsh Football League alive and kicking: Haverfordwest County, Aberystwyth Town and Maesteg Park.

Maesteg, who had finished sixth in the league, were the tournament's surprise package that year and were drawn against Aberystwyth, who they dispatched 2-0 to reach the semi-finals. Haverfordwest, meanwhile, took on Hednesford Town - then of the Midland Division of England's Southern League - and forced them into a replay following a goalless draw on Welsh soil. Hednesford thrashed the Pembrokeshire side at the second time of asking, putting four past them without reply. The English non-leaguers then triumphed in a two-legged semi-final against Colwyn Bay - who had dispatched Wrexham in the quarters - beating The Seagulls 4-2 on aggregate.

Cardiff's path to the final included a fiery confrontation with arch-rivals Swansea in the quarters. This was a grudge match in every sense of the word as The Bluebirds were seeking revenge for an English FA Cup defeat at the hands of The Swans several weeks earlier. The game took place at the Vetch Field where the visitors edged it, dumping out the holders through a lone strike from Chris Pike, the uncle of future Wales legend Gareth Bale. The team's top scorer latched onto a long ball, found space inside the box and rifled a shot straight into the bottom corner to whip the mass of Cardiff supporters behind the goal into raptures.

Maesteg's reward for reaching the dizzy heights of the semi-finals was a tie against Cardiff, and they did themselves proud in the first leg. They frustrated The Bluebirds and held them to a 0-0 stalemate, only to suffer a heavy 4-0 defeat to their full-time opponents in the return leg. The departure of Wales' largest clubs from the Welsh Cup did impact on the competition, but, as Hughes commented:

I think being unable to play teams like Cardiff City in the cup is a real shame for the domestic Welsh sides. Smaller clubs were looking at them as the big draws, but for me, Wales is Wales. You don't see the Scottish teams playing in English competitions, so why should teams from the English system be involved in Welsh competitions? The Anglo-Welsh teams made a decision to play in England and one of the longer-term consequences of that has been losing their places in the Welsh Cup and a route into Europe.

The Welsh Cup final was played at the National Stadium, and as a result humble Hednesford became the first English football side to play there. Cardiff went into the game as heavy favourites, given their status as a Football League outfit, and the match gave them the opportunity to make up for a disappointing league campaign, in which they missed out on the Division Four play-offs.

Playing in front of more than 10,000 fans, Cardiff didn't have it all their own way, but they took an early lead against the run of play when Carl Dale found the net after linking up well with his strike partner, Pike. The Welsh side had the better of the possession after taking the lead, and although Hednesford proved worthy adversaries, they held on to lift the trophy. It was a momentous cup victory for several members of that Cardiff side, particularly skipper Roger Gibbins - who'd never before won the competition in a two-decade playing career - and goalkeeper Roger Hansbury, playing his final game before retirement.

The cup final brought the curtain down on the 1991-92 Welsh football season, the last campaign where the Welsh Football League National Division and the Cymru Alliance were the pinnacles of the nation's football pyramid. After the League of Wales debuted the following summer, the two divisions became regionalised second tiers that would feed eligible clubs into the top flight, while relegated teams from the new top division dropped into them.

The launch of a new national championship would also have far-reaching implications for the Welsh Cup and the English-pyramid sides competing in it, but some of them - specifically Bangor, Barry Town, Caernarfon Town, Colwyn Bay, Merthyr Tydfil, Newport County, Newtown and Rhyl - had more pressing concerns to attend to when the FAW unveiled its League of Wales vision. The controversy these plans stoked up among such clubs is a saga in itself, but so indeed is the story behind the FAW's motivations for launching a national league. While this notion had been mulled over in the past, the governing body felt its hand was ultimately forced on the matter.

2

A League of Our Own

Proposals for a single national pyramid and league championship had been tabled at the Football Association of Wales before; but almost a century after the governing body was founded, it took an existential threat to the country's status as a sovereign football nation to kickstart these plans.

Along with its three British neighbours, Wales has held a spot on the International Football Association Board (IFAB) since the law-making body was founded and has always taken pride in fielding a national team, even if the nation's fortunes on the pitch have been mixed, at best. The FAW's right to do either of these things was purportedly called into question in the mid-1980s when a cabal of non-European FIFA members expressed their growing resentment towards the United Kingdom for hogging four seats at world football's top table.

Reports at the time suggest that African and Asian football chiefs were leading the calls for Wales, Scotland, England and Northern Ireland to merge their football associations and field a UK team, as with the Olympics (known as Team GB). Wales had more than 100 years of footballing history under its belt, yet critics claimed its case to remain a standalone team was discredited by the absence of a Welsh national league.

There were, of course, domestic football leagues in Wales before this point - such as the Welsh Football League system and the newly-launched Cymru Alliance - yet what the nation had always lacked was a national top flight to sit at the summit of its footballing pyramid, ideally with healthy sponsorship to finance it and UEFA accreditation behind it.

The fact that the strongest Welsh clubs - namely Cardiff City, Wrexham and Swansea City – were members of the English Football League was seen as hypocrisy. In the eyes of the FAW's then-secretary general, Alun Evans, the threat to the fabric of Welsh football's existence could not be overstated, and something drastic had to be

Former FAW General Secretary Alun Evans. (© Welsh Football Magazine)

done to safeguard its future. The solution, on paper, was simple: Wales needed to form a league of its own.

In practice, though, launching a Welsh national league from scratch wasn't so straightforward. Although the FAW had a strong track record of organising a UEFA-accredited football competition in the shape of the Welsh Cup, barriers including geographical constraints - specifically the poor north-south transport links - had prevented the football association from forging its own truly national championship.

Evans knew that such a dramatic shake-up of Welsh football would ruffle feathers and rattle cages, but he wasn't the only driving force behind the national championship. John Deakin, a former top-level referee, played an instrumental role in shaping the League of Wales during its formative years, having been appointed as the competition's secretary in 1992. According to Deakin, serious talk of a unified Welsh football league began around two years earlier, and it was then that the FAW first got wind of the opposition they might face.

> *The first I heard about it was a couple of years before when they started having meetings about launching a domestic league. I was still refereeing at the time and I spoke to Alun Evans about it, and I know they started sounding out the clubs and, of course, that's when the controversy started. I know the concept of a Welsh national championship had been mentioned historically, but in the two years before is when it started to be spoken about seriously.*

It is unclear just how seriously FIFA took the rumblings of discontent toward the United Kingdom having four independent football associations, though if Evans was right and the threat to Welsh football was real, this could potentially have had massive implications for the English, Scottish and Northern Irish FAs too.

Reflecting on the matter, Deakin believes that Evans was correct to fear for Wales' future as a sovereign football nation and insists that the threat against them was likely credible:

I think Alun was probably right and the threat to the Welsh national team was real. I spoke to people who had been to FIFA meetings and it was raised on several occasions. The United Kingdom comprising of four counties, each with their own footballing history, was a unique situation for the governing body and its members, but I don't think it would have gone down well with the fans if we had to merge them into a UK team.

Historically, it made sense that the likes of Swansea City, Cardiff City, Wrexham and even Newport County, were in the English league system, particularly as the north-south transport links within Wales were very poor and made the east-west (Wales – England) connections far more practical as well as being financially more lucrative. However, the question marks around Wales' right to remain an independent footballing nation was enough to convince Evans and the FAW's top brass to firm up plans for a national league.

The competition launched under the moniker of the League of Wales in October 1991 and its curtain-raising campaign was the 1992-93 season. The FAW's vision was to form a league covering the whole country, with 20 inaugural members from north, south and mid Wales on a roughly equal basis. Some joined from the Welsh Football League and Cymru Alliance divisions, while others eventually switched from England's Northern Premier League.

The League of Wales' founder clubs from the Welsh Football League National Division were Aberystwyth Town, Maesteg Park, Afan Lido, Ebbw Vale, Haverfordwest County, Briton Ferry Athletic, Cwmbrân Town, Llanelli, Inter Cardiff and Abergavenny Thursdays. They were joined by Connah's Quay Nomads, Porthmadog, Caersws, Flint Town United, Holywell Town, Mold Alexandra and Llanidloes Town from the Cymru Alliance, with, ultimately, Bangor City and Newtown joining from the English system.

While the FAW would serve as the competition's governing body, a limited company called Football League of Wales Limited was created to directly administer the league, and a sponsorship agreement with Konica Peter Llewellyn Limited was secured for its debut season, resulting, as John Deakin explained, in it being dubbed the 'Konica League of Wales' at launch.

Not long before the start of the season Konica Peter Llewellyn Limited came in and gave their backing to it, to the tune of around £55,000. That was not a large amount in the big scheme of things, but securing a headline sponsor and getting them to lend their name to the competition was more important than the money. The funds they put in weren't to be sniffed at, though - they did help the founder clubs financially.

The deal with them only lasted three years. They offered to come back in later on but at a reduced rate. There was a significant fallow period after that before we got the Mitsubishi people. Of course, in the later years, sponsorships were a lot more successful.

The League of Wales has undergone several format changes since its inaugural season, when it was practical and simple for clubs, fans and the media to understand. The 20 clubs would play each other home and away, with the team who topped the pile at the end of the season qualifying for the preliminary round of the Champions League, while the bottom two would drop into the Welsh Football League or Cymru Alliance depending on their geographical location.

As far as promotion to the League of Wales for its second season was concerned, one team would ascend from each of the two second-tier divisions, subject to their ground facilities being classed as acceptable.

In addition to the national league, a new Welsh League Cup was also established for the 1992-93 season to provide teams with another trophy to compete for. Like its English and Scottish counterparts, it's always been less coveted than its nation's primary domestic cup, but the Welsh clubs and their fans nonetheless welcomed the extra opportunity to win silverware.

Meanwhile, the Welsh Cup was to continue uninterrupted, just as it had done since it was founded in 1887 (apart from during the two World Wars

Former League of Wales Secretary John Deakin. (© Welsh Football Magazine)

and, more recently, throughout the Covid-19 pandemic). Wrexham, Swansea, Cardiff and the other Anglo-Welsh sides could continue using the competition to gain side-door entry to Europe, for the short term, at least.

The Welsh Cup, however, only retained that format for a few seasons after the formation of the League of Wales. From 1996 onwards, it was largely restricted to teams in the Welsh system. Cardiff, Colwyn Bay, Merthyr Town, Newport, Swansea and Wrexham were later invited to rejoin, but uptake among them has been poor since it was ruled that teams outside of the Welsh domestic leagues cannot use this route to qualify for Europe, as Deakin explained:

> *It was all very unfortunate. They did traditionally play in the Welsh Cup but I do understand why they were excluded given the fact that the teams that left the English system to join the League of Wales were excluded from the FA Cup. That was a pity as well, but I think, over the years, the Welsh Cup has settled down and become a very good competition in its own right.*

Although joining up with the newly-formed championship was a no-brainer for some of the founder clubs - not least because it gave them the opportunity to compete for European football - others had to be dragged, kicking and screaming, into the League of Wales.

Bangor, for example, were quite happy to remain in the lower reaches of the English football pyramid. They had, after all, crafted a history for themselves there as founder members of what is now the National League and were beaten finalists in the 1984 FA Trophy final.

Newtown AFC were in a similar position. Despite being one of the oldest clubs in Wales and a founder member of the FAW, The Robins were playing alongside Bangor in the Northern Premier League and, all things being equal, were keen to stay there indefinitely.

Rhyl were another team from the English non-league earmarked for inclusion, but the FAW's initial attempts to recruit them were met with reluctance. The Lilywhites eventually had a change of heart about membership, though not in time for the 1992-93 season and were placed in the second tier for the inaugural campaign because their application was filed late.

It was widely accepted that the 'big three' of Swansea, Cardiff and Wrexham had little to gain from jumping ship, given that they were key players in the English Football League. Had the trio joined up, they'd almost certainly have dominated the league, similarly to Glasgow's Old Firm in Scotland, not to mention had their development stifled by a lower standard of competition and comparatively lower revenue opportunities on the domestic front.

The Football Association of Wales, however, considered all other domestic teams fair game and tried to strongarm a number of them into signing up. This led to an incendiary dispute between the governing body and Bangor City, Barry Town, Caernarfon Town, Colwyn Bay, Merthyr, Newport County, Newtown and Rhyl, who became collectively known as the 'Irate Eight' due to their bitter reluctance to leave English pastures, as Deakin recalled:

> *I immediately got wind of the controversy, I'd been at an Afan Lido game where we were conducting an experiment into changes to the offside rule. We had a meeting that morning about the proposals for the League of Wales and Alun Evans informed me that the clubs in the English football system would want to continue playing there.*
>
> *At that time, he thought he could bring the likes of Colwyn Bay and Newport County with him, but of course that didn't happen. In 1992, when I took over the job, we ended up with 20 teams on board for the new division, but some of them I hadn't really heard of.*

Unwavering in their conviction that the new league was for the greater good, Evans and the FAW threatened sanctions against the rebel clubs. Bangor City, Newtown and Rhyl were, of course, the first to fall in line and join up to prevent an ugly dispute from escalating, but critics accused the governing body, including Deakin, of using dirty tactics to get them onside.

> *The highest profile club we got was Bangor City after their U-turn. From my own point of view I thought it was a pity the likes of Newport County didn't join the League of Wales because I think the competition would have made a much stronger start with them on board. Likewise, if teams like Barry Town had come in from the beginning.*
>
> *There were some clubs who were there right from the start whose position in the league I felt was not sustainable, and so it proved. I love the little town of Llanidloes, for instance, but I didn't think for one minute that it could sustain a club in the new top flight.*

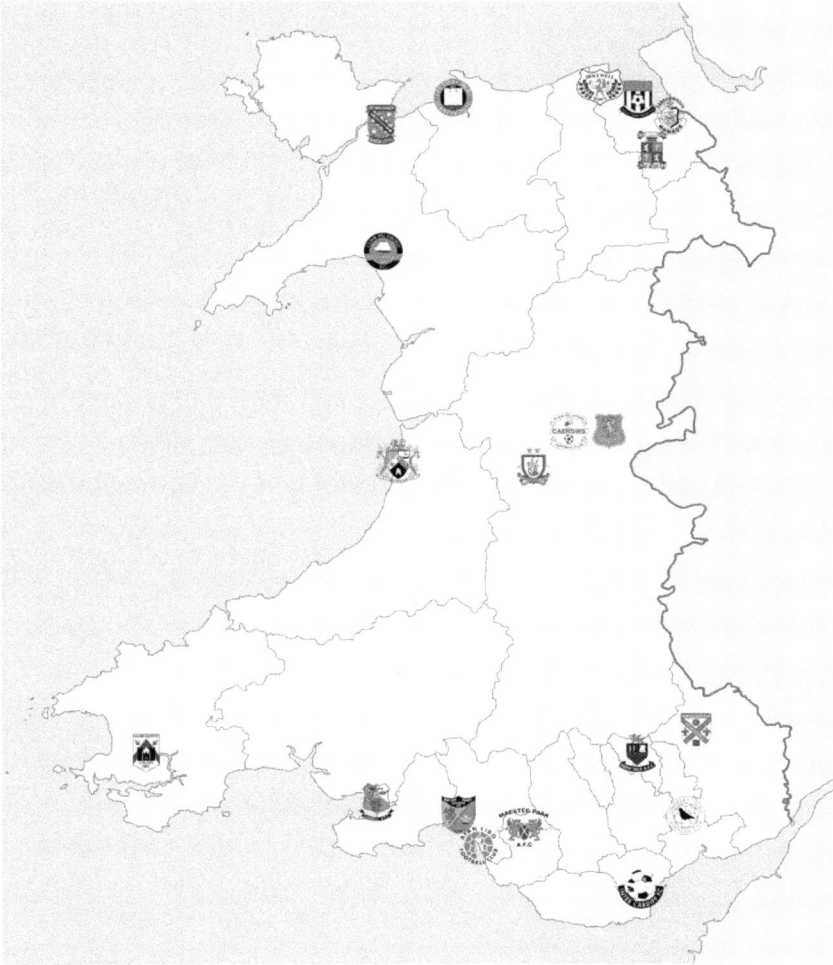

Founder clubs of The League of Wales. (© Clint Jones)

More ugliness followed when the remaining five of the 'Irate Eight' clubs were forced into exile under the threat of legal action. If they were unwilling to take part in the new league then the FAW would see to it that they couldn't play any competitive football in Wales whatsoever, even if that meant hauling them into court.

Four out of those five found temporary English homes. Barry Town spent a year as lodgers at Worcester City's St. George's Lane, and even underwent a fleeting name change to Barri Dragons before buckling under the FAW's coercion and migrating to the Welsh system.

Newport spent a year ground sharing with Gloucester City at Meadow Park and, while that was surely inconvenient at the time, things haven't turned out too badly for The Ironsides. After hauling themselves up through the English football pyramid, they won the Conference South in 2009-10 before reclaiming their English Football League status three years later, thanks to a memorable 2-0 victory over Wrexham in the Conference National play-off final at Wembley.

Meanwhile, Colwyn Bay's exile began with a lone season playing home matches at Northwich Victoria's Drill Field ground. They enjoyed some success in the English non-league in the ensuing years, climbing as high as the Conference North. A couple of relegations later, however, the club chose to rejoin Welsh football for the 2019-20 season, beginning a new chapter of their history in the regionalised second tier, Cymru North.

The most travelled of the remaining 'Irate Eight' were Caernarfon Town who spent their exile further afield than their banished brethren, playing home matches 100 miles away at Manchester-based Curzon Ashton's home turf.

The exile period was less than ideal for almost everyone involved. Not only did the dark clouds of uncertainty hang over the collective heads of each club, most of them - Caernarfon particularly - found it difficult to attract a 'home' crowd. The League of Wales, meanwhile, would have been all the stronger if the rebel clubs had chosen to pledge their allegiance to its cause.

After Barry hopped the fence into Welsh domestic football, the remaining clubs took it upon themselves to challenge the FAW's sanctions at the High Court. The court ruled in the teams' favour, allowing them to play competitive matches on home soil once again; though this became moot for Caernarfon in 1995 when they decided to join the League of Wales. Indeed, the same became true of Colwyn Bay when they returned to home soil many years later.

In hindsight, Deakin admits that he has regrets about the way the 'Irate Eight' situation was handled and remembers feeling disheartened throughout the court dispute.

Personally, I do have regrets about the way it was handled. I was brought in to do a job, and when I took over, I got wind of the full extent of the controversy, which only got worse with the 'exiles' situation. I said right from the start that making clubs play their home games in England was unsustainable, and even unlawful. That proved to be the case, of course, when we ended up in the High Court a couple of years down the line.

I gave evidence in the High Court in support of the FAW's case, but I can't say that my heart was particularly in it. I endured hours in the witness box with a guy for the exile clubs called Nicholas Stewart QC, who I have to say was a lot better than our representation. I wasn't surprised when the Football Association of Wales lost that case. It cost us a significant six-figure sum; half a million pounds that could have been better spent elsewhere.

The inaugural League of Wales trophy. (© Welsh Football Magazine)

In the long run, though, Deakin agrees that League of Wales membership was in the best interest of the majority of the inaugural member clubs. In the early years, Bangor City could be held aloft as a shining example of this as The Citizens developed and thrived in a way that would not have been possible in the lower reaches of the English football system:

I think it was in everybody's best interest. Bangor in the early years of their League of Wales membership illustrated that. I went into Europe with them to Poland. I must reiterate, if we had the likes of Colwyn Bay, and Barry Town right from the start, I think the league would have kicked off with a lot less controversy and would have been stronger.
We had to build from a low base and there were people saying to me that it won't last a year and I'd be out of a job. Twenty years later I was able to look back and say they were wrong.

Many years down the line, Evans' masterplan for a Welsh national championship was viewed in a more positive light. The former general secretary of the FAW was hailed by some as a man who put his reputation on the line for the good of the domestic game.

He passed away in 2011 at the age of 69, but the league he and his colleagues created back in the early 1990s is still going strong and is a credit to his legacy. "Alun was instrumental in the formation of the League of Wales and was a strong leader of the FAW policies," said the Football Association of Wales in tribute at the time of Evans' death.

It's easy to forget how the League of Wales was born amid a firestorm of controversy, its flames fanned by bitter legal disputes and FIFA in-fighting, yet its formation also marked an exciting new dawn for Welsh football, the founder clubs, and of course, their loyal fans.

New rivalries were forged, old ones reignited and club traditions that have stood the test of time began right here. New stars were born under its banner, budding managers who would go onto greater things cut their teeth in its dugouts - and it all started on 15 August 1992, when 20 clubs took to the field to launch Wales' first national football league championship.

3

When the Crows Soared

The League of Wales' big kick-off fell on the same date as the English Premier League's hotly-anticipated opening day. Although it lacked the glitz, glamour and huge crowds of the other new national competition across the border, that Saturday in the summer of 1992 marked the beginning of an exciting new era for Welsh football nonetheless.

The league's formation attracted media attention - occasionally for the wrong reasons amid the 'Irate Eight' controversy - but this resulted in regular coverage for the inaugural member clubs in publications like the *Western Mail* and the *Daily Post*, as well as in Wales' regional and local newspapers.

1992-93

At the start of the season, Bangor City were tipped as the title favourites, and with almost 60 years' worth of English competitive football behind them, it was easy to see why. The Citizens' attacking partnership of Steve Buxton and Lee Noble was expected to strike fear into the hearts of opposition up and down the country, while midfield lynchpin Neville Powell and veteran defender Phil Lunn added English Football League experience to their ranks.

Crowds were modest as no more than a few hundred fans turned up at each ground to watch the founder clubs that opening Saturday, and prize money was a pittance compared to other national leagues across Europe. Those 20 teams were heading into the great unknown, yet it was a huge opportunity for the Welsh game, a platform upon which it could reinvent itself.

Afan Lido forward Mitch Patton will forever hold the honour of being the League of Wales' maiden goal scorer, when his strike - during his side's 2-1 win over Connah's Quay Nomads - marked the first time a scoreboard confirmed that a goal had been scored in the new national championship.

Elsewhere, there were opening-day victories for Bangor, Haverfordwest County, Aberystwyth Town, Conwy United, Inter Cardiff, Llanelli, Cwmbrân Town and Ebbw Vale, the latter of whom hammered Holywell Town 4-1 to claim the biggest win of the weekend.

The standout match during the opening round of fixtures was contested between Newtown and Maesteg Park, who played out an action-packed 4-4 draw at Latham Park. Defender Colin Reynolds, who went on to set a record for most appearances in the Welsh top flight, scored twice for The Robins as they began their campaign with a well-earned point.

All too often, top-flight football struggles to truly surprise us. Rarely has a team outside of the so-called 'Big Six' won the English Premier League and the Old Firm have dominated in Scotland for decades. There are comparable stories in the top divisions across Europe, but the way the League of Wales' debut season played out was anything but predictable.

Before the formation of the national championship, Cwmbrân Town spent much of their time competing in the Welsh Football League system. The Crows had enjoyed minor success in the past, winning Division Two in 1967-68, lifting the Welsh Football League Cup in 1990-91 and bagging several Gwent Senior Cups. Nobody, however, expected them to overachieve the way they did in the inaugural League of Wales campaign.

Against the odds, The Crows took the league by storm and were nigh on unbeatable throughout 1992-93. They got off to an absolute flyer, winning their first three matches, the latter of which was a 6-1 obliteration of Connah's Quay Nomads at Cwmbrân Stadium. Losing just once in their opening 12 games, going down 1-0 at home to Ebbw Vale in early September, Cwmbrân barely faltered from then on. The next team to get the better of them was struggling Llanidloes Town, also by a goal to nil, in November, but The Crows bounced back from this in spectacular fashion and went on an unbeaten streak that lasted for 20 matches.

The driving force behind Cwmbrân's success was manager Tony Wilcox, who quickly established himself as a club legend. Joining The Crows in November 1991, Wilcox was an inspirational figure who maintained a close relationship with his players and coaching staff. His title-winning side was built on the bedrock of a sturdy defence, with skipper Jimmy Blackie - who went on to make a

KONICA LEAGUE OF WALES – RESULTS 1992-3

1992 August
Sat. 15 H Flint Town Utd .... W 2-0 Smith, Copeman
Sat. 22 A Conwy United .... W 1-0 Parselle
Sat. 29 H Connah's Quay Nomads ...... W 6-1 Smith (2), Goodridge, Evans, Rowlands, Parselle

September
Wed. 2 H Ebbw Vale .... L 0-1
Sat. 5 A Caersws .... W 2-1 Smith, Goodridge
Sat. 12 H Bangor City .... D 2-2 Smith (2)
Sat. 19 A Portmadog .... W 2-0 Vaughan, Parselle
Sat. 26 H Newtown .... D 1-1 Copeman

October
Sat. 3 H Mold Alexandra .... W 2-0 Evans, Clissold
Sat. 17 H Holywell Town .... D 1-1 Clissold
Sat. 24 A Afan Lido .... D 0-0
Sat. 31 H Llanelli .... W 2-1 Clissold, Goodridge

November
Sat. 7 A Llanidloes Town .... L 0-1
Sat. 14 A Aberystwyth Town .... W 2-2 Wharton, King
Sat. 21 A Abergavenny Thursdays .... D 2-2 Wharton, Goodridge

December
Sat. 5 H Maesteg Park Athletic .... W 3-1 Goodridge (2), Wharton
Sat. 12 H Llanidloes Town .... W 2-1 Payne, Goodridge
Sat. 19 A Inter-Cardiff .... D 0-0

1993 January
Sat. 2 H Afan Lido .... W 3-0 Wharton, Powell (2)
Sat. 23 H Aberystwyth Town .... W 2-0 King, Parselle

Sat. 30 H Abergavenny Thursdays ..... W 1-0 King

February
Fri. 5 H Briton Ferry Athletic .... W 1-0 Sutton
Sat. 13 A Maesteg Park Athletic .... W 3-0 Ford (2), Goodridge
Fri. 20 H Inter-Cardiff .... W 3-0 Parselle, McNeil, Clissold
Sat. 27 A Flint Town United .... D 0-0

March
Sat. 6 H Conwy United .... D 2-2 Goodridge, Ford
Wed. 10 H Haverfordwest County .... W 1-0 Ford
Sat. 13 A Newtown .... W 2-1 Goodridge, Rowlands
Wed. 17 A Ebbw Vale .... W 1-0 Ford
Sat. 20 H Caersws .... D 1-1 Ford
Sat. 27 A Bangor City .... W 3-2 Wharton, Ford, Copeman

Tues. 30 A Briton Ferry Athletic .... W 4-0 Wharton (2), Parselle, Clissold

April
Sat. 3 A Holywell Town .... W 3-1 Clissold (2), Wharton
Mon. 12 A Mold Alexandra .... L 0-1
Sat. 24 H Portmadog .... W 2-0 Dicks, G. Jones (o.g.)
Tues. 27 A Haverfordwest County .... W 5-0 Dicks, Payne, Clissold (2), Ford

May
Mon. 3 A Llanelli .... W 1-0 Goodridge
Sat. 8 A Connah's Quay Nomads ... W 1-0 Ford

	P	W	D	L	F	A	Pts
Home	19	13	5	1	37	13	44
Away	19	13	4	2	32	9	43
Total	38	26	9	3	69	22	87

The Crows' league fixtures and results from 1992-93. (© Norman Parselle)

record 378 appearances for the club - at the heart of it, and the safe hands of former Newport County stopper Pat O'Hagan between the sticks.

In front of Blackie and his water-tight rear guard was a midfield that ran like a well-oiled engine. Norman Parselle was a key part of that midfield:

It was a great group of lads I played with in that Cwmbrân team. They were probably the best I've ever played with as a footballer, but just getting to take part in the first season of the League of Wales was a highlight too. I'd played in the English system with Newport County and Forest Green but this was something new and exciting. Just getting to travel around Wales, to places like Porthmadog, with them was great, but one of the things I look back mostly fondly on is playing under the manager, Tony Wilcox.

According to Parselle, journeying across the country for away matches posed unique challenges. Although the poor transport links, that would once have severely hampered a Welsh national championship, had rapidly improved, some of the nation's winding roads weren't the ideal preparation for a 90-minute showdown in an opponent's backyard:

When we travelled up to some places in north Wales, some of our players were up the front of the bus, sick, with a bucket or a bag in front of them. Some of my teammates were used to it, but others definitely weren't.

Bouts of travel sickness aside, Wilcox took a squad of part-timers with little experience outside of the Welsh League National Division and made them greater than the sum of their parts. Consistency and organisation were the twin pillars that held Cwmbrân aloft all season, and their defensive record for that campaign is still one of the best in Welsh top-flight history. The Crows conceded just 22 times in 38 matches, an average of 0.58 goals per game, as Parselle recalled:

That defence was unbelievable. Simon King, Mickey Copeman, Jimmy Blackie, Gary Sturch and Gary Vaughan. They were fantastic, as was Pat O'Hagan in goal. If you ever talk to Mickey Copeman, that defensive record is all he ever goes on about, but to be fair to him, he has every right to be proud of it. That defence called themselves the Mean Machine after being given that nickname by one of the local newspapers.

At the opposite end of the pitch, Cwmbrân's goals were distributed fairly evenly across the squad. They lacked what could be considered a truly prolific striker and none of their forwards featured on the top goalscorers chart come the end of the season, Parselle added:

Goals were shared across the pitch, apart from that Mean Machine bunch whose only job was to keep them out. I think Simon King might have got a couple of penalties. Gary Vaughan scored one, Mickey Copeman got one, and I netted six. Wayne Goodridge, who played in midfield with me, chipped in with a few, as did Mark Smith.

Wilcox didn't have one of the league's biggest budgets at his disposal, though what he did have, according to Parselle who is now in charge of Newport County's community arm, was a far more valuable weapon in this inaugural title battle: a squad with a powerful sense of togetherness, free-flowing synergy and a work ethic that was second to none:

We only used to train once a week because Tony believed it was wrong to get family men out of their homes any more than that. We'd train at the stadium for an hour and a half, but we all used to go an hour early and do our fitness first; go on a run so we were prepared for the rest of it. We were all part-timers. We were postmen, firemen and warehouse workers, but we were a very tight-knit group and we wanted to get something from all the hard work and the travel.

For this band of brothers, the intense graft and country-spanning trips were worth it at the end of the season when The Crows won what was now the top prize in Welsh domestic football. After a stellar campaign, they were crowned unlikely champions in early May.

Parselle, who featured in 37 of Cwmbrân's 38 matches that season, recalled a sense of belief building among the squad around Christmas time, though they were under no illusions that reinforcements were needed to help them press on and challenge for the title. Despite limited resources, Wilcox managed to deliver on the transfer front by bringing in a striker who knew where the back of the net was as well as a creative midfielder:

We were doing really well that season under Tony's guidance and knew around Christmas that we could have a right go at the league title. He knew that we had to bring in some new players at that point if we wanted to go the distance, and he did exactly that. Tony snapped up Francis Ford to score goals up front, and midfield playmaker Micky Dicks, who was a very shrewd signing. Bringing those two in freshened things up and helped us kick on for the rest of the season.

Although Cwmbrân were tough to beat, there was an intense title race between them and nearest rivals, Inter Cardiff. The eventual runners-up maintained pace with The Crows for much of the campaign, and there was nothing between the pair when they met at the Cardiff Athletics Stadium in December and shared the spoils in a hard-fought goalless draw.

They were a good side with some ex-pros in their ranks, people like George Wood and Jason Gummer. If I remember correctly, it was a very close contest between the two of us going into February to March.

After 20 matches, Inter Cardiff were the league leaders, but Cwmbrân Town were only two points behind and had a match in-hand. They also had a psychological advantage over their fellow title chasers, having played them again at this critical point in the season

Cwmbrân Town's squad for their first League of Wales campaign. (© Norman Parselle)

and beaten them convincingly, 3-0, in front of a bumper crowd, as Parselle fondly remembers: ·

> *We played them around then and that was the first time a League of Wales game had more than a thousand in attendance. That was at Cwmbrân Stadium and we managed to turn them over by three goals to nil. That really put the stuffing out of them and I managed to score in that match. It was a big moment in the season, that. Putting three past our nearest rivals in front of a big crowd was a great feeling.*

At the tail end of March, Parselle was on target again, along with Andrew Clissold and Sean Wharton (twice) as The Crows clobbered Briton Ferry Athletic 4-0 to move back to the top of the league, though there was still the final stretch of the title race to go.

The contest almost went to the wire, and fate had a major part to play in the way the league was sealed and delivered. Fate, and the harsh Welsh winter, to be more precise. Cwmbrân were due to travel to Llanelli Town for an away fixture on Boxing Day, only for the game to be called off due to a frozen pitch. That match ended up being postponed until early May, and by this point, The Crows needed just one more win to clinch the title.

> *We travelled to Llanelli on Boxing Day and the pitch was completely frozen. I remember the referee saying to Jimmy Blackie: "We're going to give it another half hour because the sun is coming out, over the stand."*

To which Jimmy replied: "The sun's out in Russia and the pitches are still bloody freezing, so I can't see it changing".
So that game was postponed and we went back on a Tuesday evening in May. Wayne Goodridge scored in a 1-0 victory, and that was what won us the League of Wales.

Inter Cardiff finished just five points behind Cwmbrân, spurred on by the goalscoring exploits of forward Chris Summers, who netted 25 times that season, and they weren't the only side that had The Crows glancing nervously over their shoulders. Aberystwyth Town finished in third place, just nine points behind the champions and 12 ahead of fourth-placed Ebbw Vale.

Despite being slapped with the favourites tag pre-season, Bangor could only manage a fifth-place finish, ending the campaign on 64 points to edge out Holywell Town - who ended up being the best-performing team to come from the Cymru Alliance - directly below them. Paul Rowlands' underachieving Citizens suffered some humbling defeats along the way, including an embarrassing 6-0 reverse to Holywell in front of their own fans in October.

Meanwhile, it was a respectable mid-table finish for Afan Lido, who had played in the Welsh Football League National Division the season before, but League Cup glory made it an unforgettable campaign for them. The Port Talbot-based club were the inaugural winners of the new knockout competition, defeating Caersws 4-3 on penalties following a 1-1 draw in the final, which took place at Aberystwyth Town's Park Avenue ground.

At the bottom end of the table, Llanidloes Town and basement boys Abergavenny Thursdays were the League of Wales' first relegation casualties. The former did manage a shock 1-0 win at home to Cwmbrân before suffering the drop, though that was ultimately little consolation as they finished just two points above Abergavenny and six from safety.

While relegation amounts to a disappointing season for any club, there were mitigating circumstances behind Abergavenny's plight. Prior to the campaign, The Pennies had to provide a bond to the FA of Wales to ensure that floodlights could be installed at their ground, in accordance with the criteria for League of Wales membership. This put financial strain on the club and led to a mass exodus of players and staff ahead of the season. The squad and behind-the-scenes team

Cwmbrân Stadium – home of The Crows. (© Cwmbrân Town AFC)

they ended up with were hastily assembled, and there's no doubt that this pre-season chaos contributed to their downfall.

The relegated pair dropped into the Cymru Alliance and the Welsh Football League system respectively, and to date, neither have returned to the top flight. In fact, Abergavenny Thursdays technically don't exist anymore, having gone out of business in 2013. They've now been replaced in the Welsh pyramid by Abergavenny Town, currently a second-tier outfit.

Goals were in no short supply across the League of Wales in 1992-93. The biggest home win of the season was Ebbw Vale's 10-0 annihilation of Briton Ferry Athletic in January 1993. Prolific striker Steve Woods bagged four that day and ended the campaign as the division's top scorer, with 29 goals in 28 starts for The Cowboys.

The League of Wales' founder clubs also competed for silverware in the Welsh Cup. With the Welsh heavyweights from the English system involved in the competition, the domestic top-flight sides were unfancied and many of them did bow out in the early rounds. Connah's Quay Nomads, however, made it through to the semi-finals where they lost 2-1 over two legs to second-tier Rhyl, formerly of the English pyramid.

In the other semi-final, Cardiff City edged out Wrexham by the same scoreline and went on to lift the trophy thanks to a 5-0 demolition of underdogs Rhyl at the National Stadium.

With a title race to focus on, Cwmbrân made an early exit from the Welsh Cup, going down 1-0 at home to Merthyr Tydfil in round two. That would be little more than a distant memory come the end of the season when they were handed the freshly-forged League of Wales trophy. This was Welsh football history in the making, and it didn't stop there for The Crows.

The following season, they became the first Welsh team to compete in the Champions League, albeit the preliminary stage of it, when they took on Irishmen of Cork City over two legs. Both matches were close encounters, but the tie ended in heartache for Wilcox's men. Despite taking a 3-2 lead into the away leg and drawing first blood on the night, Cork fought back with a pair of goals to level the tie at 4-4, progress on the away goals rule and set up a glamour meeting with Turkish giants Galatasaray in the next round. Parselle's memories of the Cork fixture are not overwhelmingly positive ones, and the reason for this goes beyond the fact that the Irish side emerged victorious.

We had a meeting before the first leg against Cork and were given the chance to cancel our league opener against Connah's Quay because it was only four days before our European match. "What do you want to do lads?' Jimmy Blackie asked. "Oh, come on, let's play. I doubt anyone will get injured" I piped up, but who got injured? Me!

We beat Connah's Quay 1-0 but I did my ankle in. I did actually play in the first leg against Cork despite the injury but I was strapped up to high heaven. I lasted about 60 minutes, my ankle was swollen and I wasn't anywhere near my best, so it was bittersweet for me.

I think when I came off it was 3-1 and it finished 3-2 to us. When we went over to Cork for the second leg I wasn't fit to play. Francis Ford had the chance to score but couldn't beat the keeper from four yards, and then they go and score two in the last 15 minutes. We didn't get to play Galatasaray and they did. I just sat on the bench with my head in my hands.

It was not the last time the talismanic Wilcox would lead The Crows into Europe. In 1999, he enjoyed a career highlight when he lined up in the opposite dugout to legendary manager Kenny Dalglish, as Cwmbrân faced the Scotsman's Celtic side in a UEFA Cup qualifier.

Ahead of the tie, *The Guardian* quoted Wilcox as saying: "Pitting my wits against Dalglish is not exactly the sort of thing that happens every day. We know we have next to no chance against Celtic, but for the players it is an experience they are unlikely to savour again." As the Cwmbrân boss predicted, the Scots coasted through, winning 10-0 on aggregate, though there was no shame in that result for the Welsh underdogs. Celtic regularly pummel Scottish Premiership opposition by the same scoreline that each of the two legs finished.

The Wilcox era is regarded as the most successful in the club's history, but it didn't produce any major silverware besides that inaugural League of Wales title. A few top-five finishes, two Welsh Cup finals, plus a pair of Gwent Senior Cups were as good as it got for The Crows post-1993.

They do, however, share an unlikely record with Italian giants Juventus. Although worlds apart, the two teams are the only sides to have competed in the European Cup, UEFA Cup, Cup Winners' Cup and InterToto Cup, and since most of those tournaments have been abolished, it's safe to say that nobody else will be joining this exclusive club anytime soon.

Wilcox sadly passed away in 2003 at the age of 46 after suffering heart problems, leaving behind a proud legacy. At the time, he was one of only three managers to have led the same club through all 11 top-flight seasons, and he also set a record for number of European qualifications in the League of Wales era with five continental campaigns on his CV.

Legendary Crows boss, Tony Wilcox.
(© Cwmbrân Town AFC)

In addition to his accomplishments on the pitch, Wilcox is fondly remembered as an incredible man off it. Tributes flooded in from across Welsh football when news of his death broke and a minute's silence was held at all League of Wales fixtures the following Saturday. "Tony was the reason I became involved in football in the first place," *WalesOnline* quoted Cwmbrân's then-chairman, John Colley, as saying after Wilcox's death. "I have never met, or am likely to meet, a nicer guy. He was the most genuine man I have ever come across." Parselle, who went on to captain Cwmbrân Town under Wilcox, also remembers his old gaffer fondly:

> *Tony was a great fella, a real diamond. It's a shame he is no longer with us. He was cracking. He was an honest, family man who knew football, and knew exactly the sort of characters who would work well together and play well together.*

A part of Cwmbrân Town died with Wilcox and the club would fall upon hard times in the years after his passing. They plunged into financial difficulty and couldn't afford to keep hold of star players Jody Jenkins and Terry Green the following season. This hurt them on the field, but The Crows' ever-spiralling monetary problems threatened to snuff out their very existence.

Newport County came to Cwmbrân's rescue in the short term, arranging a benefit match between the two teams to help them financially. Despite County's charitable gesture, the stricken Gwent side struggled to replace their key players and were relegated for the first time in 2007, with a grim 5-1 defeat at the hands of Llanelli sealing their fate.

Cwmbrân were unable to arrest the decline that set in around the mid-2000s and tumbled down the Welsh football pyramid after that first relegation. Today, they find themselves in the Premier Division of the Gwent County League, the fourth tier of Welsh domestic football. Parselle believes that his former club are a great loss to the Welsh top flight, and in turn, top flight football is sorely missed in the town of Cwmbrân as well as its wider region:

> *It's a massive loss because if you look at the Welsh top flight and the spread of teams there's nobody in there from the Gwent region. When I was playing, there was Cwmbrân, there was Abergavenny and there was Ebbw Vale, and they were decent teams. I think it's really disappointing that a decent-sized Welsh town like Cwmbrân doesn't have a team in the top division, but hopefully these clubs have ambitions to one day bounce back, and in time we might see another Gwent team up there competing with the best.*

The story that unfolded for Cwmbrân since they became League of Wales founders is one of dizzying highs, European adventures and thrilling cup runs; but it's also a cautionary tale that highlights how difficult it is for clubs in the Welsh football system to get by financially.

They would not be the only club from the national championship to sink in a sea of debt.

League of Wales (1992-93)	P	W	D	L	For	Ag	Pts
1 Cwmbrân Town	38	26	9	3	69	22	87
2 Inter Cardiff	38	26	5	7	79	36	83
3 Aberystwyth Town	38	25	3	10	85	49	78
4 Ebbw Vale AFC	38	19	9	10	76	61	66
5 Bangor City	38	19	7	12	77	58	64
6 Holywell Town	38	17	8	13	65	48	59
7 Conwy United	38	16	9	13	51	51	57
8 Connah's Quay Nomads	38	17	4	17	66	67	55
9 CPD Porthmadog	38	14	11	13	61	49	53
10 Haverfordwest County	38	16	5	17	66	66	53
11 Caersws FC	38	14	10	14	64	60	52
12 Afan Lido FC	38	14	10	14	64	65	52
13 Mold Alexandra	38	16	3	19	63	69	48*
14 Llanelli AFC	38	11	8	19	49	65	41
15 Maesteg Park AFC	38	9	13	16	52	59	40
16 Fflint Town United	38	11	6	21	47	67	39
17 Briton Ferry Athletic	38	10	9	19	61	87	39
18 Newtown AFC	38	9	9	20	55	87	36
19 Llanidloes Town	38	7	9	22	48	93	30
20 Abergavenny Thursdays	38	7	7	24	36	76	38

*3 points deducted for entering administration

4

Back-to-Back Bangor

1993-94

Being branded as title favourites seemingly did Bangor City no favours during the League of Wales' inaugural season. Despite boasting one of the strongest squads in the division and holding their own in the English system for years, they struggled to live up to this billing. Season two of the new top flight was, however, an entirely different story for The Citizens.

Having finished some 23 points behind champions Cwmbrân Town, it was clear that Bangor needed to strengthen over the summer, and they did just that. Manager Paul Rowlands embarked on a recruitment drive which saw steely defender Harry Wiggins, midfield maestro Dave Barnett and goalkeeper Nigel Adkins - formerly of Tranmere Rovers and Wigan Athletic, and later in his career, manager of Southampton - arrive at Farrar Road.

Adkins, an experienced shot-stopper with a proven track record in professional football, turned out to be a pivotal signing for the club, and the story of how he became a Citizen has shades of fate about it. Following an unexpected life event, the Birkenhead-born keeper made the decision to step down from full-time football to care for his family:

My contract was up at Wigan and I was halfway through a part-time honours degree in physiotherapy. We'd just had our second child and my wife had been seriously ill, so I made the decision that I was going to go non-league and that would allow me to look after my family and complete my degree.

The summer period was going to be quite challenging for me anyway because I was working at Arrowe Park Hospital, so it was a conscious decision I made to play part-time football, and I ended up going to Bangor City in the League of Wales.

> *Why the League of Wales? Well, there was the opportunity to challenge for Europe and the club was flexible enough to allow me to finish my degree. This also gave me the chance to think about my career beyond playing football, because I'd had several injuries by this point.*

The Citizens kicked off the campaign with an eventful 3-2 victory away to League Cup holders Afan Lido and followed it up with a 6-1 mauling of Maesteg Park Athletic in their first home match of the season, with Paul Hughes and Steve Buxton both bagging braces. They then completed an impressive August with a 2-1 win over Conwy United on home soil to top the division, but back-to-back away defeats to the previous season's top two - Inter Cardiff and Cwmbrân - brought them back down to earth.

Bouncing back from this setback, Bangor went unbeaten for the remainder of September, although October proved an altogether more difficult month. It began badly with defeat at Ton Pentre, but worse was to follow when team manager, Rowlands, left the club to take the helm at his former employers, Altrincham. Bangor's board believed the ideal candidate to replace him was already on the club's books; Adkins, who explained what happened next:

> *The object for me was to just play football. I was getting paid and I was looking after my family and getting through my degree. Rolo left and went to Altrincham and, basically, the club's hierarchy came to me and said 'will you take over as manager?'.*
>
> *I was quite vocal in goal back then and I was a good communicator. I remember one of the board members, who was a school teacher, said to me 'look, we're really impressed with the way you speak to everyone and organise things, so will you take the job?'*
>
> *I didn't really want to because I knew that in management, I'd be on the phone a lot more often, and have to constantly think about players and tactics. As a goalkeeper, I only had to think about playing, but the player-manager role allowed me to keep doing that.*

Although Adkins was reluctant to take over the Farrar Road hotseat, this wasn't to be his first foray into management. While playing league football in England, he coached a Sunday League side called Renbad Rovers and gained invaluable experience with them. The future Scunthorpe United and Southampton boss guided Renbad Rovers to multiple promotions through the Birkenhead Sunday

Bangor City's title-winning team. (© Steven Humphreys)

League system, and it was at this humble club that he learned many of the fundamentals of football management:

> *When I became player-manager at Bangor City it wasn't an issue to me because, firstly, I'd been playing professional football anyway. Secondly I'd been managing at Sunday league level with Renbad, which taught me that management was all about how you speak to people and this helped me gain experience in coaching. I enjoyed all of that.*

The former Tranmere goalie was quickly installed as The Citizens' player-manager and set to work improving the squad he'd inherited. He bolstered his defence with the acquisition of Wigan duo Jimmy Carberry and Steve Appleton, while the loan signing of Dele Adebola from Crewe Alexandra was a *coup* considering he would ultimately become a highly regarded journeyman in the English Football League and score more than 150 career goals. Adkins' shrewdest signing that campaign was, however, a 21-year-old striker named Frank Mottram, who joined Bangor City in the new year from Welshpool and made an instant impact at his new club, going on to become their leading goalscorer that season.

Having fallen marginally short the previous season, Inter Cardiff proved stern title rivals for Bangor in 1993-94. At one point, The Gulls held a 12-point lead at the top of the table, but The Citizens' form from the beginning of 1994 was sublime. January saw them win six in a row, and they lost just once between then and mid-May as the battle for the title hit a crescendo.

Inter, at this stage, were still top of the pile with 81 points but had played all of their 38 league matches. Bangor, on 77 points, could leapfrog them if they won their two games in hand; but with The Citizens' goal difference lagging eight behind their rivals, this would be no mean feat. Needless to say, nerves were jangling as Bangor's fate lay in their own hands.

Adkins' men welcomed Haverfordwest County to Farrar Road on 14 May looking for a big win to set them on course for a title triumph. They achieved it, and they did it in style. For The Citizens and their fans, the fixture was the stuff footballing dreams are made of. Mottram scored a hat-trick as Bangor thrashed their opponents 9-0. Not only did it set a 'biggest away win' record for the league that would take some beating, it obliterated Inter's goal difference buffer and, as he recalled, it left Adkins' side needing only a draw from their final game:

> *There were TV cameras at the ground for that game and we were absolutely brilliant. We produced good, exciting football that day, played out from the back and just kept going. I remember Jimmy Carberry scoring our ninth from 30 yards. He just lashed it into the top corner. We were a great footballing side, and this game showcased that.*

Their final match was an away clash with mid-table Porthmadog, who had only pride to play for. The relatively short distance for Bangor fans to travel resulted in a crowd of more than 3,500, a staggering number compared to the norm for Welsh top flight fixtures, and Bangor weren't about to bottle it in front of their huge contingent of supporters. Goals from Lee Noble and Mark Rutter clinched the title and capped off a memorable season for Bangor, who finished two points clear of Inter.

According to Adkins, the reported attendance of 3,500 isn't quite accurate. Many more flocked to the ground to see Bangor bag their first league title, but a turnstile-related blunder meant that the official figure for ticket sales was far less than the actual crowd numbers:

I'm sure there were even more than 3,500 in attendance because the turnstiles broke and everyone got in. That was a special evening, that one.

It was a strong campaign all round for Bangor in all three competitions, and for Adkins who continued to produce impressive performances for his team between the sticks, despite having to juggle managerial duties with his role as first-choice goalkeeper. Mottram was also a key figure, averaging a goal a game from January and ending the season with a haul of 16 strikes.

The Citizens were beaten finalists in the second edition of the Welsh League Cup, going down 1-0 to holders Afan Lido, who prolonged their love affair with the trophy to make up for a disappointing league campaign. Adkins' side also had a good run in the Welsh Cup, dumping out Inter Cardiff in the quarter-finals to set up a two-legged semi-final against Barry Town, who were now playing in Welsh League Division One following a U-turn on their decision to remain in English football. Both legs were closely contested, with the first ending 1-1 and Barry edging the second 1-0 in front of their own fans.

This set the stage for a Welsh Cup final between Barry and Cardiff City at the old National Stadium. More than 16,000 fans turned out to watch the second-tier outfit inflict a shock 2-1 defeat on the holders and clinch the cup for the first time since 1955.

Cardiff were hardly a force in the English league system back then, but this was a massive scalp for The Linnets nevertheless. Former Swansea pair David D'Auria and David Hough were on target as the underdogs pulled off a result that sent shockwaves through Welsh football and catapulted Barry into Europe against the odds.

Meanwhile, Bangor and Inter's final league positions earned them European football the following season, and both would enter the UEFA Cup in the preliminary round. It had been a two-horse race for the most part, with third-placed Ton Pentre finishing 10 points behind the runners-up, although this was a significant achievement for the newly-promoted side from the Rhondda.

At the bottom of the table, it was a dismal and frustrating season for Briton Ferry Athletic, who were relegated on the final day, purely because they had a slightly worse goal difference than Maesteg Park directly above them. Unusually, it was not the bottom two who dropped out of the top flight in 1993-94, as 16th-placed Haverfordwest County followed Briton Ferry into Welsh League Division One after resigning from the League of Wales.

Porthmadog's prolific goalscorer, and the League of Wales' top goalscorer in 1993-94, Dave Taylor. (© Rod Davies)

Despite that 9-0 drubbing at the hands of Bangor City towards the end of the campaign, Haverfordwest would ultimately have beaten the drop by seven points, but The Bluebirds from Pembrokeshire were demoted because they were unable to find a suitable temporary venue for their home matches after accepting an offer to have their Bridge Meadow ground redeveloped.

It was an interesting season for Porthmadog and, in particular, their star striker David Taylor. 'Port' may have finished just below mid-table, but they scored goals for fun. Their final tally of 90 was just five shy of top-scoring Inter's, and Taylor claimed an astonishing 43 of those.

The forward's free-scoring heroics earned him the European Golden Shoe at the end of the season. Who'd have imagined that it would end up in Wales that year? In truth, though, an underdog trend continued as the recipients for the next two seasons hailed from the Armenian and Georgian top divisions, respectively. Somebody obviously thought this was making a mockery of the accolade, since the rules were soon changed to introduce a points system that took into account the UEFA coefficients of each league the goals were scored in.

Taylor's record stood for almost a decade, but his scoring days for Porthmadog were done. He joined Inter Cardiff in the summer and later became a journeyman in Welsh football. Also on the move from Porthmadog was Marc Lloyd Williams, who had been Taylor's main source of assists. Buoyed by their league success, Bangor targeted League of Wales domination and Adkins was keen to add to his squad that summer. Williams had caught Adkins' eye and, as the striker recalled, the Bangor manager believed he was just the man to add creativity to his ranks:

> *After previously signing for Bangor two years earlier and leaving without playing I was a bit sceptical of returning. However, due to the European ruling that you could only play a certain number non-Welsh qualified players in European competitions, I thought this could be an opportunity. I spoke to Nigel more than once and he insisted that he wasn't just signing me for the European matches but to be a prominent figure in the league campaign.*

Williams was snapped up along with right-back Kevin Jones from Wrexham and Kevin Langley, an experienced midfielder who won the old English First Division with Everton in the 1980s. It was another fruitful summer of recruitment and Bangor were all the stronger for it.

Nigel Adkins and assistant manager Steve Myers with the League of Wales trophy. (© Steven Humphreys)

League of Wales (1993-94)	P	W	D	L	For	Ag	Pts
1 Bangor City	38	26	5	7	82	26	83
2 Inter Cardiff	38	26	3	9	97	44	81
3 Ton Pentre AFC	38	21	8	9	62	37	71
4 Flint Town United	38	20	6	12	70	47	66
5 Holywell Town	38	18	10	10	74	57	64
6 Newtown AFC	38	18	9	11	52	48	63
7 Connah's Quay Nomads	38	16	11	11	59	47	59
8 Cwmbrân Town	38	16	9	13	51	46	57
9 Ebbw Vale AFC	38	16	9	13	68	66	57
10 Aberystwyth Town	38	15	10	13	57	56	55
11 CPD Porthmadog	38	14	7	17	90	71	49
12 Llanelli AFC	38	14	4	20	76	100	46
13 Conwy United	38	13	6	19	55	70	45
14 Mold Alexandra	38	12	7	19	59	75	43
15 Haverfordwest County	38	10	10	18	40	81	40
16 Caersws FC	38	9	12	17	39	56	39
17 Afan Lido FC	38	8	15	15	52	66	39
18 Llansantffraid FC	38	9	7	22	46	77	34
19 Maesteg Park AFC	38	8	9	21	43	71	33
20 Briton Ferry Athletic	38	8	9	21	53	84	33

1994-95

While the 1993-94 league title could easily have gone Inter Cardiff's way, the 1994-95 campaign was nowhere near as competitive for the club from the Welsh capital. Bangor, however, were almost unstoppable, thanks in no small part to the prolific strike partnership that Mottram instantly forged with Williams. Adkins' new strike force netted 52 times between them and, as the former Bangor manager remembered, the synergy between them helped Mottram top the league's leading goalscorers chart at the end of term:

You always need to score goals and we were fortunate enough to have Marc and Franky Mottram who could both do that. I also took a couple of lads with me from Wigan, so we had a wealth of attacking options. I knew we'd find the net plenty of times.

Reflecting on his deadly strike partnership with Mottram, Williams added:

Without a doubt, Frank Mottram was an integral part of the previous season's title-winning squad, and as a partnership we clicked straight away. Our contrasting styles of play complimented each other very well, and I'd say he's definitely one of the best I've played alongside in the league.

The Citizens lost only once in their opening 10 games to start the campaign in good stead, and they hit a purple patch around the festive period. Between Boxing Day and late February, Bangor City won eight matches in a row to cement their status as title favourites. There was little doubt that they would retain the top prize in Welsh domestic football, least of all when they moved into a 22-point lead at the top of the table.

If there was one negative for Adkins' side in the 1994-95 season, it was losing Marc Lloyd Williams to Stockport County - then of the English Second Division - in March. Bangor did receive £10,000 for the striker, a fair sum by early League of Wales standards, and were already well on the way to reclaiming the title when he departed, though there was no denying that the club would miss his flair, creativity and proven ability to find the back of the net.

Bangor's European adventure was memorable but short-lived. They were drawn against Icelandic champions ÍA Akranes in the preliminary round of the UEFA Cup and were dumped out 4-1 on aggregate. The first leg, at Farrar Road, which ended in a 2-1 loss, attracted a crowd of 3,426.

Things might have been different if Adkins' side hadn't been hamstrung by UEFA's foreign players rule. Their squad had a large contingent of Englishmen, but the player-coach was unwilling to base his summer transfer strategy around a two-legged European

Frank Mottram, the League of Wales' top goalscorer in 1994-95. (© Welsh Football Magazine)

fixture, so The Citizens' management setup had tough decisions to make on starting XIs.

The former Bangor boss also confessed to being unprepared for the first leg against Akranes. As their Farrar Road ground was council-owned, it could be difficult to secure use of it at short notice for pre-season friendlies, so warm-up opportunities were limited. A Frank Mottram consolation goal in the first leg gave Citizens fans something to pin their hopes on in the land of fire and ice, but overturning the deficit on the road was a big ask. This was one Icelandic mountain that Adkins and his charges found too steep to climb, but the Bangor boss insisted that his side were unlucky to bow out on the night:

> *We went over to Iceland and it was difficult to anticipate what Akranes were going to do with set pieces and things because there was no footage of them available. I remember we conceded from a corner and Lee Noble got sent off with the scoreline at 0-0. The pitch was a bowling green and, technically, they were absolutely brilliant.*
>
> *At half time, I told my players to just go man-to-man, go on the counter-attack and see if we can score. We were so unlucky. Honestly, we did really really well, but just fell short.*

Despite this disappointment in the UEFA Cup, Adkins' Citizens secured back-to-back League of Wales title wins in relentless fashion, and with two matches remaining, thanks to a 4-1 victory over Conwy United in April, with Buxton and Rutter scoring the goals. As Adkin's fondly recalled, an 8-0 away demolition of Connah's Quay Nomads followed and saw Bangor lifting the trophy before the final fixture of the season:

> *That season, we were by far the best team in the league. We smashed everyone. It really was as simple as that. We were a good team, and that's exactly what it was. We were a team. We didn't just hoof it, we played out from the back, had some good players, some great goalscorers, and were well organised in defence. I think we only conceded 26 goals all season.*

While Adkins was keen to highlight the camaraderie among his squad and the quality of the football they produced, one of his star players, Williams - who went on to become the league's all-time record goalscorer - was quick to hail the manager for his role in that title success, praising his recruitment and positivity on and off the field:

To be honest, he trusted the ability of the players he had, he let us express ourselves on the pitch and was forever positive with the players. He had a good balance of experienced and young players and had the contacts to bring in quality players to the club when needed.

Bangor won the 1994-95 league by nine points, with an impressive Afan Lido finishing second and securing a place in the preliminary round of the UEFA Cup qualifiers. Ton Pentre matched the previous season's accomplishment by retaining third place which, that season, came with the added bonus of entry into the qualification round of the Intertoto Cup. The Rhondda outfit also reached the Welsh League Cup final, but were beaten 2-1 by Llansantffraid FC - later to become The New Saints - at Newtown's Latham Park ground.

Inter Cardiff's first two seasons in the League of Wales were stories of 'nearly' and 'almost', but in 1994-95, they were off the pace throughout and only managed a mid-table finish. Three places and six points above them, newly-promoted Barry Town enjoyed a respectable debut in the division, and would go on to accomplish much greater things in the near future.

At the foot of the table, Maesteg Park racked up the lowest points total the competition had seen so far, with just 12 on the board. The Park, who had only won twice all season, dropped into Welsh League Division One, while 19th-placed Mold Alexandra fell into the Cymru Alliance.

In the Welsh Cup, none of the League of Wales sides made it past the quarter-finals as their neighbours from the English leagues dominated the competition. Bangor did, as Adkins recalled, do themselves proud by taking eventual winners Wrexham to a replay in the last eight following a 2-2 draw at Farrar Road, but The Dragons edged the replay 1-0 via a Kieron Durkan goal to set up a semi-final against Merthyr, who had knocked out Ton Pentre in the quarters:

I remember the Wrexham game at our place was a full house. There was a big crowd to spur us on in that cup quarter-final. The pitch was really muddy, I seem to recall, but I saved a penalty and we should have beaten them on the night.

We went to their place for the replay and it was another good game, which they narrowly won 1-0. We gave a great account of ourselves against a strong Football League side and these were memorable matches for me even though the outcome wasn't what we wanted.

Farrar Road, the home of Bangor City until 2011. (© MadSproute)

In the other quarter-finals, Swansea City hit Porthmadog for eight without reply and Cardiff City edged past Llandudno 1-0 on their way to the final. In the semi-finals Wrexham beat Merthyr 4-1 over two legs but there was only one goal in it between arch rivals Cardiff and Swansea. The Bluebirds reached the showpiece courtesy of a stunning strike from Paul Miller - a deft lob from just inside the opposition's half - in the first leg at the Vetch Field.

The final took place at the National Stadium in front of over 11,000 fans with Wrexham securing the trophy thanks to a 2-1 victory courtesy of a double from Gary Bennett, his first coming from the penalty spot. This was a record 23rd Welsh Cup victory for The Dragons, but it would be their last.

The following season, only clubs playing in the Welsh system were eligible to enter the cup and this meant that fans of Cardiff and Swansea would never see their teams feature in the competition again. Wrexham, along with some of the English non-leaguers, did make another appearance 15 years later when the rules were briefly relaxed, but failed to recapture the glory their fans were accustomed to in the historic tournament.

As for Adkins, he left Farrar Road in February 1996 and completed his training as a physiotherapist before joining Scunthorpe United in that capacity. He got the chance to test his managerial mettle in the English Football League when Brian Laws left The Iron's dugout in 2006, and a successful career that has included stints with Southampton, Reading, Sheffield United, Hull City and Charlton Athletic continued to blossom over the border.

Adkins, who was inducted into Welsh Premier League Hall of Fame in 2013, became the first manager to coach in both the English and Welsh top flights when he guided The Saints to promotion from the Championship as runners-up in 2012 - and, today, he remains a shining example of the calibre of manager that Welsh domestic football has helped produce.

League of Wales (1994-95)		P	W	D	L	For	Ag	Pts
1	Bangor City	38	27	7	4	96	26	88
2	Afan Lido FC	38	24	7	7	60	36	79
3	Ton Pentre AFC	38	23	8	7	84	50	77
4	Newtown AFC	38	20	8	10	78	47	68
5	Cwmbrân Town	38	20	7	11	69	49	67
6	Flint Town United	38	20	3	15	77	60	63
7	Barry Town	38	16	11	11	71	57	59
8	Holywell Town	38	16	10	12	62	55	58
9	Llansantffraid FC	38	15	10	13	57	57	55
10	Inter Cardiff	38	14	11	13	58	43	53
11	Rhyl FC	38	16	5	17	74	69	53
12	Conwy United	38	14	7	17	60	65	49
13	Ebbw Vale AFC	38	12	9	17	51	57	45
14	Caersws FC	38	11	11	16	57	64	44
15	Connah's Quay Nomads	38	12	7	19	57	79	43
16	CPD Porthmadog	38	11	7	20	57	73	40
17	Aberystwyth Town	38	9	12	17	57	75	39
18	Llanelli AFC	38	10	6	22	64	104	36
19	Mold Alexandra	38	10	4	24	57	90	34
20	Maesteg Park AFC	38	2	6	30	23	113	12

5

The Professionals

1995-96

The League of Wales was always diminutive in stature compared to many of its continental counterparts, yet throughout its early years it was quickly gaining traction. This was plain to see in 1995 when one of its member clubs took on full-time professional status.

Good times were rolling for Barry Town following their move back to the Welsh system in 1993, and while their first season in the top flight was unspectacular, bigger things were on the horizon when they stepped up to professional football for the 1995-96 campaign, and this marked the beginning of a decade of dominance for the club that is known to some as The Linnets, and others The Dragons.

Forward Paul Giles was named as player-manager for the new season with his older brother, David, as his assistant, and under their stewardship Barry Town's squad of full-timers were unstoppable. The new management team turned heads during the close season with a host of transfer *coups* from the English Football League, including striker Tony Bird from Cardiff City, goalkeeper Mark Ovendale from Northampton Town and midfielder Gary Barnett from Leyton Orient.

Midfielder Darren Ryan, who joined The Dragons from Chester City the following year, shared his experiences at Jenner Park and offered insight into the appeal of Barry Town for ex-Football League professionals during the mid-90s:

> *The level of professionalism at the club was so high and the quality of the players was really good, and I can say that having played in the English Football League. Having the chance to compete for Europe was also a big pull for me. I hadn't done it before, so that was a big part of the appeal, along with being able to stay in the full-time game.*

The difference in class between Barry and their rivals was often apparent on the pitch as Giles' men coasted to the 1995-96 league

Barry Town in action at Newtown during the 1995-96 campaign. (© Welsh Football Magazine)

title. By early February, the final standings were taking shape and The Linnets looked unmovable at the summit following a lengthy unbeaten spell. Flint Town United had an outside chance of catching them, but had played two games more, and early pace-setters Ebbw Vale had fallen to midtable after eight straight defeats.

It was plain sailing for Barry from here as they glided across the finish line. Ovendale conceded just 23 times as the team won 30 out of their 40 league matches, tasting defeat only three times along the way: going down 1-0 at Bangor, as well as losing at home to Cemaes Bay and Flint Town, the latter of which was a 5-1 drubbing that went down as one of the shock results of the season. The Dragons ended the season 17 points ahead of runners-up Newtown, who would join Barry in the UEFA Cup qualifiers. Meanwhile, Conwy United finished third and booked a spot in the Intertoto Cup qualifiers, inspired by the performances of 38-goal striker Ken McKenna. Dethroned champions Bangor were seven points worse off in fourth, marking a disappointing campaign for them.

At the other end of the table, there was a catastrophic decline for Afan Lido. Despite finishing second the season before, and winning the first two editions of the League Cup back-to-back, Lido finished in 20th place in the newly-expanded 21-team top flight and dropped into the Welsh League Division One - along with bottom club Llanelli - where they'd remain for two years.

The League Cup was won by Connah's Quay Nomads, marking their first silverware of the League of Wales era. The Nomads had progressed to the knockout stages from a group with Rhyl, Flint and Holywell, but their league form suffered as they edged towards the final. They did arrest their decline in the weeks leading up to the big event, putting them in good stead for the final against Ebbw Vale, who they had narrowly pipped to 10th in the league. The two teams contested the trophy at Caersws' Recreation Ground with The Nomads coming out on top, 1-0, thanks to a second-half strike from Peter Hughes.

Meanwhile, Barry were courting double honours, going all the way to the final in the Welsh Cup, which no longer included those previously dominant Welsh teams who played over the border. After wrapping up the league comfortably several weeks earlier, Giles' squad of full-time pros were huge favourites to add the coveted trophy to their 1995-96 honours list.

Their opponents in the final were Llansantffraid FC, back then football minnows from a border village with a population of 1,000 who had just finished 12th in the League of Wales. That Welsh Cup final was the last to be played at the National Stadium and the result was one of the biggest upsets the competition has ever seen. Just as Barry had stunned Football League neighbours Cardiff to clinch the trophy two years earlier, Llansantffraid defied the odds and beat The Linnets 3-2 on penalties following a 3-3 thriller in front of 2,666 fans.

Goalkeeper Andy Mulliner was the hero for Llansantffraid, bouncing back from putting through his own net during normal time to save Dave Withers' spot-kick in sudden death and secure cup glory for the underdogs, as well as an unlikely ticket into Europe. Speaking about that shock defeat to a village team, Darren Ryan, who joined Barry that summer, said:

> *Although the Llansantffraid defeat came shortly before I joined Barry, it was still being talked about after I arrived. I don't think it went down very well with the owners. I remember we drew them again in the cup the following season and the owners made a point of telling us to ensure there wasn't a repeat result.*

It was a season of highs for Barry, but there were lows too, and the tragedy the team endured off the pitch was far more significant than cup final heartbreak. Chairman Neil O'Halloran passed away in October 1995, and in April of the following year, young midfielder Matthew Holtham was killed in a road traffic collision on his way back from an away fixture.

The club paid tribute to the pair in the best possible way: by going from strength to strength on the pitch and making history. O'Halloran's widow, Paula, took over the ownership of the team and was hands-on in running

Barry Town players celebrating their 1995-96 title triumph. (© Welsh Football Magazine)

the club. One of the first big decisions she had to make was naming a new manager following the departure of Giles at the end of the season.

League of Wales (1995-96)		P	W	D	L	For	Ag	Pts
1	Barry Town	40	30	7	3	92	23	97
2	Newtown AFC	40	23	11	6	69	25	80
3	Conwy United	40	21	13	6	101	58	76
4	Bangor City	40	21	6	13	72	65	69
5	Flint Town United	40	19	9	12	76	57	66
6	Caernarfon Town	40	16	13	11	77	59	61
7	Cwmbrân Town	40	14	15	11	58	49	57
8	Inter Cardiff	40	14	12	14	62	62	54
9	Caersws FC	40	15	9	16	81	97	54
10	Connah's Quay Nomads	40	13	14	13	68	63	53
11	Ebbw Vale AFC	40	14	11	15	59	56	53
12	Llansantffraid FC	40	14	10	16	66	57	52
13	CPD Porthmadog	40	13	11	16	56	62	50
14	Aberystwyth Town	40	13	9	18	60	68	48
15	Cemaes Bay FC	40	13	7	20	63	80	46
16	Holywell Town	40	12	7	21	53	74	43
17	Briton Ferry Athletic	40	11	9	20	64	91	42
18	Rhyl FC	40	11	9	20	47	83	42
19	Ton Pentre AFC	40	8	16	16	46	65	40
20	Afan Lido FC	40	9	9	22	33	71	36
21	Llanelli AFC	40	8	9	23	50	88	33

1996-97

The Dragons' hierarchy had big ambitions and set their sights on competing in Europe. Although successful during their time at Jenner Park, the Giles brothers were not seen as the men to fulfil those ambitions and a change in the dugout was deemed necessary. A move, as Ryan recalls, that the brothers didn't see coming:

> *I came in after they had left, but I can tell you that Paul and David Giles made a very big impression at Jenner Park. I got to know both of them when I moved to the town and I played with, and for, Paul Giles afterwards. They are great guys with massive personalities, and they were absolutely devastated about being dismissed.*

Once again, Barry recruited from within and named Gary Barnett as player-manager. The veteran midfielder had extensive Football League experience under his belt, enjoying spells with Oxford United, Fulham, Huddersfield and Leyton Orient before joining The Dragons, but he was an outsider for the managerial hotseat given his lack of coaching experience.

O'Halloran's decision to take a punt on Barnett proved to be a smart move. His appointment ushered in a golden era for Barry Town, who broke record after record under his watch. Ryan, who is now a youth coach at Wolverhampton Wanderers, was one of Barnett's first recruits, and the former Chester man was full of praise for his old Linnets gaffer.

> *Gary's man management was one of his biggest strengths but he was a top coach as well. He knew exactly how he wanted us to play and you could see that in our games. We played some great football at times, with an emphasis on dominating possession. He knew how to get the best out of individuals, as did his assistant, Richard Jones, who he worked well with. Gary dealt with the challenges of being a full-time coach really well.*

The 1996-97 season was a significant one for the League of Wales. For the first time since its formation, results were featured on the Press Association's vidiprinter service, which saw the scores appear on televised football shows including the BBC's *Final Score* and Sky Sports' *Soccer Saturday*. This was a boost for the competition that helped raise its profile.

Around the same time, video game developers began to include the Welsh top flight in their products, with *Sensible World of Soccer* among the first to feature the clubs, and management sims, such as the *Championship Manager* series, going on to do the same, but it was Barry's feats that season which truly put the League of Wales on the footballing map.

In the summer of 1996 Barry became the first team from the new league to win a European qualifier when they defeated Latvia's Dinaburg 2-1 on aggregate. All of the goals came in the away leg, with Chris Pike and Craig Evans on target, as Barry made history on the continent. The significance of the result was not lost on Ryan, or his Barry teammates:

I've got great memories of that European campaign. Not many Welsh teams have pulled off results like we produced against that standard of opposition. I think the teams we faced were surprised at just how good we were. We had a few ex-Football League players in our ranks and were full time, but our opponents were taken aback nonetheless.

Next up for The Linnets was Hungarian outfit Vasutas, who were red-hot favourites to progress from the preliminary matches to the first round of the competition. Things went to script in the first leg in Budapest as Barry Town went down 3-1, but a spirited performance at Jenner Park saw Barnett's men pull off an unlikely fightback. They won the return fixture by the same scoreline to force extra time and penalties, and triumphed 4-2 in the shootout. Pike and Evans were on target again, with David O'Gorman also finding the net for the battling hosts in normal time.

If a team from England had pulled off a European comeback of this magnitude, it would have whipped the media into a frenzy. The back pages would likely have been awash with headlines proclaiming it a "miracle", but Barry's accomplishment received little publicity, as Ryan recalled:

The stand-out result was that Vasutas one. We were 3-1 down from the first leg and lost Gary Lloyd through suspension. But we went into the return leg on the front foot and overturned that deficit before putting them out on penalties. That was a great night and it deserved to make headlines!

The yellow-clad army did earn some press coverage as they marched proudly into the first round to play fellow Celts Aberdeen, managed by Roy Aitken. Needless to say, The Dons were expected to steamroller their Welsh opponents, but Barry made a fight of the first leg. Richard Jones scored in the first half at Pittodrie to cancel out Dean Windass' opener, and although it finished 3-1 to the hosts, The Linnets earned plaudits for their performance.

The return leg was a thrilling affair at a packed, rain-drenched Jenner Park. Barry fought tooth and nail and proved Aberdeen's equals on the night. They looked to have edged the match 3-2 when Tony Bird netted late on, only for David Rowson to score at the other end a minute later to level things at 3-3 and knock Barry out by a respectable 6-4 on aggregate. Ryan Commented:

> *The Aberdeen nights were incredible too. We narrowly lost up there. Richard Jones scored an absolute wonder goal but we conceded two really sloppy ones in the second half. I think that tie was ultimately lost in that first leg, but we gave a great account of ourselves at Jenner Park when we drew 3-3 with them. We should have won that match. They were great experiences in Europe and I think they set us up to go on to achieve what we achieved that season.*

Memorable European nights became a running theme at Jenner Park throughout the club's golden age, but, as Ryan points out, life was peachy for Barry fans on the homefront too. In fact, their 1996-97 campaign was flawless as they pulled off a clean sweep of the main domestic trophies, bringing home the league title, the Welsh Cup and the League Cup.

Milestones were passed and records tumbled along the way. Barry won the league with an unprecedented haul of 105 points, 19 more than perennial bridesmaids Inter Cardiff in second. They also set a record for goals scored with 129 - 42 of which were netted by top scorer Tony Bird - but would break it by five in '97-98 as their runaway success continued.

En-route to the league title, Barry were involved in the first televised League of Wales match, a home showdown against Caernarfon Town which attracted a record crowd of 2,746 to Jenner Park. As Ryan recalled, Barry coasted to a 5-2 win to consolidate their position at the top of the table:

That Caernarfon Town game originally got cancelled because of a frozen pitch. I remember us trying to get the match on but it was pushed back. The rearranged fixture was our first televised League of Wales game.

That was a great day and a good spectacle to show how the league was improving. Having a full-time team in there made it a good advert for the competition. We went on to sign Eifion Williams, who played against us in that match, based on how he performed that season.

An open-top bus tour to celebrate Barry Town's treble-winning 1996-97 season. (© Welsh Football Magazine)

Bangor City - who had an indifferent league campaign by their own standards, ultimately finishing eighth - were Barry's opponents in the League Cup final and held The Linnets to a 2-2 draw after extra time, but Barnett's men were victorious on penalties, winning 4-2. Barry went on to defeat the same opponents in the '97-98 final, once again on penalties. Ryan - who scored Barry's equaliser in extra time to force a 2-2 draw in the first of those two finals - admits that Bangor City were hard done by to finish the 1996-97 season empty handed:

> *If I'm being honest, they should have beaten us in that League Cup final at Aberystwyth as they were the better team. We won on penalties in the end, but Marc Lloyd Williams caused us all sorts of problems that day. They deserved to win it.*

Barry's opposition in the Welsh Cup final was the League of Wales' inaugural winners, Cwmbrân Town. The teams clashed at Cardiff's Ninian Park in front of more than 1,500 fans. It was the first time the final had been contested there since the 1950s, and it was a close fought affair. The Linnets took an early lead through Cohen Griffith, but Chris Watkins equalised in the second period. Yet Barry, at the peak of their power, weren't about to let a domestic treble go begging, and they forced a winner with 20 minutes left, Griffith again being the goalscorer, as Ryan fondly reminisced:

> *Winning the treble was amazing. Cwmbrân pushed us really close in that cup final. It wasn't a great game but we managed to get over the line. We were lucky that we always had players on the bench who could come on and make a difference. I think Cohen Griffith might have come on as a substitute in that game and scored two. We also had Chris Pike and Tony Bird, and that shows our strength in depth.*

League of Wales (1996-97)		P	W	D	L	For	Ag	Pts
1	Barry Town	40	33	6	1	129	26	105
2	Inter Cardiff	40	26	6	8	80	32	84
3	Ebbw Vale AFC	40	23	9	8	87	40	78
4	Caernarfon Town	40	23	9	8	81	58	78
5	Newtown AFC	40	22	5	13	74	49	71
6	Total Network Solutions	40	19	12	9	78	54	69
7	Conwy United	40	20	8	12	66	44	68
8	Bangor City	40	20	5	15	82	62	65
9	Cwmbrân Town	40	19	8	13	71	61	65
10	Porthmadog FC	40	18	8	14	64	60	62
11	Connah's Quay Nomads	40	16	9	15	62	64	57
12	Cemaes Bay FC	40	13	10	17	62	72	49
13	Aberystwyth Town	40	13	8	19	67	82	47
14	Caersws FC	40	11	9	20	53	77	42
15	Flint Town United	40	11	8	21	48	76	41
16	Carmarthen Town	40	11	7	22	41	79	40
17	Welshpool Town	40	10	9	21	50	80	39
18	Ton Pentre AFC	40	12	3	25	59	99	39
19	Rhyl FC	40	10	8	22	51	71	38
20	Holywell Town	40	7	8	25	52	81	29
21	Briton Ferry Athletic	40	5	1	34	39	129	16

1997-98

The 1997-98 season saw a league-and-cup double for Barry as they won the League of Wales - with a points total of 104, only one less than the previous term - and the League Cup thanks to that

Barry Town were presented with the 1997-98 league trophy by former FAW president Brian Fear during a presentation dinner. (© Welsh Football Magazine)

aforementioned penalty-shootout victory over Bangor. They were, however, knocked out of the Welsh Cup at the semi-final stage by Connah's Quay Nomads.

The Nomads went on to lose the final to Bangor 4-2 on penalties after a 1-1 draw at Wrexham's Racecourse Ground. The Citizens, who were then managed by former Everton star Graeme Sharp, edged the shootout to ensure the Scot's single season in charge ended on a positive note with major silverware in the bag and European qualification secured.

Other highlights from Barry's 1997-98 campaign included a two-legged European clash against Ukrainian giants Dynamo Kyiv - which ended 6-0 to Kyiv on aggregate and saw top-class international players like Serhiy Rebrov and Oleh Luzhnyi visit Jenner Park - and their debut in the Invitation Cup, later to become the Premier Cup, a new competition founded by the FAW.

The FAW Premier Cup was an annual addition to the domestic football calendar. The idea was to have a cup competition where the Welsh teams playing in England, that were now excluded from the Welsh Cup, could compete with the best the League of Wales had to offer.

Barry Town's Eifion Williams receiving the 1997-98 Golden Boot. (© Welsh Football Magazine)

The inaugural edition featured two groups of four teams followed by a knockout stage. Barry finished top of Group A, ahead of Bangor, Swansea and Conwy United, recording an impressive 2-1 victory over the Football League-based Swans along the way, but their campaign came to an end at the quarter-final stage, losing 1-0 to Merthyr at Jenner Park. Chris Summers scored the decisive goal in extra time. Reflecting on the 1997-98 season, Ryan commented:

That was a hit and miss season for me. I got sent off in Europe against Kyiv in the second leg for something stupid and then we lost to Merthyr Tydfil in the Premier Cup. Our exit in the semi-finals of the Welsh Cup was another tough one to take, but I have to give credit to Connah's Quay for the way they played in that game. They really did their homework on us and stopped us. They went through and deservedly so, but obviously doing the double that season helped us put that result behind us.

The number of clubs in the League of Wales fluctuated during this period, either because of teams hopping the fence from the English system, or clubs folding. At the end of the 1997-98 season, four clubs - Porthmadog, Flint Town, Welshpool Town and Cemaes Bay - were relegated as the FAW reduced the division to 18 teams. That was the plan, at least, but Ebbw Vale were later expelled from the top flight due to financial difficulties that ultimately forced them to fold, which meant that the 1998-99 campaign would only feature 17 clubs.

League of Wales (1997-98)	P	W	D	L	For	Ag	Pts
1 Barry Town	38	33	5	0	134	31	104
2 Newtown AFC	38	23	9	6	101	47	78
3 Ebbw Vale AFC	38	22	11	5	94	55	77
4 Inter Cardiff	38	23	5	10	58	28	74
5 Cwmbrân Town	38	22	7	9	78	47	73
6 Bangor City	38	20	8	10	72	54	68
7 Connah's Quay Nomads	38	18	12	8	75	54	66
8 Rhyl FC	38	17	10	11	61	49	61
9 Conwy United	38	15	8	15	66	59	53
10 Aberystwyth Town	38	13	12	13	64	63	51
11 Caersws FC	38	14	4	20	64	71	46
12 Carmarthen Town	38	11	11	16	57	72	44
13 Caernarfon Town	38	12	7	19	57	66	43
14 Total Network Solutions	38	9	15	14	54	67	42
15 Rhayader Town	38	11	6	21	55	78	39
16 Haverfordwest County	38	10	8	20	54	87	38
17 Porthmadog FC	38	10	5	23	55	77	35
18 Flint Town United	38	9	7	22	50	77	34
19 Welshpool Town	38	6	7	25	55	97	25
20 Cemaes Bay FC	38	2	3	33	30	155	9

1998-99

Amid these ups and downs, all-conquering Barry continued to dominate like a shark in a goldfish pond, and made it four league titles on the bounce in 1999, though not by anywhere near the same points total in the newly streamlined division. They ended the campaign with 76 points, which was still 13 more than second-placed Inter Cardiff could muster.

There was another milestone for the club in this period as defender Gary Lloyd became the first League of Wales player to earn a call-up to the Wales senior squad, when he was an unused substitute in a fixture against Belgium. At the time, some dismissed Lloyd's inclusion as a publicity stunt by national team head coach, Bobby Gould, but Ryan begs to differ:

I disagree that it was a publicity stunt. A few league clubs came in for Gary. He was a really good technical player. It was great for the league, but he thoroughly deserved to be in the squad. It's a shame he didn't kick on from there and win full international caps.

For me, Gary should have played in the English Football League and he did have a few opportunities to go there. A couple of clubs came in for him, but it wasn't worth his while to move somewhere so far away from where he was living at the time when we were making a good full-time living at Barry. He was a really good player, though.

However, it wouldn't be long until a player from the division would receive a senior international cap, though it wouldn't be in the iconic red shirt of Wales. That honour went to Bangor City striker Samuel Ayorinde, who earned two full caps for Nigeria during his career, one of which while he was playing for The Citizens.

One of the undisputed highlights of Barry Town's golden era was an awe-inspiring unbeaten run that spanned 51 league matches - nine more times than Brian Clough's legendary Nottingham Forest side managed in the late 1970s. It began with a 1-0 win over Llansantffraid in 1997-98 and rolled on until three games into the 1998-99 campaign when Afan Lido brought it to an abrupt halt, emerging as unlikely 2-0 winners at Jenner Park.

Along the way, they bested some opponents by jaw-dropping scorelines, including a 10-0 dismantling of Llansantffraid in 1997 and a 12-0 victory over Cemaes Bay in early 1998.

Their record unbeaten run may have ended, but Barry's trophy-winning feats continued while Barnett was at the helm, adding another League Cup to their collection by thrashing Caernarfon 3-0 in the final, and also bringing home the FAW Premier Cup at the second time of asking after stunning Wrexham 2-1 in the final at the Racecourse Ground.

The Premier Cup final, which took place on 23 May, was closely contested. The two teams went into the break goalless, but Barry were quick to shatter the deadlock in the second period. Justin Perry opened the scoring for the Welsh champions before Karl Connolly drew the Football League side level from the penalty spot with just over 15 minutes left to play. The winning goal came in the 84th minute, and it arrived via an unlikely source. Centre-back Lee Barrow had the final say that day, nodding home a late corner to make it 2-1 to The Dragons and add yet another cup to Barry Town's rapidly-growing honours list.

The only domestic trophy they didn't get their hands on that year was the Welsh Cup, which went to Inter Cable-Tel - the moniker Inter Cardiff assumed for a short time after entering a sponsorship agreement - following a penalty-shootout victory over Carmarthen Town.

During this period of extended dominance, some referred to Barry Town as "The Manchester United of Wales", while others hailed the League of Wales champions as the best team in Wales, including those playing in the English league system. Ryan agrees with this, and points to some of The Dragons' European scalps and victories over the Welsh clubs competing in England as evidence to back up such bold claims:

The Barry Town squad in 1999, with the League of Wales Cup, FAW Premier Cup and League of Wales trophy. (© WikiCommons)

When we beat Swansea City in the FAW Cup, I remember their manager, Jan Molby, saying on the TV afterwards, 'they've got better players than us'. The fact that we played Football League clubs in the Premier Cup and beat them shows how good we were. It was a credit to us and our manager that we built such a strong squad.

There would be more silverware and European glory to come for Barry, but the thing about golden eras is that they always come to an end; and sadly, this has proven especially true for Welsh domestic teams who've attempted to go full time. For the clubs' fans, this period is unforgettable, but the hardships and injustices that followed also live long in their memories.

	League of Wales (1998-99)	P	W	D	L	For	Ag	Pts
1	Barry Town	32	23	7	2	82	23	76
2	Inter Cardiff	32	19	6	7	61	26	63
3	Cwmbrân Town	32	17	6	9	73	44	57
4	Aberystwyth Town	32	16	9	7	59	47	57
5	Caernarfon Town	32	13	11	8	45	46	50
6	Newtown AFC	32	13	10	9	45	35	49
7	Conwy United	32	14	7	11	54	49	49
8	Total Network Solutions	32	12	11	9	55	42	47
9	Carmarthen Town	32	13	8	11	46	46	47
10	Caersws FC	32	12	8	12	49	55	44
11	Bangor City	32	11	6	15	44	49	39
12	Connah's Quay Nomads	32	10	8	14	43	46	38
13	Haverfordwest County	32	9	7	16	43	60	43
14	Afan Lido	32	7	10	15	28	46	31
15	Rhayader Town	32	5	11	16	29	54	26
16	Rhyl FC	32	7	2	23	40	80	23
17	Holywell Town	32	3	9	20	38	86	18

6

The Company Men

1999-2000

As the turn of the millennium approached, a new power emerged in Welsh domestic football, and it came from an unlikely source. Llansantffraid is a humble Welsh village in Powys, a few miles from the border and the English county of Shropshire, but its football team, Llansantffraid FC, earned a prominent dot on the sporting map following that shock victory over Barry Town in the 1996 Welsh Cup final.

Prior to this, Llansantffraid had enjoyed a meteoric rise through the league system, starting in the Montgomeryshire Amateur Football League and clawing their way up three divisions to the League of Wales in 1992-93, while bagging a Welsh Intermediate Cup along the way.

It was quite the journey for the villagers, and a rewarding one too. After the dust from their glorious giant killing of Barry Town had settled, the club secured a shirt sponsorship agreement with Oswestry-based telecommunications firm, Total Network Solutions (TNS), and this eventually evolved into something much bigger and far more lucrative, as Mike Harris - the founder of TNS - explains:

> They were looking for a shirt sponsor and my company said "okay let's give it a go". They were based locally to us, no more than seven miles away, so we gave them a helping hand. The following year, they came back and asked us to renew our sponsorship, but from our perspective, local advertising on the shirt of a team from what was then a relatively small league was not something we were going to do again.
>
> They were disappointed we declined to renew, so we suggested changing their name to our company name as a counteroffer. We didn't expect to ever hear from them again, but within about two hours I had a phone call from Llansantffraid's club president, Mike Hughes, who said: "I've spoken about it with the committee, and we'll go with it", so we put together a deal that changed the name of the team to Total Network Solutions.

Treflan, the original home of Llansantffraid FC. (© David Luther Thomas)

Bankrolled by telecoms cash, TNS manager Graham Breeze led his players into Europe for the first time, taking on Polish outfit Ruch Chorzów in the Cup Winners' Cup. The village team fought well in the first leg, and snatched a late equaliser through Leslie Thomas to draw 1-1. Despite losing 5-0 in the away leg, and being eliminated by six goals to one on aggregate, the people of Llansantffraid were proud of their football team's accomplishments.

When the club entered that sponsorship agreement, they officially became Total Network Solutions Llansantffraid FC. There are high-profile examples of football teams named after their sponsors around the world, from Philips-backed PSV Eindhoven in the Netherlands to Red Bull's portfolio of clubs in various countries; but this was a first for football in Britain.

A year later, the village's name was dropped altogether from their moniker and the team was renamed Total Network Solutions FC, or TNS, an abbreviation that was necessary when playing in Europe due to UEFA's regulations on third-party sponsorship. According to Harris, the big rebranding didn't go down well with everyone:

If you're successful at doing something, your competitors are going to slag you off. When we were a small village team who got turned over on a regular basis, people were like "oh aren't they a nice little old team". But as soon as we were a threat to them, the way the rest of Welsh football perceived us changed very quickly.

I think there was a certain amount of jealousy towards us when we started to grow into a force. Locally, within the community, some people bought into it and others didn't. You're never going to please everybody, but at the end of the day, football requires money to operate. No football club at any level competes solely with what they get through the gates.

It was a calculated risk by the club's board to allow that name change, and ultimately, it was a very wise move on their part because the success they strived for came about.

Llansantffraid's Welsh Cup-winning side of 1996. (© Phil Blagg)

Over the next few seasons, the money invested in TNS helped the club amass a squad with professional experience, although they were not yet full-timers at this point. Veteran midfielder Tony Henry, formerly of Manchester City, was appointed as manager in 1997, and he quickly assembled a team that was capable of challenging Barry Town's throne.

Defender Timothy Alexander had played for Wimbledon early in his career, Darren Ryan - recruited from Barry Town - had featured for Chester, Shrewsbury and Stockport, and striker Gary Powell began his career at Everton, though never made a senior appearance for them.

The Total Network Solutions FC side of 1999-2000 packed impressive pedigree and proved capable of going toe-to-toe with the League of Wales' all-conquering champions. This was evident throughout the season as Henry's side kept up the pace with The Linnets week in, week out, matching or bettering their results almost every weekend.

It was the closest title race so far and it all came down to a nail-biting final round of fixtures. The two contenders were in action on different days, with TNS up first, taking on Rhayader Town away from home on 24th April. They edged the match 1-0 to move two points ahead of Barry in the standings, but The Dragons still had one more match to play, a crunch clash away to Connah's Quay five days later. Nothing but a win would do for Barry and a crowd of 688 showed up to witness the title decider, a much bigger attendance than the 200 or so that typically frequented Deeside Stadium back then.

Having secured four titles in a row, The Linnets were expected to make it five out of five, but there was a shock on the cards that day. A brace from Nomads forward Stuart Rain stunned Barry, sealed a deserved victory for the hosts and handed a first league title to TNS, as Harris recalled:

> Even coming second would have been an achievement, so a lot of us went out the night before to celebrate. We went on to Connah's Quay to watch the Barry game the day after, clinging onto the very slim chance that we might get something out of it.
>
> When The Nomads went 1-0 up, we all thought "it doesn't really matter. Barry Town will surely turn this around between now and the final whistle". I remember there was quite a serious injury on the pitch. There was a player down for about five minutes, but they seemed to add a lot more stoppage time on than that.
>
> Five o'clock came and went and we were still playing football. The results from the English system had already come in by this point. Maybe the official didn't want the fairy tale of Total Network Solution winning the league at the expense of all-conquering Barry Town to come to pass, but low and behold, Stuart Rain scored his second of the game and it happened! There were so many TNS fans there that day. We filled their stand and brought a good atmosphere to the ground. About 300 of those attending were probably from Llansantffraid. It was a very passionate day that brought a lot of joy to many people. It all fell into place.

This would be far from the only trophy the club would win with the help of Harris' resources, but for the businessman, the 1999-2000 league title still holds a special place in his heart:

> That first league title stands out for me because it was one nobody predicted. It was well documented that we were looking to improve and become a better team, but winning the league didn't look like a reality until the final six or seven weeks of the season. Our budget was £2,000 a week back then. That paled in comparison to the likes of Barry Town and Bangor City. I think it was only the eighth biggest budget in the league.

The final-day drama propelled TNS into the first qualifying round of the Champions League, while Barry had to settle for a place in the UEFA Cup qualifiers. Although the top two were often head and shoulders above the rest, the chasing pack weren't a million miles behind them. Cwmbrân Town, who finished third, notched up 69 points, only five fewer than Barry.

The Crows were strong all season and their league campaign was boosted by the rich form of striker Chris Summers, who claimed the Golden Boot with 28 strikes. It was his goals that proved decisive for Cwmbrân as they finished level on points with Carmarthen Town directly below them, pipping the fourth-placed team to a spot in the Intertoto Cup qualifiers.

Cwmbrân also made it to the Welsh Cup final, having knocked Barry out on penalties in the semis following a 1-1 draw. Their opponents were Bangor City, and they may have fancied their chances given The Citizens' recent track record of falling at final hurdles. Bangor had even lost that season's League Cup final under humiliating circumstances, suffering a 6-0 thrashing from Barry Town to gift The Linnets their only silverware of 1999-2000.

As was often the case for Cwmbrân, though, another trophy to add to their inaugural League of Wales title was a bridge too far. Bangor opened the scoring courtesy of Paul Roberts midway through the first half at Wrexham's Racecourse Ground, and that was ultimately the decider.

A haul of just one domestic trophy was disappointing by Barry's own high standards, but they were not ready to fade into the night just yet. A change in the dugout saw former Crystal Palace and Arsenal player Peter Nicholas take charge of The Linnets for the 2000-01 season, and he wasted no time restoring the glory days at Jenner Park.

	League of Wales (1999-00)	P	W	D	L	For	Ag	Pts
1	Total Network Solutions	34	24	4	6	69	37	76
2	Barry Town	34	23	5	6	98	34	74
3	Cwmbrân Town	34	21	6	7	71	37	69
4	Carmarthen Town	34	22	3	9	68	42	69
5	Llanelli AFC	34	21	3	10	76	46	66
6	Aberystwyth Town	34	19	4	11	70	46	61
7	Connah's Quay Nomads	34	17	6	11	57	35	57

League of Wales (1999-00)		P	W	D	L	For	Ag	Pts
8	Newtown AFC	34	14	6	14	48	41	48
9	Bangor City	34	15	3	16	56	61	48
10	Afan Lido FC	34	12	10	12	45	43	46
11	Rhyl FC	34	13	5	16	40	60	44
12	Caersws FC	34	11	8	15	49	50	41
13	NEWI Cefn Druids	34	13	2	19	44	63	41
14	Rhayader Town	34	9	7	18	35	48	34
15	Inter Cardiff AFC	34	8	6	20	30	62	30
16	Haverfordwest County	34	6	11	17	37	65	29
17	Conwy United	34	6	5	23	33	96	23
18	Caernarfon Town	34	1	8	25	21	81	11

2000-01

It was a fruitful summer of recruitment for Nicholas, who snapped up goalkeeper David Forde - who would go on to earn over 20 caps for the Republic of Ireland - from Galway United, as well as talent from across the border. Lee Phillips made the short trip from Cardiff, Luke Staton was recruited from Bolton and Jamie Moralee was signed from Colchester.

Boasting a CV that also listed stints with Crystal Palace, Watford and Belgian club Royal Antwerp, Moralee was a major *coup* for The Dragons and the League of Wales, and he speaks fondly about his time at Jenner Park:

I was plugging away at Colchester United and I got a call from Peter Nicholas, who I knew well from my Crystal Palace days. Peter told me he'd taken the Barry Town job and was preparing the squad for an upcoming UEFA Cup campaign. He explained that they had a fantastic owner but the team had failed to win the league the previous year.

He was actively trying to entice players with English Football League experience to Barry and put a strong team together, with the aim of trying to surpass what they'd achieved before. The objectives were to go further in Europe and win the league title again.

He told me Barry Town was the biggest club in the league and located in a great part of the country. I was considering the move and drove up to south Wales about four days later to have a look at their setup and the area. I signed a two-year contract straight away.

One of the highlights of Nicholas' first season at the Barry helm was a plumb European qualifier against Boavista of Portugal. Despite a 5-0 loss, over the two legs, there was no disgrace in 2-0 and 3-0 reverses against that standard of opposition and, as Moralee recalls, those great European nights under the lights would forever be remembered by Barry fans:

> *I made my debut against Boavista. Those games were great. They were*
> *the champions of Portugal at the time, having toppled Porto, Benfica and*
> *the other big teams in their division. They were a top team. I played for*
> *some decent-sized clubs in England, but never got the opportunity to play*
> *in European ties like that one.*
> *To finally get that chance in my late 20s was, for me, something that really*
> *topped off my career. I started at Palace and ended up playing at every level*
> *in England, but never in European competitions. The chance to do this at*
> *Barry was hugely appealing to me.*
> *Barry Town helped me accomplish my remaining career goals, ones I'd*
> *held since I was a young lad in London, just starting out in football.*

Europe was both brief and memorable, yet Barry's accomplishments on the domestic front in 2000-01 were more significant. The club began the season strongly, losing only once in their first five matches and remained consistent after that, quickly becoming involved in a two-horse race for the title with the previous year's beaten cup finalists, Cwmbrân Town.

This was another intense title showdown in which there were just three points between the champions and the runners-up at the end of the season. Barry gained a psychological advantage in mid-April when they held firm to beat Port Talbot 2-0, while Cwmbrân lost ground after going down at home to Carmarthen Town by the same scoreline.

The Crows' title hopes were quashed in the next round of fixtures by a 2-0 loss at Llanelli, which rendered Barry's final fixture of the season against Newtown meaningless as far as the title race was concerned. The Linnets lost 2-0 on the day of their victory celebrations.

As for TNS, their fans may have questioned whether they would be one-season wonders just 12 months on from their title triumph as they failed to mount any kind of challenge to Barry in the league, or even maintain pace in the race for European qualification. They

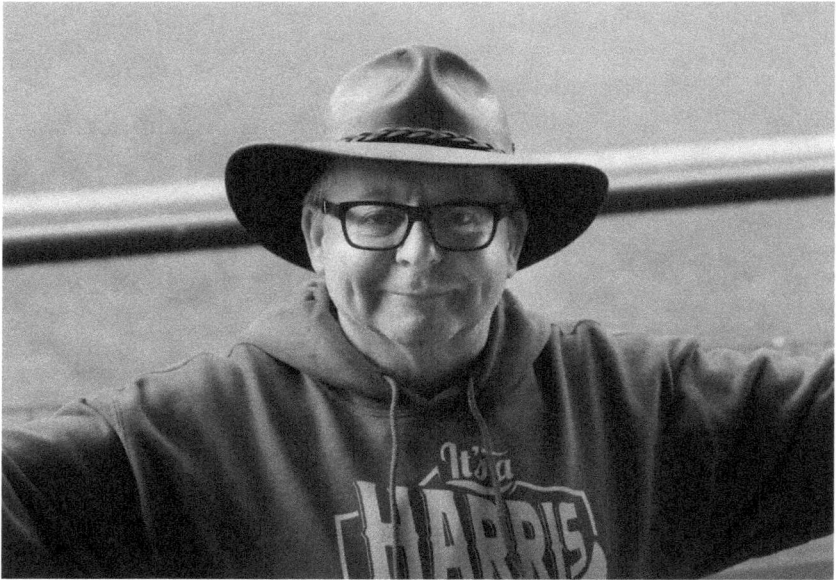

TNS owner Mike Harris. (© Brian Jones)

did, however, make it to the 2001 Welsh Cup final where Barry Town awaited them. The two teams had developed a rivalry of sorts by this point and there was no love lost between them when they prepared to lock horns at the Racecourse Ground.

Just over 1,000 fans turned out for this one and it was broadcast live on BBC Wales. Goals from Moralee and Gary Lloyd won it for Barry, completing their league-and-cup double as well as a clean sweep of victories in their fixtures against TNS that season.

For Moralee, this was an emotional match for reasons that extend beyond the football pitch. The striker had suffered a bereavement not long before the cup final, losing his aunt with whom he was very close. He paid a moving tribute to her after opening the scoring, as he explained:

> *Scoring in that game is a memory that will never leave me. About three or four games before that cup final, we had just cemented the league, so we were going for the double. I lost my aunt around then, my mum's twin. Peter Nicholas told me to go back to London to be with my family and let him know what frame of mind I was in later in the week.*
>
> *I went to London midweek and called the gaffer on Saturday, ahead of the final on Sunday. I said "listen boss, I've seen my family and I think I need*

to play in memory of my aunt". I had a T-shirt made up with the words "that's for you, Carole" printed on it, to unveil if I scored.

As it happens, I netted the opener. I'm not someone who would usually harp on about the quality of my goals, but this was a volley I'm really proud of. I took my shirt off and displayed the T-shirt in my aunt's memory. We went on and won it 2-0 and that was our first double accomplished.

After just 12 months at Barry, I not only experienced a league-and-cup double, but also achieved my dream of qualifying for the Champions League.

Barry were now back to their best, but had been denied a treble by a plucky Caersws side who held them to a 1-1 draw in the League Cup final before triumphing in the penalty shootout. The Bluebirds went on to finish a respectable fifth in the table.

For any teams in the Welsh leagues with full-time aspirations, prize money is highly sought after to help with the wage bill and operating costs. As double winners, Barry were fine on this front but Total Network Solutions, the business, saw a poor return for their investment in 2000-01, which led to a management shake-up midway through the season, with forward Ken McKenna taking on the role of player-manager to replace Andy Cale.

Park Hall – the home of TNS. (© Welsh Football Magazine)

Despite an indifferent campaign, there was no denying that big-money sponsorship had created a new challenger in Welsh football. TNS had prised open Barry's cast-iron grip on the top flight the season before and went on to greater success in the years to come.

Their business model, however, was not well replicated by other clubs. The same year that Total Network Solutions sponsored Llansantffraid, another telecoms firm, CableTel, provided backing to Inter Cardiff and the team spent several seasons playing as Inter CableTel AFC.

Inter became overly reliant on their sponsor's funds, and when CableTel abruptly withdrew their cash in 1999, a period of decline set in. They ended the season one place above the relegation zone, and in 2000-01 they finished bottom of the table, dropping into Welsh League Division One. Although they'd eventually rise again years later, after merging with Cardiff Metropolitan University's football team (known as Cardiff Met), this was a turbulent period for The Gulls which highlights the pitfalls of being too dependent on single-source corporate sponsorship at this level of football.

League of Wales (2000-01)		P	W	D	L	For	Ag	Pts
1	Barry Town	34	24	5	5	84	30	77
2	Cwmbrân Town	34	24	2	8	71	34	74
3	Carmarthen Town	34	17	7	10	68	39	58
4	Newtown AFC	34	18	4	12	48	37	58
5	Caersws FC	34	16	9	9	72	39	57
6	Aberystwyth Town	34	15	10	9	64	42	55
7	Rhyl FC	34	16	10	12	74	52	54
8	Total Network Solutions	34	15	9	10	64	47	54
9	Connah's Quay Nomads	34	14	8	12	45	47	50
10	Haverfordwest County	34	14	7	13	56	55	49
11	Afan Lido FC	34	13	8	13	42	37	47
12	Rhayader Town	34	10	10	14	54	65	40
13	NEWI Cefn Druids	34	11	5	18	60	70	38
14	Bangor City	34	10	7	17	56	84	37
15	Oswestry Town	34	10	6	18	40	74	36
16	Port Talbot Town	34	10	5	19	49	77	35
17	Llanelli AFC	34	9	2	23	57	97	29
18	Inter Cardiff AFC	34	3	4	27	26	104	13

2001-02

The 2001-02 season marked the end of an era for the Welsh top flight as it was the final campaign to play out under the League of Wales banner. It was also the 10th anniversary of the competition and it began brightly for Barry Town. In the summer before their domestic campaign kicked off, the club became the first League of Wales side to win a Champions League tie when they defeated Azerbaijan champions FK Shamkir 3-0 over two legs. Their reward for this feat, as Moralee fondly recalls, was a dream two-legged clash with Portuguese giants FC Porto:

We had reached a stage in the Champions League that no other Welsh domestic team had ever managed to get to, the fixture before the group stage. I remember watching the draw for the round where we got Porto from the changing rooms. Our chairman and manager flew out to Geneva for the draw, and out of the pot came Porto!

What a feeling that was for everyone at the club, especially those who had been foraging for years in the League of Wales. To get to play a club like Porto was massive for those lads, but also for everyone connected to the club. At that moment, I knew I'd made the right decision signing for Barry. No disrespect to Colchester, but they couldn't offer me something like this.

What came next is arguably the most famous day in the club's history. On 1 August 2001, Barry took on the Portuguese champions in the second leg of this tie at Jenner Park and defeated them by three goals to one. Lee Phillips, Michael Flynn and Gary Lloyd were on target that day to forever secure their statuses as Linnets legends.

Granted, Barry had lost the first leg in Portugal 8-0 and their opponents made no fewer than 10 changes for the second leg, but this was a remarkable accomplishment nonetheless. In the Porto team that day were Ricardo Carvalho and Hélder Postiga and their career trajectories only make Barry's feat seem more impressive in hindsight, including for Moralee:

That first fixture was the debut of Carvalho, who went on and had a fantastic career at Chelsea. Deco scored a hat-trick in that 8-0 defeat. We were up against players like him, Jorge Andrade and Postiga. They were knocked out of the Champions League after putting us out but went on to win the UEFA Cup, beating Celtic in the final.

They were an unbelievable team and I wasn't surprised when they won the Champions League under Mourinho after that. When we beat them 3-1 at Jenner Park in that second leg, I think that goes down as one of the shock results of all time in European competitions.

Barry remained dominant throughout the final League of Wales season too, winning it by seven points while also retaining the Welsh Cup, but TNS proved worthy adversaries and grew under the stewardship of McKenna. He guided them to second, just one point ahead of third-placed Bangor City, whose title bid was almost single-handedly powered by striker Marc Lloyd Williams as he ended the campaign with an astonishing 47 goals.

The Welsh Cup final that year was a firecracker between Barry and Bangor. The match started with a bang as Linnets skipper Jon French hit a superb half-volley on the turn that made the net bulge. Mike Flynn doubled their lead before the break, but Bangor hit back, reducing the deficit when Clayton Blackmore's free kick was headed home by Huw Griffiths. Moralee then extended Barry's lead again, but there was more drama to come and Barry Town were never allowed to relax. The usually-prolific Williams hit the post and missed a penalty in the second half, before Moralee netted his second of the afternoon in stoppage time to make it a somewhat flattering 4-1 to The Linnets:

I got two late goals in that one at Aberystwyth. It was a tough game as we had Marc Lloyd Williams to stop, who was scoring for fun at the time. Me and him probably got about 30 goals that season, and there was this narrative before the game that pitted us against each other and questioned who was going to do the business on the day.

We had the added pressure of going for a double-double too. We had that momentum going into it, knowing that we were the champions and everyone wanted to beat us.

It was a very tight game, with penalty shouts here and there. I felt it could have gone either way at 1-1, but we took it away from them at the death. I got a couple of late goals and we won 4-1. Scoring in two cup finals running, winning the league again and playing in Europe; I was thinking things really couldn't be going any better for me in south Wales right now.

So, the curtain came down on the League of Wales era with double-winning Barry in the ascendancy. TNS had emerged as credible contenders to their throne, while Bangor headed up the chasing pack along with Caersws, who retained the League Cup thanks to a 2-1 win over Cwmbrân, and finished fourth to claim their place in the Intertoto Cup once again.

A new age for Welsh domestic football was about to begin, but few would have predicted the seismic changes to the status quo that came with it.

	League of Wales (2001-02)	P	W	D	L	For	Ag	Pts
1	Barry Town	34	23	8	3	82	29	77
2	Total Network Solutions	34	21	7	6	65	33	70
3	Bangor City	34	21	6	7	83	38	69
4	Caersws FC	34	18	4	12	65	44	58
5	Afan Lido FC	34	18	4	12	42	36	58
6	Rhyl FC	34	17	5	12	53	45	56
7	Cwmbrân Town	34	17	4	13	66	53	55
8	Connah's Quay Nomads	34	14	9	11	56	46	51
9	Aberystwyth Town	34	14	9	11	53	46	51
10	Carmarthen Town	34	13	9	12	51	37	48
11	Caernarfon Town	34	12	8	14	64	64	44
12	Port Talbot Town	34	12	7	15	44	55	43
13	Newtown AFC	34	9	11	14	35	44	38
14	NEWI Cefn Druids	34	8	8	18	49	79	32
15	Llanelli AFC	34	8	7	19	41	64	31
16	Oswestry Town	34	8	6	20	39	84	30
17	Haverfordwest County	34	6	10	18	45	76	28
18	Rhayader Town	34	3	6	25	29	89	15

7

A New Era Dawns

2002-03

It was the end of an era for Welsh domestic football. The nation's top flight ushered out its League of Wales branding when the 2001-02 campaign concluded and became known as the Welsh Premier League, a name that would stick for the next decade and beyond.

A new sponsorship agreement was secured for the relaunch, with automotive firm JT Hughes Mitsubishi becoming only the second business to lend its name and backing to the competition during its first decade, following in the footsteps of Konica.

Although there was a shake-up on the branding front, the transition to the Welsh Premier League was a change in name only, for the most part. The division retained its previous format as well as an 18-club line-up and, as the campaign played out, it became clear that Barry Town, TNS and, to a lesser extent, Bangor City, were still the teams to beat.

Continuing to progress towards full-time professionalism under manager Ken McKenna, TNS were selective in the summer transfer market and bolstered their midfield with the acquisition of journeyman Gary Brabin from Chester City and Simon Heal from Haverfordwest County.

Barry Town's camp, meanwhile, was a hive of activity. Manager Peter Nicholas left Jenner Park in September 2001 to serve as Colin Addison's assistant at Swansea, which paved the way for veteran defender Kenny Brown to step up and become head coach of the first team. During his first pre-season, Brown sought to add depth to his squad and did a spot of cross-Atlantic shopping to bring in English midfielder Ian Bishop from Miami Fusion. In addition, Nicky Burke and Nathan Cotterrall joined from Port Talbot and Cwmbrân Town respectively, while striker Raith Plant was a summer capture from Llanelli Town.

While Brown secured back-up for several key positions, the new Linnets boss, as Jamie Moralee recalls, kept the core of his team intact and fully understood that his job was to maintain a winning status quo:

> *Kenny was an older player who had been around the leagues and could play anywhere across the back four. He was in the twilight of his playing career but had seen from the inside how things were evolving and how it worked. The players kind of ran the dressing room and the older lads who had played at a higher level helped create an environment that ran on autopilot. What Kenny did well was recognise that the dynamic didn't need changing. He left it the way it was and let the lads continue to build that ruthlessness in the dressing room.*

There were tough European campaigns for the previous season's top two before the Welsh Premier League's inaugural term gained momentum, with TNS losing 12-2 on aggregated to Amica Wronki of Poland in the UEFA Cup qualifiers, and Barry conceding six without reply over two legs against Latvia's Riga-based Skonto FC in the first qualifying round of the Champions League. Bangor and Caersws also fell at the first hurdles on their continental journeys that summer.

Despite many tipping TNS and Barry to contest a two-way title fight, Bangor threw down the gauntlet in front of the dominant duo with a strong start to the new campaign. They were the early pacesetters by October following an unbeaten start that saw Citizens head coach Peter Davenport named as manager of the month for both August and September. A quartet of their players also headed up the top goalscorers chart at this early stage, with Lee Hunt, Kenny Burgess, Eifion Jones and Paul Roberts all netting for fun.

Barry and TNS were, however, as consistent as ever from this point and early challenges from Connah's Quay and Port Talbot quickly fizzled out. Bangor's title ambitions almost went the distance, with Davenport's men never allowing the top two out of their sights, but a 2-1 defeat away to The Nomads on 15 April derailed their title hopes. George Horan and Tommy Mutton were on target to put Connah's Quay on course for a top-five finish, but as Jamie Moralee explained, Barry's main competitor was TNS:

> *I wasn't aware of any existing rivalry between ourselves and TNS, but that season I knew there was a lot of new money coming into them and there's no doubt that they were our main competitors, along with Bangor City.*

Barry Town striker Adebayo Akinfenwa in action in May 2003. (© Welsh Football Magazine)

> *The contests between us and TNS were always fierce and I think a rivalry of sorts did develop over time. The competition between us in 2002-03 was intense, but in the three seasons I was at Jenner Park, I'm happy to say I never lost a league title to them.*

The Welsh Premier League's first season went to the wire from a mathematical perspective, but overturning The Linnets' superior goal difference on the final weekend seemed an impossible task for TNS. The outcome of the title race appeared to be a foregone conclusion after the previous round of fixtures, during which Barry edged out Cwmbrân 2-1 to move within touching distance of their seventh league title. However, Barry had to do it the hard way as Mark Dunn had given The Crows an early lead from close range, but Ade Akinfenwa - a powerhouse of a striker who went on to play starring roles for clubs across the English Football League – scored twice to turn the game on its head.

Only a major slip-up from Brown's men on the concluding weekend could have handed the title to TNS, but Barry turned on the style in their final-day showdown with Aberystwyth Town on their home turf. The hosts ran riot and hit their opponents for five, with Jamie Moralee netting twice and Jon French, Tom Ramasut and

Akinfenwa also adding their names to the scoresheet as The Linnets secured yet another first-place finish in style, as the former Barry forward recalls:

> *The title wasn't done until the wire that season. Everyone on the outside was hoping we'd lose on the final day, but we just had this mentality about us. Even on an off day, we'd find a way to win. We had a desire and will to succeed and get the job done.*
>
> *We were expecting a tough match - there were decent players at Aberystwyth back then, like big Gary Finley, and they had really quick wingers. On their day, they could hurt teams. It was a potential banana skin for sure, but we went out, got the job done and the rest is history. We had bagged another league title and reached the Champions League again.*

Elsewhere, a relegation also appeared to have been decided on the final day as Oswestry Town's 1-1 draw with Caernarfon condemned 17th-placed Welshpool Town to the drop. However, the mid Wales club were handed a lifeline when Welsh League Division One runners-up Neath were denied a top-flight licence because their ground did not fit the criteria for one. This allowed Welshpool to lodge a successful appeal with the FAW, the outcome of which resulted in them being reinstated into the Welsh Premier League for the 2003-04 season, meaning that only bottom club Llanelli were relegated.

Meanwhile, Rhyl FC were beginning to establish themselves as a dark horse in domestic competitions, ending the season strongly, not far from the European places. Under the guidance of coach John Hulse, The Lilywhites secured a top-six finish and won the League Cup, defeating rivals Bangor City 4-3 on penalties following a 2-2 draw in the final.

It was, however, Barry who dominated the local backpage headlines come the end of the season. Making history was what the Jenner Park outfit did best during their golden era, and towards the tail end of it, they did it again. The Linnets met Cwmbrân Town on 11 May to contest the 2002-03 Welsh Cup final at Llanelli's Stebonheath stadium, and with this match came the opportunity to seal an unprecedented third league and cup double on the bounce.

It was a hard-fought cup final in which Barry were forced to come from behind to cover themselves in glory. An early penalty from Ramasut fired them in front, but a pair of quick-fire goals within 10 minutes of each other gave The Crows the lead at the break.

Cwmbrân fans had become accustomed to heartbreak in the decade that followed their inaugural League of Wales title win, but the outcome of this one was crushing even by their standards. The Crows looked to have done enough to get their name on the trophy in the closing stages, only for Lee Jenkins to pounce with just minutes left to force extra time.

Neither team could find an opening in the half hour that followed, but everyone in the stadium knew where the cup was heading when Cwmbrân missed their first two spot-kicks in the resulting shootout, leaving French to bury the winning penalty and send the cup back to Barry, to the relief of Moralee:

That was a close one. We equalised in the 86ᵗʰ minute through Jenkins and then won on penalties. I remember Gary Lloyd played a blinder that day. He was a big player for us. The idea of a left-back from the Welsh top flight being called up for the Wales senior team today, like he did, is almost unthinkable, but the level of football we were playing and the publicity we were attracting made it possible for Gary.

Was that treble double-winning Barry Town the greatest side the Welsh top flight has ever seen? Moralee seems to think they're right up there, and it's hard to disagree:

Those three years when we won three doubles on the bounce, that was a team I believe was top class and I think it stands up alongside any Welsh side in history.

Even those who plotted to dethrone them, like TNS' Mike Harris, held them in high esteem and had a great deal of respect for them, describing Barry as the "benchmark" to match. He also downplayed the notion of a toxic rivalry between the clubs:

We saw them as the benchmark we had to beat. There was mutual respect between us. Our title win in 2000 proved we were fair rivals to them, but we never got a hatred feeling towards them - we only ever saw them as a team to emulate or go beyond.

Although the glory days seemed to be alive and well for Barry Town on the pitch, the dawning of the Welsh Premier League era brought uncertainty for them off it. Financial problems had been mounting for more than a year, and after Paula O' Halloran stepped aside as chair of the club, former Scarborough FC official Kevin Green took up the role of chief executive and was charged with stopping the monetary rot at Jenner Park.

Securing prize money was vital for Barry since their operating costs and wage bill were higher than other Welsh Premier League clubs' because of their full-time status. Progressing further in European competitions was set as a priority due to the lucrative TV rights funds that were up for grabs, but this was a big ask for any Welsh domestic side. The Dragons were, however, still incredibly tough to beat, as Moralee explained:

There was a lot of stuff going on behind the scenes during my third year at Barry Town. There was talk about the new ownership being less interested in football and wanting to get involved in other projects. This was all bubbling away in the background, but we were still winning on the pitch even though I heard that there were financial problems and some of the lads weren't getting paid. There was always talk of a takeover.

There were a lot of team meetings and there were times when we considered not playing that week because some of us hadn't been paid. But it never quite came to that - we carried on playing and we carried on winning. Through all that madness, we still won the league.

Green did come up with initiatives to raise the club's profile, one of which was the head-turning recruitment of FA Cup winner and former England international John Fashanu as Barry Town chairman midway through the 2002-03 season. The ex-Wimbledon striker was seen as a missing puzzle piece for The Linnets, a figurehead whose presence had the potential to grow the club's stature and fend off the threat to their dominance from TNS, on the field and, as Moralee remarked, other threats off it:

When Kevin Green came in before Fashanu, he was presented as one of those guys who could act as a firefighter and keep things going while warding off the administrators. We thought that if we could progress in the Champions League, it would create a big opportunity for new ownership to take the club over. We were being fed all of that, but we just wanted to crack on and do the best for the club and ourselves.

A PR stunt it may have been, but Fashanu's appointment was welcomed by most Barry fans. He talked a good game upon his arrival too, revealing ambitious plans to position the club as a kindergarten for budding African talent. Through his Winners Worldwide agency, Fashanu set his sights on recruiting emerging stars from countries such as Nigeria to set up with EU work permits, before developing and selling them on at a profit to bigger clubs in Europe.

It was a strategy that aimed to benefit Barry on the pitch in the short term and help them turn a profit beyond that. Their regular European outings would give these players a shop window to showcase their talents, so in theory, everyone involved would benefit.

In a statement published by *The Guardian* in March 2003, the former England star described his partnership with Barry Town as a "marriage made in heaven". Fashanu claimed to have secured a first-refusal agreement with Manchester United for their youth players and promised lucrative TV rights deals with networks in China and Nigeria. The fans were dubious about this. Many questioned what kind of following a Welsh team who attracted little more than 400 fans to their home matches each week would find among armchair supporters in Africa and Asia; and they were right to be sceptical.

He failed to deliver on most of his bold promises, despite managing to briefly recruit a few Nigerian players, including Akinfenwa, who is of Nigerian descent, and Abiodun Baruwa, a goalkeeper who had five full international caps for the Super Eagles to his name. Both players' time at Jenner Park was brief and so, indeed, was Fashanu's.

Barry's celebrity chairman may have succeeded in generating press coverage for the club, but ultimately, he did little to resolve their increasingly precarious financial situation or settle the unpaid and unexplained debts he inherited from previous regimes. Following an early exit from Europe at the hands of Macedonia's Vardar Skopje in the 2003-04 season - and after just eight months in the role - Fashanu stepped down from his post with a press statement that was published in the *Western Mail* in August 2003: "I love the club and its people, and will keep promoting the club to the best of my ability. I and my board members want to take this club to another level. Stepping down as chairman of the club is only a temporary measure for the next six months or so. It's been a hard decision, but I will keep in close contact with them. I'm exhausted with the work I have at the moment, and something has to give, I simply cannot be in two places at the same time."

The Barry Town's squad celebrate their title-winning 2002-03 season. (© Welsh Football Magazine)

Fashanu's decision to step away from Jenner Park ultimately proved to be more than "temporary" and, by this point, Barry were in dire financial straits. Administration soon followed. The professional squad that had helped The Linnets dominate Welsh football and make history gradually disintegrated like a sandcastle against an ever-crashing tide, as Moralee recalled:

Every day we went in and there was uncertainty. Some of the lads had mortgages and kids and were not being paid. We couldn't believe what was happening. We just wanted to play football and enjoy it. I felt for the fans when we were told the club was going into administration.

We were told all contracts would be null and void. Everyone had to jump ship from here and I ended up going to Forest Green Rovers because the manager there, former Swansea City boss Colin Addison, knew me from the Welsh Premier League.

It was hard to replicate what we had at Barry - the success, the camaraderie, but it also proved hard to sustain it. I look back at the three seasons I had at the club and they go down as some of the best years of my career without a shadow of a doubt. It was the best. It ended, but the way it ended didn't stop us from accomplishing things in that final season I was there, so there's no bad feelings from me.

While Barry Town were in the midst of a financial meltdown, TNS' stock was growing considerably. In June of that year, they announced plans for a merger with fellow Welsh Premier League side Oswestry Town FC, who were actually based in the English county of Shropshire, and were facing bankruptcy before the deal came about.

The union was controversial as some of Oswestry's shareholders claimed to have been kept in the dark while it was happening. The two clubs also had trouble convincing UEFA to ratify the agreement due to it spanning two different countries. Despite having the FAW's backing, the deal was originally rejected, only to be approved by UEFA on appeal.

A new era for TNS was about to begin and, with Barry Town in crisis, the scene was set for the newly-forged Llansantffraid-Oswestry alliance to take The Linnets' place at the pinnacle of Welsh domestic football; but 2003-04 saw a surprise contender to the throne arise.

Welsh Premier League (2002-03)		P	W	D	L	For	Ag	Pts
1	Barry Town	34	26	5	3	84	26	83
2	Total Network Solutions	34	24	8	2	68	21	80
3	Bangor City	34	22	5	7	75	34	71
4	Aberystwyth Town	34	17	9	8	54	38	60
5	Connah's Quay Nomads	34	18	5	11	55	46	59
6	Rhyl FC	34	17	7	10	52	33	58
7	Afan Lido FC	34	14	10	10	44	34	52
8	Caersws FC	34	15	6	13	57	52	51
9	Cwmbrân Town	34	14	8	12	51	40	50
10	Newtown AFC	34	12	6	16	48	54	42
11	Port Talbot Town	34	11	6	17	36	51	39
12	NEWI Cefn Druids	34	11	5	18	37	51	38
13	Haverfordwest County	34	10	5	19	40	68	35
14	Caernarfon Town	34	8	10	16	43	53	34
15	Carmarthen Town	34	9	5	20	33	66	32
16	Oswestry Town	34	6	10	18	36	67	28
17	Welshpool Town	34	7	7	20	30	62	28
18	Llanelli AFC	34	4	5	25	42	89	17

8

Rise and Fall

2003-04

The Welsh Premier League's 2003-04 season was all about the redistribution of power. Barry Town's days as the division's top dog were now effectively over and this spelled opportunity for the likes of TNS and Bangor City, the new title hopefuls. It was, however, rank outsiders who capitalised the most from The Linnets' downfall; initially, at least.

Rhyl FC were a club with a storied history that included local honours, Welsh Cup success and impressive feats in the English FA Cup back when they plied their trade across the border. Over the years, they had developed top-drawer talent such as midfield warhorse Barry Horne, who went on to play for Everton and Wales, and Lee Trundle, a striker who shone at Wrexham, Swansea City and Bristol City off the back of his time at Belle Vue.

Welsh legends have also been drawn there to see out the twilight years of their playing careers, a notable example being iconic Everton goalkeeper Neville Southall, who turned out three times between Rhyl's sticks in 2001 and played the final games of his career for the north Wales club. The 92-cap-winning Wales international explained how he came to sign for an up-and-coming team near to his home town of Llandudno:

> *To be honest, I'd pretty much given up on playing first-team football by then. I spoke to the owner a couple of times and I hadn't been playing much at all around then. I didn't really plan to make the move there, it just sort of happened. It was similar to when I joined Torquay United in the English league - I just walked in there and went with the flow.*

Although the veteran shot-stopper had dabbled in coaching before this point - notably during a stint as Wales' caretaker manager in 1999 - his contract at Rhyl was strictly a playing one.

I only signed up as a player. Coming from the level I'd been playing at, there was advice I could pass onto my teammates, but I had to be really mindful about that. I had a similar experience at Torquay. By advising the other players it can look like you're undermining the manager. I was a veteran player, but I had to think about how it might look if I was talking to the players. It didn't happen at Rhyl, to be fair, but the situation at Torquay was on my mind.

The year before Southall arrived at Belle Vue, Rhyl had been bought by local businessman Peter Parry, who had captained the club when aged just 17 before his playing career was cruelly cut short by a brain haemorrhage. The arrival of Parry and the investment he pumped into The Lilywhites had a transformative effect on the team and kickstarted an exciting new era for the club, as Southall recalled:

Peter had great ambition for Rhyl and was investing a lot of money in them. Like any ambitious owner, he wanted to build a club and put together a winning team. In the old days, the club was well run but when an owner arrives and wants to be ambitious, that comes with risks, which Peter was willing to take. All clubs are like this to an extent.

Southall's time at Rhyl was brief and, although it was cut short by injury, the goalkeeping great looks back on it as a positive experience and takes heart from the fact he got to finish his illustrious career in Wales, having begun it there with Llandudno back in 1973:

It was mostly a good experience. I started my playing days in the Welsh leagues and finished them there as well; so that was nice. I picked up an injury in the end, did my calf in and the manager didn't play me after that, which was understandable. At the time, I came away feeling that Rhyl was a great club, a typical seaside team. It was good to see what the Welsh top flight was like from the inside. Clubs like Rhyl back then were stepping stones to what the competition has become now.

After the turn of the Millenium, long-term Lilywhites fans had more than their fair share of tales to tell. They'd witnessed legends like Southall taking to the park at the end of their playing careers, enjoyed minor trophy success, and watched promising homegrown talent emerge; yet it all paled in comparison to their glorious 2003-04 campaign.

Rhyl FC's quadruple-winning squad of 2003-04. (© Welsh Football Magazine)

The team's supporters and hierarchy were confident they had the right man in charge. English coach John Hulse, who joined the club in 2002, marked his debut campaign with League Cup glory, guiding Rhyl to that famous penalty-shootout victory over arch rivals Bangor City in the final, and this was coupled with a satisfactory top-six league finish.

Hulse, in turn, had belief in his squad and made only minimal changes to it that summer, signing Chris Adamson from Newtown but otherwise making do with the players at his disposal. This included fan-favourite striker Andy Moran and midfielder Marc Limbert, whose only previous appearance for The Lilywhites came in the 2003 League Cup final.

The new campaign began with a straightforward 2-0 victory over Cefn Druids at Belle Vue. Moran and Limbert were both on target, in front of a modest crowd of 273. In hindsight, Rhyl fans could have been excused for tempering their expectations the following weekend when they lost at Haverfordwest County by two goals to one, with Moran netting their consolation.

Who would have guessed that Hulse's side wouldn't lose a single league match for the rest of the campaign? In fact, Rhyl didn't lose many more than that across all competitions.

One man who was at Belle Vue week in, week out to witness the dawning of this golden era was journalist Dave Jones. He regularly covered Rhyl's matches for local papers, and later became one of the most prominent reporters of football in north Wales for the *Daily Post*:

> *I really didn't expect Rhyl to achieve such runaway success in 2003-04. Although they had won their first major Welsh football trophy in 50 years the season before, when they lifted the League Cup, it was still a surprise to me when they pulled off something truly unprecedented that season.*

A 2-1 win at home to Port Talbot Town in their next league fixture was the beginning of a 19-match unbeaten run. It came to an end in mid-November when the club faced a strong Newport County side in the FAW Premier Cup. Rhyl, who had defeated title favourites TNS 3-2 in the league just two days earlier, lost 3-0 to The Exiles.

Buoyed by the free-scoring antics of Moran and the impressive form of players like Limbert, Chris McGinn and Gary Powell, Hulse's side almost finished the calendar year undefeated from this point. The only blemish on their form guide was a 1-0 defeat away to TNS in the first leg of the League Cup quarter-finals, which turned out to be a moot result when they triumphed in the return leg 3-1 to progress by three goals to two on aggregate.

What was it about this Lilywhites side that made them so formidable on the pitch? According to Jones, the intense camaraderie among the squad was the fire in their engine room:

> *Experience and togetherness were key to the team's success. Many members of that squad had played football at a very good level in England, which obviously helped. The foundations of that team were built in 2002-03 when the League Cup was won.*

In the winter transfer window, Rhyl snapped up striker Lee Hunt from Bangor City, and this turned out to be shrewd business by Hulse. The big centre-forward, who hails from Merseyside, wasted no time forming a deadly partnership with Moran up top, as Jones explained:

> *A bit of fine tuning to the 2003-04 squad in that transfer window was sufficient to carry them on to great things. The group was packed with experience, including ex-Football League players such as Steve Walters and*

Gary Powell, but the key move was signing Lee Hunt in December as a strike partner for Andy Moran.

Times were good at Rhyl heading into 2004. With a fantastic strikeforce and a creative midfield, the club was on the hunt for silverware on all fronts. This was a stark contrast to champions, Barry Town, who began the season with an interim management team following their collapse into administration. With the last vestiges of their professional setup now departed, The Linnets were forced to recruit a squad from the lower reaches of Welsh football.

Most of Barry's new players were signed from teams like N&M Construction of the South Wales Amateur League, five levels down from the Welsh Premier League, and the gulf in quality between this new-look team and the rest of the top flight was plain to see. Losing their opening four league games, it was the beginning of a grim run of form which included an 8-0 thrashing away to Caernarfon Town. The Linnets had gone from dominating Welsh football, boasting a fully professional squad and making history in Europe, to finding themselves on the wrong side of results like this; and things would soon get much worse.

Barry travelled to Rhyl in mid-September and were hammered 4-0, with defender Tim Edwards bagging a double and Steve Walters and Limbert one each. Their winless run continued long beyond this and was showing no signs of ending as the festive season approached. December brought little in the way of goals or points, but it did yield new ownership for Town when local businessman Stuart Lovering bought the club after outbidding Shamrock Travel owner Clayton Jones. Lovering came along when Barry needed a saviour, and in fairness to him, his successful acquisition did prevent the club from going out of business there and then.

In hindsight, however, to say his tenure was a period Linnets supporters would rather forget is putting it lightly. The general consensus among Barry fans is

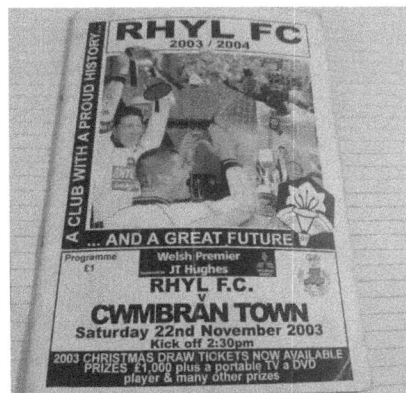

A matchday programme from Rhyl vs Cwmbrân Town in 2003. (© Andy J Havelot)

that almost every decision Lovering made during his time at Jenner Park flew in the face of the club's best interests, whether that was banning the official supporters club from fundraising at the ground or threatening to withdraw the team from the Welsh football system altogether.

Long-time Barry Town secretary Dave Cole had the following to say about Lovering's takeover in a retrospective interview published by *Dai Sport* in 2019: "Stuart Lovering bought Barry Town in the December and, at first, people were grateful. He had saved the club. If he had not come in at the time we would have ceased to exist. For six months it was great and supporters were getting behind the team. Then he started coming up with plans which were far beyond a club of this size. Then, wham! It all fell apart."

Just how spectacularly it fell apart is a whole other story, but The Linnets' long wait for a first win of the season continued for another two months after Lovering's arrival, finally coming in February 2004. Barry defeated fellow strugglers Welshpool Town in dramatic fashion, clinching a 5-4 victory in the 98th minute thanks to a penalty from youngster Luke Sherbon.

Lovering made his first managerial appointment not long after this, and it was a good one, on paper. Experienced coach Colin Addison - who had managed teams in the English Football League as well as in Spain, South Africa, Kuwait and Qatar - was brought in and tasked with saving this inexperienced Barry side from relegation, but it was a daunting challenge.

Meanwhile, TNS were steadily growing in stature, though their merger with the now-defunct Oswestry Town became drawn out and still wasn't finalised when the season began. Early into the new campaign, they were handed a glamorous tie in the UEFA Cup preliminary round when they were drawn against Kevin Keegan's Manchester City.

Back then, City were not the formidable juggernaut they are today, having only won promotion back into the English Premier League in 2002. Compared to TNS, though, they were a team of Goliaths and the result of the first leg at the City of Manchester Stadium reflected the chasm between them. The Sky Blues registered a comfortable 5-0 win, with Trevor Sinclair, Shaun Wright-Phillips, Sun Jihai, David Sommeil and Nicolas Anelka on the scoresheet.

Although TNS were a distant second best, this was a tie which helped them raise their profile in the game significantly. Not only

TNS played Manchester City in the first competitive fixture at Eastlands. (© Phil Blagg)

were they City's opponents for the first competitive match at their new City of Manchester Stadium, they were also given live broadcast coverage by ITV.

The return leg was played at the Millennium Stadium in Cardiff and more than 10,000 supporters showed up to watch TNS put up an admirable fight before going down 2-0. It has to be said that 9,000, at least, of those in attendance were there to see The Sky Blues, yet this was, nevertheless, invaluable exposure for the Welsh Premier League club.

Moreover, Keegan was full of praise for TNS after the match in the Welsh capital, complimenting them on their dogged defending across the two legs: "Football is full of variety. You have to give credit to TNS for the way they defended so determinedly," *WalesOnline* quoted him as saying. "I don't know who's going to win the Welsh league this year, but I will tell you this - that team will have to go some to beat TNS."

Ken McKenna's side took heart from their high profile matches against Manchester City and this spurred them on to maintain their solid form on the domestic front. There was little between the division's only professional outfit and Rhyl throughout the campaign, and the two teams contested what was arguably the most exciting title race since the Welsh national championship began.

Rhyl, who had already knocked TNS out of the League Cup, dealt a crippling blow to the Llansantffraid outfit's league title ambitions in early April when they defeated them 1-0 following a hard-fought 90 minutes. Moran scored the only goal of the game late on, taking his total for the season to an eye-watering 41 across all competitions.

Just days earlier, The Lilywhites had defeated a heavily-fancied Swansea City side 2-0 at Belle Vue to reach the FAW Premier Cup final. A huge crowd of 2,379 turned out for that one, but even more flocked to their ground to see them beat TNS - a club record 2,741.

Hulse's side did drop points in their next league fixture, a 1-1 draw away to Cwmbrân Town, but remained in pole position in the title race. TNS, however, refused to let Rhyl get comfortable at the summit and battled to the very end, winning three games in a row to take the contest to the final weekend when both title contenders were playing away.

Rhyl were at Porthmadog and TNS travelled to Welshpool Town. It was The Lilywhites' title to lose, and sure enough, they got the job done, winning the match 2-0 via goals from Moran and Powell to render TNS' 5-0 win at Welshpool moot and secure their first Welsh Premier League crown.

Although this crop of Rhyl players could collectively be described as something special, the *Daily Post's* reporter, David Jones, was one of many observers to lavish high praise on Hulse for masterminding their debut title triumph:

> *John Hulse was a very shrewd and experienced campaigner who knew exactly how to get the best out of his players. Hulse had been number two to Lee Williams at Belle Vue in 2001-02 and the good work began there, but the club's golden era was ushered in when he became first-team manager for the 2002-03 season.*

Rhyl's celebrations went on into the night, but couldn't continue any longer than that as, two days later, more silverware was at stake when they defended their League Cup title on 3 May against Carmarthen

Town at Newtown's Latham Park ground. It was a one-sided final that secured double honours for Rhyl thanks to Moran's fifth hat-trick of the year, and a McGinn strike.

The double became a treble by the end of an eight-day period that Rhyl fans now look back on as the stuff of legend. On 9 May, the club returned to Latham Park for the Welsh Cup final to face TNS, with McKenna's men desperate to avoid a trophyless season.

It was a tight final and a scrappy one for large periods. Poor finishing from both sides kept it goalless by the end of 90 minutes, but the breakthrough came just one minute into extra time. Rhyl won the cup courtesy of a deflected strike that Limbert claimed, though the decisive touch that guided the ball into the net came from TNS defender Chris Taylor.

After the game, Hulse hailed his heroic charges in an interview with BBC Wales. "The character of the side showed through today, they were magnificent," he said. "After 90 minutes I just told them to keep their discipline and shape and carry on doing what they're good at."

Winning trophies was indeed what his Rhyl side were good at, and they had the chance to bag yet another one on 12 May when they faced Wrexham in the FAW Premier Cup final. The Lilywhites had home advantage but were still clear underdogs. Sadly, for Rhyl fans, their incredible trophy-bagging spree faltered, with The Dragons coasting to a 4-1 win. A Moran strike and a £50,000 runners-up cheque offered some consolation for Rhyl, though.

More tangible consolation came less than a fortnight later when the club added regional honours to their magnificent haul, defeating Halkyn United 6-1 in the North Wales Coast FA Challenge Cup final, with hat-tricks from McGinn and Powell. It was a quadruple trophy-winning season that exceeded all expectations, as David Jones noted:

John Hulse had put together a good squad, but it surpassed all expectations, winning the league title, Welsh Cup and retaining the League Cup, as well as landing the lesser regarded, by some at least, North Wales Coast FA Challenge Cup. Had they made it a five-timer by winning the FAW Premier Cup too, I think it might have been regarded among Welsh football's greatest ever achievements.

Rhyl were on cloud nine, but a shadow was cast on The Lilywhites' most successful season in the summer when leading goalscorer Andy

Moran was handed a drugs suspension after testing positive for the banned substance nandrolone - this gave him the unwanted record of becoming the first footballer in Britain to be suspended from domestic competition for failing a dope test.

The striker denied knowingly taking it and claimed the test findings were the result of contaminated food supplements. The FAW, however, stripped him of that season's Golden Boot award and banned him from competitive football for seven months, and instead awarded the honour to second-highest scorer, Graham Evans of Caersws, who became the first player to win it on three separate occasions.

It was a blemish on an otherwise impeccable campaign for Rhyl, though their historic quadruple wasn't the only major headline to come out the 2003-04 season. Despite Addison instilling some fight in them, Barry Town didn't leave the foot of the table all season and ended up four points short of safety. They were relegated to the Welsh Football League Division One.

The Linnets, or at least a rebooted version of them, would eventually return to the top division, but the club and its fans would have to go to hell and back to get there.

Welsh Premier League (2003-04)	P	W	D	L	For	Ag	Pts
1 Rhyl FC	32	23	8	1	76	26	83
2 Total Network Solutions	32	24	4	4	77	28	76
3 Haverfordwest County	32	17	11	4	40	23	62
4 Aberystwyth Town	32	18	5	9	59	39	59
5 Caersws FC	32	15	10	7	63	41	55
6 Bangor City	32	16	6	10	72	47	54
7 Cwmbrân Town	32	15	3	14	51	44	48
8 Connah's Quay Nomads	32	11	9	12	58	55	42
9 Caernarfon Town	32	11	9	12	65	65	42
10 Newtown AFC	32	12	5	15	43	50	41
11 Port Talbot Town	32	11	6	15	41	51	39
12 Porthmadog FC	32	11	3	18	41	55	36
13 NEWI Cefn Druids	32	11	2	19	44	59	35
14 Afan Lido FC	32	8	8	16	31	54	32
15 Welshpool Town	32	6	7	19	35	71	25
16 Carmarthen Town	32	3	11	18	28	69	20
17 Barry Town	32	3	7	22	30	77	16

9

Dancing in the Streets

2004-05

TNS' merger with Oswestry Town was a long-running saga but with completion now in sight, the 2003-04 Welsh Premier League runners-up were dreaming of a bright future. Managing director Mike Harris had big plans to move the club from its Treflan home in Llansanffraid to a new stadium in Oswestry by 2005, and lay solid foundations to progress further in Welsh football, albeit in a ground located in England.

The idea behind the union was to appeal to fans from a wider geographic region, spanning Llansantffraid in Powys and Oswestry in Shropshire. Despite TNS' recent success and Town's rich history, both clubs had suffered from poor attendances since the league began; but Harris felt an amalgamation of the two teams could draw support from each side of the border.

This wasn't the only factor that influenced the agreement, though. TNS had always planned to build their new ground on the other side of the border, but the FAW took issue with this; unsurprising given the battle it waged with the Welsh clubs who wanted to remain in the English system when the national championship was formed. The governing body could have been accused of inconsistency if it had allowed a Llansantffraid team to play its matches in England, but a merger between TNS and Oswestry laid this problem, and the pressing issue of their relocation plans, to rest since the latter club was already sanctioned to host Welsh football in England, as Harris explained:

The success we enjoyed was originally born out of the village of Llansantffraid, but since then, the rules of the game and the criteria for it have continually changed. The ground criteria for clubs in the top flight and in Europe was never going to be fulfillable in Llansantffraid. The pitch was owned by the council and it was part of the school's sports facility - the ground was not in a position to meet the criteria for many reasons.

For starters, there wasn't enough space to put stands behind the goal and completely enclose the ground. These factors meant that we would not have qualified for a top-flight licence in the modern era and ultimately would have been relegated as a result. We had to find a solution over time and that was what led to us buying Oswestry Town when they went into financial decline. They had a ground which was fit for developing. It had the space we needed but the team was going bankrupt. In the purest world, it was an ideal situation because they wanted our financial help and welcomed the merger.

As part of the merger it was agreed that the new-look team would play an equal number of games in the traditional green and white of Llansantffraid, and the blue of Oswestry, to respect both teams' heritage.

A trophyless 2003-04 was a disappointment for the conjoined club since they were now the only full-time outfit in the Welsh top flight following the fall of Barry Town. They did, however, enjoy a significant reputation boost thanks to Sky Sports presenter Jeff Stelling.

"They'll be dancing in the streets of Total Network Solutions tonight," quipped Stelling after *Soccer Saturday*'s results round-up announced a 4-0 victory for the Llansantffraid club over Porthmadog. TNS themselves describe this as the moment they were "immortalised".

Stelling's gag was a reference to broadcaster Sam Leitch's infamous blunder in the 1960s, when he proclaimed on national television that "they'll be dancing in the streets of Raith tonight," while reporting on a victory for Scottish side Raith Rovers. There would be no cutting of shapes in Raith that evening, despite the result, since the club is actually based in the town of Kirkcaldy.

TNS boss Ken McKenna was given the green light for mass recruitment ahead of the 2004-05 campaign and brought in eight players that summer. Their biggest *coup* was striker Marc Lloyd Williams, who arrived as part of a triple swoop from Aberystwyth Town, alongside defender Gary Finley and midfielder John Lawless, a product of Liverpool's youth academy.

TNS' season began in familiar fashion: with a European exit. They lost 4-1 on aggregate to Swedish side Östers in the first qualifying round of the UEFA Cup. McKenna's men held firm for much of the first leg in Scandinavia, only to be undone by a pair of late goals.

TNS' top goalscorer for 2003-04, Michael Wilde, finds the net in Europe. (© Phil Blagg)

The return leg was played at Wrexham's Racecourse Ground and the Welsh Premier Leaguers made their opponents work for their place in the next round. Michael Wilde, the club's top goalscorer in 2003-04, hit a consolation strike for TNS to add respectability to the aggregate scoreline. Reporting on the match, the *Daily Post* opined that TNS were "beaten but not disgraced" by superior opposition, which just about summed up the tie.

TNS made a great start to their domestic campaign, going 18 matches undefeated against Welsh opponents. This emphatic run was inspired by the incendiary strike partnership Wilde and Williams struck up and included plenty of highlights along the way. Among them was a 2-1 win away to defending champions Rhyl, a 6-0 demolition of Airbus UK on the road, and a 7-0 thrashing of Connah's Quay Nomads at Deeside Stadium. Their winning streak finally came to an end, however, on New Year's Day 2005 at Welshpool Town when the hosts registered a shock 5-2 win over the league leaders.

By this point, the league's only full-timers had firmly established themselves as odds-on favourites for the title, but holders Rhyl did not surrender their crown so easily. Their campaign began with a somewhat disappointing 7-1 aggregate defeat to Skonto FC of

TNS celebrate winning the Welsh Cup in 2005. (© Phil Blagg)

Latvia in the first qualifying round of the Champions League, though they were worthy adversaries to TNS in Welsh competitions, as Mike Harris recalled:

> *Rhyl were our diehard competitors that season, a time I like to refer to as the Milkshake Era. They were a proper team who came from traditional British football with a loyal and passionate following. It was always beers in the afternoon, a load of abuse during the game, and hopefully some sensible conversations about it afterwards.*
>
> *There was a lot of rivalry at the time between myself and Rhyl owner Peter Parry. He was successful in his business back then and was able to provide good funding for them.*
>
> *It was a hard-fought battle. When we played them over the Bank Holiday that season, I think there were over 1,000 people packed into their stadium. The BBC televised that match as well. It was a good occasion and it was even better that we came out on top.*

Not only did The Lilywhites remain hot on TNS' heels in the league for most of the season, the two sides also met in the Welsh Cup semi-final and FAW Premier Cup quarter-final, with the Llansantffraid-Oswestry outfit narrowly beating them in both tournaments.

In the league, Rhyl kept up the pressure on TNS until mid-April, but Mike Harris' team had the chance to bag their second league title by beating Carmarthen away, and they held their nerve, edging the match 1-0 thanks to Marc Lloyd Williams' strike in the 40th minute. Rhyl did all they could at Caernarfon Town that day, winning 4-1 via doubles from Andy Moran and Lee Hunt, but ultimately lost their grip on the league title.

In the final standings, Rhyl finished four points behind TNS, who lost only one more league match following that earlier upset at Welshpool. That was a narrow 1-0 reverse away to Bangor City in March, a result which helped The Citizens ultimately claim third spot.

It was by no means a poor season for Rhyl, but it was one of heartache. John Hulse's side had the chance to add a League Cup crown to their haul of runners-up medals on 2 May when they met Carmarthen Town in the final at Newtown's Latham Park ground.

Having won a quadruple the season before, Rhyl were the favourites but Carmarthen had been the competition's great entertainers, beginning their League Cup campaign with an 11-4 aggregate win over Llanelli AFC in the preliminary round. The first leg ended 1-1, but incredibly, it rained goals in the second as Mark Jones' side won 10-3 on the day.

Carmarthen then beat Bangor 7-5 over two legs in the first round proper before edging close contests against Cwmbrân Town and Porthmadog to set up the final against Rhyl. However, despite scoring for fun *en route* to the final, Carmarthen couldn't find the net in normal time at Latham Park and neither could The Lilywhites. The Old Gold won the match 2-0 in extra time through strikes from Richard Kennedy and Omar Abdillahi, the goals just three minutes apart.

This was a first major honour for Carmarthen, who finished sixth in the league, and they had the chance to add to it less than a week later when they met TNS in the Welsh Cup final, at Stebonheath Park in Llanelli, in front of just over 1,100 spectators. Carmarthen proved tough opponents for the newly-crowned league champions to overpower, but their players began to tire as the game entered its final quarter. John Lawless had looked dangerous all afternoon for TNS and he proved to be the match winner, pouncing 15 minutes from time to sink The Old Gold and make it a league-and-cup double for TNS, as Harris recalled:

They frustrated us a lot in that final. They were very difficult for us to break down and the windy conditions on the day didn't help matters. We didn't get too many chances, but Lawless managed to break away, round the keeper and score.

The Welsh Cup had quite a journey that day! It went back on the team bus with us, had a few beers and a few bumps and finished its evening in a curry house. I think one of the goats on the side of the trophy ended up with a bit of naan bread in its mouth.

Harris' TNS were finally fulfilling their ambitions and potential, and the biggest game in their history, a matter of weeks later, certainly caught the attention of the football world.

Welsh Premier League (2004-05)	P	W	D	L	For	Ag	Pts
1 TNS	34	23	9	2	83	25	78
2 Rhyl FC	34	23	5	6	70	31	74
3 Bangor City	34	20	7	7	73	44	67
4 Haverfordwest County	34	17	12	5	50	28	63
5 Caersws FC	34	19	5	10	67	39	62
6 Carmarthen Town	34	17	10	7	60	34	61
7 Cwmbrân Town	34	15	8	11	52	47	53
8 Aberystwyth Town	34	15	8	11	45	40	53
9 Welshpool Town	34	14	9	11	55	46	51
10 Newtown AFC	34	13	7	14	49	55	46
11 Porthmadog FC	34	11	12	11	38	39	45
12 Connah's Quay Nomads	34	9	9	16	48	58	36
13 Port Talbot Town	34	6	11	17	36	49	29
14 Llanelli AFC	34	8	5	21	42	84	29
15 Caernarfon Town	34	7	7	20	28	72	28
16 Airbus UK	34	5	9	20	36	76	24
17 NEWI Cefn Druids	34	5	7	22	30	72	22
18 Afan Lido FC	34	6	6	22	29	52	21*

*3pts deducted

2005-06

Liverpool FC had conquered Europe that season, pulling off their legendary 'Miracle of Istanbul' comeback against AC Milan to lift the 2005 Champions League trophy. Their defence of club football's most prestigious crown began in front of a packed Anfield on 13 July, and their opponents were none other than TNS.

The tie came about under bizarre circumstances. Liverpool's place in the following season's Champions League was not guaranteed because they had finished fifth in the English Premier League and it was unclear whether UEFA would allow them to defend their title or place them in the less prestigious UEFA Cup.

Harris, as he explained, saw an opportunity and offered Liverpool the chance to take on TNS in a one-off preliminary tie, a potential side door for The Reds to enter the Champions League:

> *I saw an opportunity to put our club on the map there, but I believe in sporting merit. I don't think any club should be in a competition purely because of their name, but if you win the Champions League, why shouldn't you be able to defend it the next season?*
>
> *I think UEFA overlooked the fact that the winner of the Champions League might not even qualify for the competition the following season. It was a circumstance Liverpool couldn't do anything about, so I saw a chance to potentially set up a tie that would light up people's imaginations. We had to get knocked out by somebody - why not the champions of Europe?*

The offer ended up being entirely moot because Liverpool reached a compromise with the governing body and were allowed to defend the trophy after all. They would start off in the first qualifying round, and by the strangest twist of fate, were drawn against TNS. Harris had secured the match he wanted:

> *As it happens, we got the big draw anyway, and the press really bought into it. The Liverpool matches rank among the biggest and best I've been involved in.*

Becoming the first team to play Liverpool in Europe since The Reds' momentous night in Istanbul was a big deal for TNS, even bigger than the UEFA Cup tie which saw them become Manchester City's first competitive opponents at Eastlands.

The first leg took place at Anfield in front of more than 44,000 supporters, and Reds manager Rafa Benítez gave the Welsh champions the respect they deserved by fielding a strong starting XI. The Liverpool line-up that night was awash with world-class talent, including Steven Gerrard, Xabi Alonso, Jamie Carragher and Fernando Morientes.

Liverpool's Dietmar Hamann taking a penalty kick against TNS in their Champions League qualifier. (© Phil Blagg)

TNS' team may have been assembled for a tiny fraction of the cost of Liverpool's, but many of those who took to the field that evening are now undisputed club legends. Among them was Wilde, Tommy Holmes, Martyn Naylor, Nicky Ward, Scott Ruscoe and Steve Evans. The latter pair eventually went on to join the club's coaching and managerial setup.

Predictably, there was no fairy tale on Merseyside that night, with Liverpool comfortably winning the match 3-0 thanks to a Gerrard hat-trick. The England international was also on target twice in the return leg played at the Racecourse Ground, with Djibril Cissé adding another.

Despite losing 6-0 on aggregate, TNS earned widespread praise for their performances in both matches against the Champions League winners. The tie will always be special to the club's fans and it was more memorable for some of their players than others. Lawless, a life-long Liverpool fan, took to the field against his beloved team when he came on as a sub in the first leg at Anfield, and goalkeeper Gerard Doherty saved a penalty from Dietmar Hamann in the second leg.

TNS goalkeeper Gerard Doherty was singled out for praise during his side's Champions League qualifier against Liverpool. (© Phil Blagg)

Doherty was singled out for plaudits for his performances across the two legs, and Benítez was quick to acknowledge how difficult the shot-stopper made things for his side at home and away. "The goalkeeper saved a lot of goals, and for me, he was the best player in the two games," said the Spaniard in the aftermath of the second leg.

TNS started their 2005-06 league campaign slowly with two away draws, 2-2 at Porthmadog and 1-1 at Port Talbot Town, but this was the beginning of another lengthy unbeaten run. They did not taste defeat in the league until the 23rd match of the season, in which they were beaten 2-1 away to Carmarthen Town thanks to a Nathan Cotterill brace.

By this point, however, TNS held a massive 16-point lead at the top of the league and were already being hailed as champions-elect, despite another season of credible opposition from Hulse-led Rhyl and a new contender, Llanelli AFC, who had announced plans to go full-time.

During the early months of 2006, however, came a dramatic shake-up for TNS. Total Network Solutions, the business, was acquired by British Telecom. This meant that the club's sponsorship deal had to come to an end, but more significantly, they'd need a new name, as Harris explained:

> *BT had expressed an interest in buying my company the year before. We were growing continually and taking large contracts from under their noses. They put an offer in front of me which was too good to refuse. When they acquired the business, they didn't want to be involved with the football club too, so this meant we had to rebrand.*

Following an audacious bid to sell the team's naming rights on eBay, a TNS supporter approached Harris with the perfect solution to their identity crisis.

> *One of the fans came up with the idea for the new name. They pointed out that 'Llansantffraid' means 'The Parish of Saint Ffraid', and Oswestry is named after King Oswald, who also was a saint. It made perfect sense to call ourselves The New Saints as this also allowed us to continue with the TNS abbreviation.*

All change it may have been on the branding front, but it was business as usual on the pitch for The New Saints. They lost just one more league game that season - a 2-0 reverse against Aberystwyth - and were 18 points better off than runners-up Llanelli after the final match. Rhyl had to settle for a third-placed finish, with Carmarthen rounding off the top four.

It was a decent season for Port Talbot Town who finished in fifth place, and their prolific striker, Rhys Griffiths, in particular. The towering forward's haul of 28 goals earned him the Golden Boot and almost propelled his team into Europe. The Steelmen finished only a point behind Carmarthen, who would be Wales' representatives in the Intertoto Cup for the 2006-07 season.

Port Talbot also reached the League Cup final but were routed by The New Saints. Ward opened the scoring early on for the league champions before Wilde took centre stage and scored a hat-trick to help TNS to a comfortable 4-0 win, and double honours.

It didn't all go The New Saints' way that season, however. They made an early exit from the Welsh Cup, beaten 1-0 by Llanelli in round four, and left the likes of Bangor City, Rhyl, Port Talbot and Carmarthen Town to all march on to the quarter-finals of the competition. The 2006 final came with added spice as arch-enemies Rhyl and Bangor were the last teams standing. The Racecourse Ground was the venue for this grudge match and more than 1,700 supporters made the journey to Wrexham to witness it.

It was The Lilywhites who came out on top thanks to a contentious penalty from Moran and a 12-yard drive from Gareth Wilson. Tempers boiled over throughout and Bangor ended the match with 10 men due to Chris Priest's red card in the wake of the penalty incident. "We could have been 2-0 up at half-time," commented Hulse to BBC Wales after watching his side secure the trophy "but to be fair to them, when they went a man down early in the second half, they made a good spirited game of it when they might possibly have caved in. I thought we missed a couple of decent chances after the break as well, but a 2-0 win was very pleasing in the end. It was definitely a penalty, but I didn't see why the lad was sent off. If something like that happens, it's normally for swearing at the referee."

Welsh Premier League (2005-06)	P	W	D	L	For	Ag	Pts
1 The New Saints	34	27	5	2	87	17	86
2 Llanelli AFC	34	21	5	8	64	28	68
3 Rhyl FC	34	18	10	6	65	30	64
4 Carmarthen Town	34	17	6	11	62	42	57
5 Port Talbot Town	34	15	11	8	47	30	56
6 Technogroup Welshpool	34	15	9	10	59	48	54
7 Aberystwyth Town	34	14	10	10	59	48	52
8 Haverfordwest County	34	12	14	8	49	36	50
9 Bangor City	34	14	3	17	51	54	45
10 Caersws FC	34	11	12	11	44	56	45
11 Porthmadog FC	34	12	8	14	57	59	44
12 Gap Connah's Quay	34	10	8	16	36	46	38
13 Caernarfon Town	34	9	10	15	47	55	37
14 Elements Cefn Druids	34	7	11	16	42	58	32
15 Airbus UK Broughton	34	8	8	18	35	60	32
16 Newtown AFC	34	10	6	18	42	61	31
17 Cwmbrân Town*	34	8	8	18	42	73	19
18 Cardiff Grange Quins	34	4	4	28	23	110	15

*13pts deducted

2006-07

The Welsh Premier League was in danger of becoming predictable. The New Saints lost only twice in their first 20 games and were threatening to run away with the title for a third season on the bounce. On top of that, this was the second campaign of an extended period where TNS, Rhyl and Llanelli would make up the top three.

Rhyl were runners-up, finishing only seven points behind The Saints, but cursed the amount of draws they racked up. The Lilywhites actually lost one game fewer than The New Saints, suffering defeat only three times but playing out nine stalemates.

Llanelli were an emerging threat to TNS' position at top dogs. The Carmarthenshire club also claimed the signing of the season when snapping up the prolific Griffiths from Port Talbot, who continued his free-scoring antics throughout the campaign, breaking the 30-goal barrier to reclaim the Golden Boot and help his side to a third-placed finish.

At the other end of the table, the Welsh Premier League lost one of its former champions when Cwmbrân Town suffered the drop. In what was an agonising season, the club ended up with just 20 points on the board and a one-way ticket to Welsh League Division One.

Double honours were becoming a habit for TNS and this season didn't buck that trend. In March, they brought home the FAW Premier Cup by defeating Newport County of Conference South by a goal to nil. Steve Beck was on target that day to help TNS become only the second team from the Welsh top flight to get their hands on the trophy.

It was an eventful edition of the Premier Cup all round. In the quarter-finals, Port Talbot claimed one of the biggest scalps the competition had ever seen when they downed Swansea City 2-1 in front of 2,641 home supporters. Ex-Swans midfielder Andrew Mumford struck the winner in extra time to fire The Steelmen into an historic semi-final against Newport. It wasn't to be for Port Talbot but the honour of Welsh domestic football was maintained by TNS when they overcame Newport in the final, as Mike Harris recalled:

For me, that victory over Newport was as big as the European matches against Liverpool. We also beat Cardiff in the semi-finals on our way to lifting that trophy, and were named as Team of the Year at the BBC Awards because of our feats in the competition.

The other domestic cups had surprise outcomes and added diversity to the list of trophy winners during the Welsh Premier League era. The League Cup went to Caersws, who stunned Rhyl on penalties following a 1-1 draw in the final, while Carmarthen won the Welsh Cup for the first time by edging a 3-2 thriller against Afan Lido at Stebonheath Park.

Despite TNS making it a hat-trick of consecutive league titles, Caersws and Carmarthen's 2007 cup victories proved that it was still possible for outsiders to achieve trophy success in Welsh football. This meant that other clubs could dream of pipping The New Saints to silverware, and it wasn't long until someone did exactly that in the league too.

Welsh Premier League (2006-07)	P	W	D	L	For	Ag	Pts
1 The New Saints	32	24	4	4	81	20	76
2 Rhyl FC	32	20	9	3	67	35	69
3 Llanelli AFC	32	18	9	5	72	33	63
4 Technogroup Welshpool	32	17	9	6	54	33	60
5 Gap Connah's Quay	32	16	8	8	49	40	56
6 Port Talbot Town	32	15	6	11	42	39	51
7 Carmarthen Town	32	14	8	10	57	50	50
8 Aberystwyth Town	32	13	9	10	47	37	48
9 Bangor City	32	14	6	12	55	47	48
10 Haverfordwest County	32	10	9	13	49	46	39
11 Porthmadog FC	32	8	11	13	40	52	35
12 Airbus UK Broughton	32	7	8	17	40	67	29
13 Elements Cefn Druids	32	7	7	18	41	66	28
14 Caersws FC	32	6	9	17	34	59	27
15 Caernarfon Town	32	6	8	18	41	73	26
16 Newtown AFC	32	6	6	20	30	63	24
17 Cwmbrân Town	32	4	8	20	36	75	20

10

A Town Painted Red

The town of Llanelli's footballing history is a fascinating one. Rewind to the 1950s and the Carmarthenshire community's favourite pastime was rugby, but their local football team was beginning to make a name for itself after securing a spot in the English Southern League.

After the Second World War, Llanelli AFC benefitted from an influx of Scottish players, who had relocated to the market town in search of work. Among them was none other than Jock Stein, a true legend of the game who found success as player and manager at Celtic before going on to coach Leeds United and the Scottish national team.

The attention players like Stein generated enabled Llanelli to turn professional for a spell in the '50s, during which they competed at the business end of the league table and enjoyed decent runs in the FA Cup. The Reds' first stint as a full-time outfit was, however, short-lived as the FAW did not grant them permission to continue playing in the Southern League. It would take more than half a century, but Llanelli AFC eventually became a full-time professional football club once again. This happened in 2005 during a time when The Reds had firmly established themselves as one of the Welsh Premier League's top sides.

Chairman Robert Jones - the uncle of Hollywood star Catherine Zeta-Jones – had put the club up for sale for £350,000 and they were snapped up by investment company Jesco Group. Incoming chairman Nitin Parekh restored the club's full-time status and revealed ambitious plans to grow Llanelli in stature, which began to unfold with the appointment of former Atlético Madrid and Real Betis striker Lucas Cazorla Luque as director of football.

Luque brought Spanish flavour and flair to Stebonheath Park, signing a handful of his compatriots over the summer. Forwards Rudi Torres, Francisco Rodríguez and Jacob Mingorance were snapped up, along with midfield pair Efrén Fernández and Iván Nofuentes.

The Reds also made a statement of intent during that transfer window when former Swansea defender Stuart Jones signed on to become their first full-time player since the Stein era. Interviewed by *The Independent*, Parekh outlined his vision for the club: "I sat down with one of my directors and we thought about what sort of football we wanted to play. We

Llanelli boss Peter Nicholas with Terry Lewis. (© Terry Lewis)

wanted flair, the sort of style which would bring people through the turnstiles".

Llanelli's Spanish imports certainly brought style, though perhaps not as consistently as the fans would have liked. Torres netted twice on his debut - a 5-0 demolition of Bangor City - but his stay at Stebonheath wasn't a long one. Scottish outfit Hamilton Academicals poached him away from The Reds the following January, securing his services in a five-figure deal.

Fernández did appear to be a promising capture, until he suffered a leg break against Aberystwyth Town 10 games into his Llanelli career, keeping him out for the season. Rodríguez, meanwhile, only made a handful of appearances and found the net just once in the league, his sole strike coming in an away win over Cefn Druids.

Nofuentes was a minor success story and the driving force behind much of Llanelli's attacking play during the 2005-06 season. His pace and creativity were great assets for The Reds, and he wasn't too shabby in front of goal either, netting 15 times. The winger returned to Spain the following summer after helping his side to a second-placed league finish.

The cream of Llanelli's Spanish crop, however, was Mingorance; a creative spark in their midfield and a talented playmaker. The former Málaga man was named in the 2006 Welsh Premier League team of the year, but it was during the following season that he really shone, scoring 19 times and linking up well with top scorer Rhys Griffiths throughout the campaign.

Griffiths had joined the club following that white-hot season with Port Talbot, in which he won the Golden Boot and Player of the

Season awards. The prolific striker explained why Llanelli was the right move for him at the time:

> In every way, joining Llanelli was the perfect move for me. It was great to join a fully professional club, not least because I'd just bought my first house around then. They were an ambitious team who were eager to challenge. The target was to win the league and get into the Champions League, or at least qualify for Europe that season.
> I'm not sure what the chairman's motivation was, but they were certainly doing things properly. It was a very professional setup where players were sometimes training twice a day and having lunch together - everything was as it should be for full-timers.
> I felt like I prepared myself well for full-time football. I was always doing it the right way and training regularly, so this was a good opportunity for me.

To a large extent, the group of Spaniards who had mostly departed Llanelli at the time of Griffiths' arrival were fair weather players, quite literally. The technical abilities they honed back home were best suited to high quality playing surfaces and warmer weekends, and not so much rain-drenched pitches of Wales. Looking back on the impact they made at the club, though, Griffiths was full of praise for one of them in particular:

> There were only two Spanish players who stayed for the 2006-07 season. One of them was Mingorance, and he is one of the best I've ever played with. He was a left-footed player who lacked fitness, if I'm totally honest, but for an hour he was brilliant every game.

Like the majority of his compatriots, director of football Luque, didn't stick around at Llanelli for the long haul. His contract was cancelled the following February due to "irreconcilable differences over future strategy" and Peter Nicholas - a former Wales international who was part of his staff - took sole control of first-team affairs in the role of manager. "The board stresses the need for continuity and consistency in management strategy and will continue to execute its plan for the club," Llanelli's hierarchy said in a statement issued in the wake of the Spaniard's dismissal. "The board would like to thank Lucas for his contribution and for making the team a competitive force in the League. Llanelli AFC remains committed to its professional status and has continued to invest heavily on and off the pitch."

The Llanelli board lived up to its promises and continued pumping money into the club, but it was clear that The New Saints would prove difficult to dethrone. After securing their third consecutive league title in 2007, they moved into their newly renovated stadium, Park Hall, in Oswestry, giving them the infrastructure to match their success and future ambitions.

TNS had a significant head start on Llanelli, who were newcomers to the world of full-time professional football, and that was reflected in the points gulf between the two at the end of the season. The Reds amassed 13 points fewer than the league champions and were six behind second-placed Rhyl. This campaign did give them something to build on, although they ultimately failed to achieve their lofty ambitions, as Griffiths explained:

It wasn't really seen as a successful season overall. We expected to challenge for the league. We went to Bangor in mid-December and were top at the time, but we lost there and I think we went down 1-0 at Port Talbot over Christmas too. The wheels came off during that period. We gave TNS the chance to pull ahead of us and they took it.

We also lost in the semi-final of the Welsh Cup to Carmarthen, which was a game we should have won as well. We went from, at one point, looking like the double was on, to not winning anything, although getting back into Europe was very important financially.

Despite their disappointment in the league, Llanelli did, however, pull off one of the greatest European victories ever achieved by a Welsh Premier League side when they dumped Swedish club Gefle IF out of the UEFA Cup. An inspired 2-1 win away was followed up with a goalless draw at home to set up a tie against Odense BK of Denmark. The Reds lost 6-1 on aggregate, but their pride was more than intact.

Another positive was the *coup* they pulled off when they landed Griffiths in the run-up to the season. The striker picked up where he left off at Port Talbot Town to top the league goalscoring chart once again and, as he recalled, he was also on target in the memorable win in Sweden:

That was my debut in the Gefle game. I remember we were 1-0 down at half time and the fact that this wasn't good enough really highlighted the intent of the club.

We got an absolute hammering off Peter Nicholas during the interval, and then in the second half we went out full of fire. I equalised with a diving header, which actually came off my ear and lobbed the keeper, then Mingorance scored a great individual goal and we won it 2-1 on the night. The home leg finished 0-0, but we should have won that comfortably.

As a result of this European success Llanelli fans had every reason to believe their team could run champions The New Saints even closer the following season, though few would have predicted just how memorable the campaign would be for the ambitious Stebonheath Park outfit.

2007-08

It began on a somewhat sour note when fan-favourite Mingorance - the sole survivor of the club's Spanish revolution - left abruptly after becoming involved in a wage dispute. For all of their natural talent, it was difficult to argue that the midfielder and his fellow countrymen were missed, given the scintillating form Llanelli enjoyed home and away all season.

Under the savvy management of Nicholas, The Reds were steely and consistent, winning 27 out of their 34 league games, which was enough to help them bag their first Welsh Premier League title with a seven-point lead over second-placed TNS at the end of the campaign.

There were many factors that made this Llanelli side so difficult to beat. Firstly, they were awe-inspiring in front of goal, netting 99 times in the league. That's an average of nearly three goals per game, which was almost to be expected with Griffiths up front. He was once again the division's top marksman with 40 strikes to his name. Griffiths was a match-winner in every sense and this was one of seven consecutive campaigns in which he won the Golden Boot. What's more, the striker has gone on to become the second-highest goalscorer in the history of the competition, behind Bangor City legend Marc Lloyd Williams.

With such dedication to attractive, attacking football, most teams would be at risk of shipping almost as many goals at the other end of the pitch, yet the Llanelli class of 2008 were as defensively solid as they were deadly in the final third. With an experienced rear guard comprising Wyn Thomas, Stuart J Jones and former Wales international Andy Legg, The Reds only conceded 35 goals in their

34 Welsh Premier League matches; the division's fourth-best defensive record. Their nearest rivals, The New Saints, only let in five fewer.

The decisive result in the title race came in early March when Llanelli and TNS went head-to-head at Stebonheath. A win would have sent the visitors top, but The Reds would not be moved that evening. Craig Jones proved to be their key man on the night, setting up Llanelli's first two goals in a sublime 4-0 win before scoring himself in the second half.

While Llanelli's professionalism and efficiency at both ends of the pitch are obvious reasons they were so successful during this era, according to Rhys Griffiths - who has since gone into management himself, and is now in charge of Penybont - Peter Nicholas' tactical prowess and rousing team talks played an important part in that title triumph too:

> There's good and bad in every manager I've had and Peter was no different. I thought he was very good at half time and before games. He showed real intensity during his team talks, the Gefle game I mentioned being a good example of this.
> Tactically, he was decent. For instance, in that pivotal game against The New Saints when we won the league, he chose to play Andrew Mumford behind me up front, and that really paid off as Andrew scored twice on the day.

Stebonheath Park, home of Llanelli FC. (© Welsh Football Magazine)

Peter always signed well and put a lot of faith in his senior players to run the changing room for him. That's really important - and I've found that myself since I went into management.

In mid-March, Llanelli had the chance to lift the first silverware of the Welsh domestic season when they lined up against Newport County in the FAW Premier Cup final. Playing with home advantage, as the game took place at their own Newport Stadium, marking the second time the final was staged there, County won the trophy for the one and only time through a late goal from Craig Hughes, in front of almost 2,000 fans. However, the decision to play the game in very poor conditions still rankles Griffiths:

That game against Newport should never have been played. The weather that day was horrendous and we were up against it because the match took place at their ground. Credit to Newport, though. They handled the conditions a lot better than us.

They were what I'd described as a 'streetwise' team, while we had a squad of young players. They had the likes of Jason Bowen, Lee Jarman and Steve Jenkins adding experience to their ranks, and they just ground out a 1-0 win.

I remember having a great chance to score just after half time and I totally fluffed it. I'll never forget that, but like I said, it was disappointing that a showcase game like this was allowed to go ahead under those conditions.

This proved to be the last edition of the FAW Premier Cup as the competition was folded after the BBC withdrew its backing in 2008. The broadcaster's decision came amid dwindling interest in the cup and claims that the teams from the English system weren't taking it seriously. Griffiths still sees that decision as one that impacted the domestic clubs far worse than those playing in England:

That competition has been a big loss to the Welsh domestic game because of the potential for giant killings and prize money. We beat Wrexham in the quarters and they were still in the Football League then. We were 2-0 down and came back to win 4-2.

There was a lot of money in that competition. We got £50,000 for coming second and Newport County got £100,000 for winning it. At one time, the top goalscorer - which was me that year - earned £10,000.

However, just as as the BBC was losing interest in Welsh Premier League clubs, another broadcaster ramped up its coverage of domestic football. S4C's *Sgorio* had been airing live games from Europe's top leagues since the late 1980s and, from 2008, they began showing live matches from the Welsh Premier League every weekend. *Sgorio* has gone on to become one of the Welsh top flight's greatest assets and now regularly broadcasts live games and highlights shows live to air and via the internet.

Nicholas' side may have lost a cup final, but they were in the driving seat in the title race, and with TNS and Llanelli due to meet again on the final day, many were tipping the contest to go to the wire. There was, however, a twist in the tale before then.

Llanelli had been incredibly consistent after that victory over The New Saints, winning seven of their next eight matches, which gave them the opportunity to wrap up the title at Connah's Quay Nomads on 12 April, but they ended up winning the league without kicking a ball.

The previous evening, TNS were expected to see off an Airbus UK side that was set to finish in the bottom half, but The Wingmakers registered a surprise 2-0 win. Although this rendered The Reds' trip to Deeside meaningless, where the outcome of the league was concerned, Llanelli won the match regardless, with Griffiths scoring the only goal of the game. "It's good it's all settled and we don't have to go to the wire," a delighted Nicholas told reporters ahead of the match against Connah's Quay. "Full credit to the players and staff and with three games to go, we can start to enjoy ourselves."

Llanelli's title success saw their manager become the first coach to win the Welsh national championship with two different clubs, having previously won it with Barry Town.

Nicholas also added a League Cup to his personal honours list in late April when Llanelli reached the final of the competition on away goals following a 2-2 aggregate draw with Aberystwyth Town. This set up a final against Rhyl FC, who had overcome Bangor 3-1 over two legs.

The match took place at Newtown's Latham Park where first-half goals from Andrew Mumford and Chris Holloway sealed victory and a maiden League Cup for Llanelli, as Griffiths recalled:

We played Rhyl five times that season. We played them twice in the league. We played them in the League Cup final, the Welsh Cup semi-final and the

Premier Cup semi-final - and we managed to beat them every time. As much as I look back with a bit of pride at that League Cup victory, at the time, it was all about the Welsh Cup, the final of which was coming up a week later.

Meanwhile, TNS, who were denied a record-equalling fourth Welsh league title in a row, reclaimed some pride on the final day of the season when they beat Llanelli 3-0 at Park Hall. It was a dead-rubber fixture and the outcome of it may also have been influenced by the fact that The Reds had an upcoming Welsh Cup final against Bangor City to prepare for.

Nicholas' team returned to Latham Park on 4 May to face The Citizens, hopeful of making it triple honours following their league title and League Cup success. It proved to be a chaotic final where neither side did themselves proud defensively, though it was enjoyable for the neutrals and, ultimately, the Bangor faithful too, but their team did it the hard way. A Griffiths strike just before the hour mark gave Llanelli a 2-1 advantage and that's the way it stayed until the last minute when Christian Seargeant pounced to force extra time.

Play was halted for eight minutes due to a pitch invasion from a section of the Bangor support in the wake of Seargeant's equaliser. There were even reports that some of the Llanelli players were

Bangor City celebrating victory in the 2008 Welsh Cup final. (© Tomos Lewis)

assaulted when fans stormed the pitch, and after the final whistle. The drama continued into extra time, and through a Marc Limbert penalty and a goal from substitute Karl Noon, Bangor got their hands on the famous trophy for the sixth time.

All in all, those in attendance saw six goals, three red cards (one of which was shown to Griffiths), an injury-time equaliser, and a pitch invasion at Latham Park. Value for money; less so if you happened to be a Llanelli supporter or one of their players, as Griffiths explained:

To be honest, that game was horrendous. By then, I think we'd probably played about 60 games that season because we did well in every competition and in Europe.

They had a man sent off early, but that seemed to galvanise them to defend for their lives and we just didn't perform that well. That opening goal I still claim to this day, but it was officially given as an own goal. The second goal I scored and I was really pleased with, and we should have seen the game out from there.

When they equalised, that pitch invasion happened and they knocked over the keeper - I'll be honest, we were hoping the game would be abandoned because we were out on our feet. When Thomas got sent off and the 10 versus 11 advantage was gone, they were much stronger than us in extra time. I knew it was game over when it went to 3-2.

One of the centre-backs had been winding me up all game, and I said to him "If you wind me up again, I'm going to smack you". So he did, and I did. I got sent off and they won 4-2 in the end. I felt like I let the team down, because getting sent off in such a big game was poor.

In Llanelli AFC, The New Saints appeared to have met their match. Another fully professional outfit had arrived on the scene and they had the financial clout and calibre of players to permanently replace them at the summit of the Welsh football pyramid.

A great rivalry might have developed between the two full-time clubs had Llanelli not suffered the same fate as many Welsh league champions and succumbed to financial ruin. The club was unable to replicate the success of 2007-08 the following season and Nicholas left his post. Griffiths believes there was more to his departure than meets the eye:

I think Peter probably got sacked for things that, to this day, I don't know about. I'm not suggesting it was anything too untoward going on there,

Llanelli's title-winning side of 2007-08. (© Terry Lewis)

perhaps just some arguments with the chairman. I don't think it was football-related anyway.

Andy Legg was named as player-manager to replace Nicholas in the dugout and the former Wales international did enjoy some success; initially, at least, as Griffiths reflected on the change in management:

Peter got sacked and Leggy got his job. It wasn't a shock at the time because there were rumours that he was going to leave, but I was disappointed because I always got on with Peter. I was his captain after all. Andy brought Steve Jenkins with him when he took over, and he was brilliant - I've still got a lot of time for Steve. He was a really good coach.

Highlights of Legg's time in charge include a memorable first-leg win over Scottish Premiership side Motherwell in the new Europa League - dampened only slightly by a 3-0 defeat in the return leg - and a first Welsh Cup triumph in 2010-11. This came thanks to an impressive 4-1 victory over Bangor City in the final at Parc y Scarlets, the home of rugby union side Llanelli RFC and a second home of sorts for The Reds when playing in Europe. However, the promise of the Nicholas era had diminished, according to Griffiths:

We still had largely the same team during that period, a really good side who continued in the same vein, always up there competing and we went on to win the Welsh Cup, but we were probably not quite as good as we should have been, to be honest.

Legg left the club in November 2012, five months before it was wound up due to unpaid tax debts of £21,000 and Llanelli AFC became yet another ambitious Welsh club who had flown too close to the sun, but such teams have a way of coming back from the dead. They were reborn as Llanelli Town that same year and recognised by the FA of Wales as an official continuation of the previous team, albeit with part-time status, but had to begin this new chapter of their existence in Welsh Football League Division Three; a small price to pay considering the alternative was extinction.

Llanelli did fight their way back up into the Welsh Premier League but were relegated in 2019 and, as a result, are currently playing their football in Cymru South.

Welsh Premier League (2007-08)	P	W	D	L	For	Ag	Pts
1 Llanelli AFC	34	27	4	3	99	35	85
2 The New Saints	34	25	3	6	85	30	78
3 Rhyl FC	34	21	6	7	60	24	69
4 Port Talbot Town	34	17	8	9	57	48	59
5 Bangor City	34	15	10	9	62	31	55
6 Carmarthen Town	34	15	9	10	59	47	54
7 Neath FC	34	15	9	10	57	52	54
8 Haverfordwest County	34	14	5	15	61	59	47
9 Aberystwyth Town	34	13	7	14	57	45	46
10 Technogroup Welshpool	34	12	10	12	49	52	46
11 Airbus UK Broughton	34	11	9	14	36	44	42
12 Elements Cefn Druids	34	12	2	20	45	66	38
13 Newtown AFC	34	9	10	15	47	66	37
14 Caernarfon Town	34	10	6	18	42	74	36
15 Gap Connah's Quay	34	9	7	18	42	85	34
16 Porthmadog FC	34	7	6	21	48	70	27
17 Caersws FC	34	6	8	20	37	72	26
18 Llangefni Town	34	7	3	24	39	82	24

11

The Dream Team

2008-09

When Rhyl FC won an unlikely quadruple in 2004, it was an underdog story for the ages. Manager John Hulse had modest resources to work with, but he squeezed every drop out of that group of players, dared them to dream and inspired them to greatness. More silverware and European adventures would follow in the Hulse era, which remains the most successful period in the club's history; though it came to an abrupt end in May of 2008.

Hulse announced that he was vacating his post just weeks before The Lilywhites were due to begin an Intertoto Cup campaign against Irish side Bohemians. The news came out of the blue and left Rhyl fans reeling. Little more than a month earlier, the outgoing manager had expressed his excitement about a sixth consecutive European campaign with the club.

Although nobody saw it coming, The Lilywhites legend insisted that his departure was amicable and he spoke fondly of the club and its fans when announcing his decision. "I've had six great years with Rhyl but I felt it was best for everyone that the change is made now," he said in a statement published by the *Daily Post*. "People will look for all sorts of reasons but the plain fact is that I believe it's time to move on. I told the club last Wednesday and initially agreed to stay on until after the Bohemians matches, but on further reflection I decided to make the break now. I've had a great relationship with the people at the club and with the fans, who have been fantastic, and I'm sure I'll always be assured of a warm welcome at Belle Vue in the future."

Rhyl's first competitive matches since Hulse's exit were forgettable ones. That two-legged tie against Bohemians finished 8-3 to the League of Ireland outfit, but with a new management team of Allan Bickerstaff and Osian Roberts soon in place, things were looking up.

By this point, ongoing investment, prize money and European football revenue had built up and this gave Bickerstaff and Roberts a generous transfer war chest to harness. They invested these funds wisely, assembling a squad packed with the kind of professional experience Rhyl needed to close the gap on full-timers Llanelli and The New Saints.

New recruits Neil Roberts, Gareth Owen, Danny Williams and striker Jamie Reed were former Wrexham stars, while Matthew Williams was a product of Manchester United's youth academy. Veteran defender Greg Strong, a journeyman with experience in both the English and Scottish professional leagues, rounded off a successful summer of recruitment. Strong outlined why Rhyl was an enticing place to see out his playing career following a spell with Dundee:

> *I'll be honest, I didn't really know a lot about Rhyl at the time but I did a bit of research and was invited down for a chat. Once I saw Neil Roberts, Gaz Owen and some of the other guys and had a good talk with them, I realised it was a move I should consider. It was Neil who told me how ambitious the club was and explained that they were looking to get into the Champions League.*
>
> *As soon as those words 'Champions League' were mentioned, that sealed it. I was a bit of a journeyman in my career, but that was a competition I'd never played in. The opportunity excited me, and it was the same for a lot of players who joined Rhyl back then.*

High-profile new signings seemed to be arriving by the day at Belle Vue. Dave Jones, a prominent Welsh Premier League football reporter, wrote about the club extensively at the time and often referred to the squad Bickerstaff and Roberts built as "The Dream Team": "[It was] an incredibly exciting time to be a reporter. I was getting invited down to the ground on a regular basis to interview the next big signing." he wrote on his website, *Grassroots North Wales*, in a retrospective account of The Lilywhites' 2008-09 campaign.

There was a real buzz around the club and this put them in good stead for their opening league game, a home showdown with Newtown. Roberts and Reed got their Rhyl careers off to a flyer with debut goals and Greg Stones added another in a 3-0 win.

Rhyl didn't drop a point until 21 September when they visited Neath FC, who had announced plans to go full-time in the summer

Greg Strong and his Rhyl FC squad. (© Rhyl 1879)

and a player development partnership with Swansea City. Goals from Stones and Reed had given Rhyl a 2-0 lead at the interval, but a second-half fightback from the hosts saw the spoils shared in a 2-2 draw.

The Lilywhites lost a league match for the first time on 15 November. Port Talbot Town were the visitors to Belle Vue that day, and came away with a surprise 3-2 win.

Despite this wobble in front of their own fans, Rhyl were running away with the title and would ultimately lose just one more league game all season - a 4-3 reverse at home to Cefn Druids in December. They never looked like being caught by title rivals Llanelli and The New Saints - who went on to finish second and third respectively - at any point in the campaign. It was a season awash with highlights and memorable victories, but for Strong, one game from early in the campaign stands out as the best result and performance of them all.

On 30 August, champions Llanelli travelled to Belle Vue and were humbled by a 5-1 clobbering thanks to goals from Danny Williams, Jamie Reed and Josh Johnson, as well as a Neil Roberts double. Stuart J Jones netted a consolation for The Reds, but their free-scoring marksman, Rhys Griffiths, was kept at bay that afternoon, as Strong recalled:

> *I had heard about Rhys Griffiths and how nobody could handle him in the league. I think it was myself and George Horan who were playing centre-half at the time and I certainly thought going up against Rhys was a challenge. I'm sure George did as well, but in that game we made a really big statement. We absolutely ran all over them in every department. We were better than them on and off the ball. We were fit, strong, and we understood the game. They didn't have any answers to what we threw at them. I think it was after that game that people realised we were a real team.*

The league was won in spectacular fashion in mid-April when Rhyl beat The New Saints 2-1 at Belle Vue, in front of more than 1,500 spectators. Alex Darlington had fired TNS ahead but Neil Roberts equalised in the 34th minute, before Mark Connolly latched onto a misplaced pass from Saints midfielder Barry Hogan and slotted in a title-clinching winner.

Although Strong was delighted to seal the title, he admits to having fonder memories of another victory over The New Saints, which came earlier in the campaign:

> *It was great to get over the line at that point, but this game doesn't stick in my mind as much as our away win to TNS earlier in the season. I think that was 3-0 and a win like that on their turf was unheard of at the time. They were full-time and rarely lost at all.*
> *We really did play well on the day and that was another eye-opener for people. We went there with no fear, even though people had told us all kinds of stories about them footballing teams to death. We were excellent on the day and it was a very comfortable victory.*

Rhyl kicked on and stretched their impressive run to the end of the season, defeating Cefn Druids 4-2 to extend their unbeaten streak to 18 games, 17 of which were wins. What's more, their final points total of 90 was the highest amassed by a Welsh Premier League champion since Barry Town won the competition with 104 on the board in 1998.

Llanelli were only seven points behind come the end of the season, but that emphatic 5-1 win Rhyl registered against them early in the season served as a bold statement of intent that set a precedent in the balance of power between the league's title hopefuls. The Golden Boot did, however, return to Stebonheath Park thanks to another prolific season for Rhys Griffiths, who netted 31 Welsh Premier League goals in 2008-09.

Third place was seen as a disappointment for TNS, though they did not finish the season trophyless having lifted the League Cup in early April thanks to a 2-0 win over Bangor City, in which John Leah and Conall Murtagh scored either side of half time.

At the other end of the league table, Caernarfon Town looked dead and buried midway through the campaign and finished the season bottom with 20 points. They were relegated to the Cymru Alliance, with Bala Town replacing them in the top flight. Second-bottom Caersws were only five points better off, though they did not join Caernarfon in the drop. They survived relegation due to Welsh League Division One champions Ento Aberaman (Aberdare Town) failing to meet the FA of Wales' ground regulations for the top flight.

With the league campaign ending on 25 April, there was still the not-so-small matter of the Welsh Cup final to resolve. Bangor City had the chance to make amends for losing the League Cup final to TNS the previous month, while their opponents Aberystwyth Town were looking to turn an unspectacular season into a great one by nabbing some silverware.

Bangor, the holders, were odds-on favourites to retain the trophy for a second year running, and the bookmakers didn't get this one wrong. The Citizens emerged 2-0 winners at Parc y Scarlets, with Les Davies and Christian Seargeant on the scoresheet.

On the way to the final, Bangor had knocked out league champions Rhyl in the fourth round of the competition, triumphing 4-2 on penalties after a 1-1 draw. They had also got the better of The Lilywhites in the League Cup earlier in the season, dumping them out at the quarter-final stage. They needed extra time for that one, ultimately winning the tie 3-1. For Strong, losing two cup ties in one season to such bitter rivals still stings to this day:

We wanted to win everything and I remember being as mad as I ever was during my time at Rhyl when we lost away at Bangor in the Welsh Cup. They were down to 10 men and we absolutely battered them for most of the game. For whatever reason, whether we were sloppy with our finishing or it was a bit of luck on their part, we couldn't make our dominance count despite creating so many chances.

Then it went to penalties and we lost in the shootout. I remember being livid because we should really have won the game comfortably. That was a really, really bad night.

While Rhyl's 'Dream Team' couldn't reproduce the cup success of their 2004 predecessors, the way they stormed what was expected to be a competitive league holds a special place in the hearts of their supporters. This team was a far cry from the unfancied minnows who bagged a quadruple against the odds. The professional pedigree they boasted even had them fancying their chances of causing an upset or two in Europe the following season.

Their Champions League qualifying campaign began with a tantalising tie against Serbian giants Partizan Belgrade. Osian Roberts - who had reduced his role in the management of Rhyl by this point due to his commitments as FAW Trust technical director - took full control of the team for the first leg at Belle Vue as Bickerstaff had a long-standing family commitment. He was upbeat ahead of the match and confident of giving the Serbs a game: "Obviously we have to be organised to deal with things such as set pieces, tactics and their general shape, but I'm more interested in getting our players to play," he said in a pre-match statement published in the *Daily Post*. "If each player can get an eight or a nine out of ten then it could be a night to remember for Rhyl fans. If we're going to lose then let's do so having a right good go at them."

Rhyl attempted to take the game to Partizan and managed a respectable 11 shots on target in the first leg, but they were thoroughly outmatched on the night. The visitors, who were then managed by former Watford and Fulham boss Slaviša Jokanović, won the game 4-0 thanks to three first-half goals and a header from Nenad Đorđević after the break. It was a tough game, as Greg Strong admitted:

It was a good experience but those defeats were tough to take. We had our pride and were used to winning week in, week out. In the first leg, I thought that we held our own. I know it finished 4-0, but I thought we were alright. We hit the post at 1-0 but didn't create a lot of clear-cut chances because they were tough to break down. I do think we were competitive for spells of the match and it wasn't an easy game for them.

The away leg took place in front of 10,000 spectators in Belgrade, and Rhyl were Welsh lambs to the Serbian slaughter in the nation's

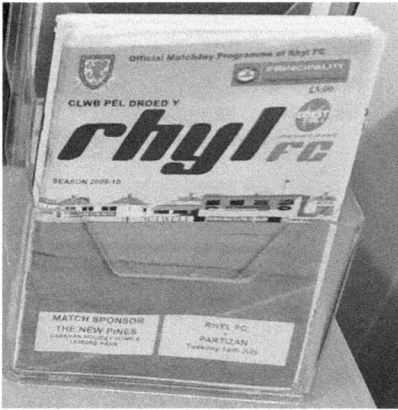

The official programme from Rhyl's European clash with Partizan Belgrade. (© Rhyl 1879)

capital. Their hosts didn't hold back that night, and as Strong recalled, their new signing Cléo helped himself to a hat-trick as Partizan breezed to an 8-0 triumph, a record European victory for them:

In that second leg at their place, they gave us a footballing lesson and just ripped us to pieces. I think on that day they made us look like what we were - a group of ageing footballers.

Eyebrows were raised when Bickerstaff was absent from The Lilywhites dugout in the first leg, and later that month, Rhyl announced that they were parting company with their manager before the 2009-10 league season had even begun. His exit came hot on the heels of reports that the club had slashed his transfer budget for the upcoming campaign.

Strong was installed as player-manager and had little more than a fortnight to prepare for the first league game of the season. The squad he inherited from Bickerstaff had also been reduced to 14 players as part of the cost-cutting measures implemented by the board. With limited coaching experience behind him, the former Dundee and Motherwell defender admitted to having reservations about taking the job:

It was after the Champions League tie that they asked me to take over, and I'll be honest, I did have doubts about it. I wasn't on the coaching staff there and it wasn't something I was looking at doing. I was coaching at Bolton's academy at the time, though.

I was surprised to hear that Bickerstaff was gone because we won the league the season before. I think it was a personal dispute or contractual problem that led to that. Peter Parry gave me a phone call and said "We're not going to interview for the job and would like to offer it to you." I was shocked because there were coaches already on the books at the club.

It's not in my nature to step away from things, so right away I said "Yeah, I'll do it". I literally learned on the job because I didn't prepare myself in any kind of formal sense.

Hampered by difficult circumstances, Strong couldn't emulate the previous season's success and his side were off the pace in the title race. Initially on course for a top-three finish, Rhyl ultimately finished sixth, but with only three points between them and third-placed Port Talbot.

Missing out on Europe was frustrating for Strong and The Lilywhites, but they had much bigger problems come the end of the season. On 17 May 2010, Rhyl's licence to play in the Welsh Premier League was revoked. Although they insisted that they met the criteria for the top flight, the club was penalised for failing to submit their accounts on time.

Upon appeal, however, it transpired that The Lilywhites' financial situation did indeed prevent them from meeting the requirements, and they were demoted to the Cymru Alliance. "Rhyl FC are to step back from the Welsh Premier League after the FAW rejected the licence application," read a statement from the club, issued after their unsuccessful appeal. "Financially, the club has had a very difficult second half to the season. The manager, the players and all non-playing staff have been magnificent throughout this difficult period. We have taken steps to rationalise the operations and we are actively seeking new sponsors. We had hoped to remain at the top of Welsh football whilst working through the residual financial issues. Now we will continue to rebuild the club's finances and get back to the WPL as soon as possible."

An unexpected relegation just one season on from winning the top prize in Welsh domestic football forced Strong to consider his future, but the close relationships he had forged with his players and staff ultimately convinced him to stick around at Belle Vue:

> *When we were relegated I was left with a decision to make about whether I wanted to stay on and manage in the lower division, but at that time I'd built up some really good relationships at Rhyl. I'd been at the club a few years and when you move over to the management side, you get close to and speak a lot more with the people behind the scenes and you see what it means to them. I decided to stay on and try to help the club get back up to the top flight.*

Going from champions to relegation in the space of 12 months is a dramatic downward spiral by any standards, but this wasn't the last the Welsh Premier League would see of Rhyl FC. Their bid to make an immediate return to the top division appeared to be going to plan, until Strong received bad news from the club's hierarchy:

Things were going well in my first year at the helm, and then I was called to a meeting where I was told we weren't going to apply for a Welsh Premier League licence for the next season. This knocked me for six because I felt like we were very close to getting back to where we were. Being told that made me question my future. It was all down to finances, which I understand in hindsight, and rightly or wrongly I decided to see things out and stick around.

Rhyl twice finished runners-up in the Cymru Alliance before winning promotion in style in the 2012-13 season. During that campaign, Rhyl didn't lose a single league match and became the first team to win the Cymru Alliance while remaining unbeaten. As Strong outlined, his men also scored a staggering 100 goals while securing promotion back to the top flight:

We saw the 2011-12 season through and the following year I was told we would be going for the licence. When we did get promoted back up, we went the entire season unbeaten and I think that makes us the only team to ever achieve this in the second tier.

We got a great set of players together that season despite having a tiny budget, and I had a lot of loyalty to those lads. What it showed me was that if you get a group of people who are all committed to the same cause, it can take you a long way. Obviously they need a bit of quality about them as well, but that squad was second to none.

I had lads who were working in Carlisle but they'd journey to Rhyl for training and then head back home again. The money wasn't even worth them doing that. It was actually costing them to come! What an incredible group of players they were!

Unfortunately for Rhyl fans, their return to the Welsh Premier League wasn't the stuff of fairy tales. After three unremarkable seasons, they were relegated again in 2016-17. This was followed by another three years in the Cymru Alliance before their financial woes intensified with the outbreak of the coronavirus pandemic and the resulting postponement of all Welsh football. With no income and scant investment coming in, Rhyl's board took the decision to cease all activity and a formal winding up order followed, making the two-time Welsh champions the first British club to fold as a result of the Covid-19 pandemic.

It was a sad day for Welsh football. Even though the impact of coronavirus was partly to blame for Rhyl's demise, it was disheartening to see yet another Welsh Premier League champion suffer this fate, especially one with a history stretching back to 1878. Strong agreed:

> *I think Rhyl are really missed in the top flight because when I was there, it was always a ground the opposition relished coming to. The pitch was always good and it was usually one of the higher crowds in the division. I still feel for the people who put a lot of work in getting the club to the top - not the ones who pushed their faces to the front and wanted people to hear about what they'd done - but the ones who were always in the background and would do anything for that club.*
>
> *It's sad because there were days when we'd get 2,000 into Belle Vue for the Bangor and Prestatyn games - it was alive and it was a really good place to be. It was on the way up and it's just a shame that bad decisions were made and they ended up where they are.*

This may be a depressingly familiar scenario for clubs in the Welsh domestic leagues, but there is a silver lining to this tale and others like it. Phoenix clubs are a running theme in Welsh football, and they are proof that teams like Rhyl can never truly die. They are so ingrained

Phoenix club Rhyl 1879 in Ardal NW League action during the 2022-23 season. (© M Langshaw)

in the hearts of their supporters and the towns they're based in; and this often gives them a route back from the abyss, albeit in a different form than before.

In The Lilywhites' case, that form was CPD Y Rhyl 1879, a spiritual successor to the former Welsh Premier League champions founded by members of the club's staff and the Rhyl Fan Association (RFA) to uphold the legacy and traditions of the original team. If CPD Y Rhyl 1879 are to ever return to the top flight, their journey back will be a long one, beginning in the lower reaches of the Welsh football pyramid.

Their fans, however, have every reason to be upbeat. Not only have the new club's directors secured the use of the Belle Vue ground for their home matches, the team that arose from Rhyl's ashes won the North Wales Coast East Football League Premier Division in 2022 and, at the time of writing, are among the favourites for promotion in the 2023-24 Ardal North West campaign.

Welsh Premier League (2008-09)	P	W	D	L	For	Ag	Pts
1 Rhyl FC	34	29	3	2	95	29	90
2 Llanelli AFC	34	26	5	3	98	38	83
3 The New Saints FC	34	20	11	3	79	27	71
4 Carmarthen Town	34	19	5	10	62	47	62
5 Port Talbot Town	34	16	8	10	57	48	56
6 Bangor City	34	16	7	11	58	40	55
7 Haverfordwest County	34	16	7	11	53	39	55
8 Aberystwyth Town	34	12	10	12	51	50	46
9 Gap Connah's Quay	34	12	5	17	49	65	41
10 Newtown AFC	34	10	10	14	46	54	40
11 Technogroup Welshpool	34	11	7	16	48	70	40
12 Airbus UK Broughton	34	12	3	19	47	57	39
13 NEWI Cefn Druids	34	9	7	18	57	74	34
14 Neath FC	34	10	4	20	43	65	34
15 Prestatyn Town	34	8	9	17	48	70	33
16 CPD Porthmadog	34	10	2	22	57	91	32
17 Caersws FC	34	6	7	21	38	61	25
18 Caernarfon Town*	34	8	8	21	32	73	20

*3pts deducted

12

The 'Super 12'

There were ups and downs for the Welsh Premier League and its member clubs in the first two decades of its life. For all of the thrills and promise it brought, poor attendances and the ever present threat of the financial abyss were a blight on the competition; and in April 2008, the Football Association of Wales agreed that a radical shake-up was needed.

The governing body summoned the top flight's 18 clubs to vote on its proposals for sweeping change across the length and breadth of Welsh domestic football. The plans, drawn up by then-FAW secretary John Deakin, involved dissolving the Premier League in its current format and replacing it with a First and Second Division comprising 10 teams each. As Deakin explained:

I didn't think that having 20 clubs was sustainable, financially for one thing. I saw the finances of these clubs and some of the lesser known teams were struggling. It would have been a novelty if a club had rung me up one day and said they were well off. A lot of clubs were asking "When are we getting this money; when are we getting that money?" They were relying on it to carry on, and too many were under threat of extinction.

Although some would claim that changes were long overdue, Deakin acknowledged that the FAW's hand was essentially forced on this one due to the new licensing requirements tabled by UEFA:

I thought those new licensing regulations were a good idea. Looking back at their impact over time, I think they have improved the standards of the league infrastructurally, on the sporting side because of the academies, and also financially, but the financial requirements were stringent and if clubs couldn't meet them, they couldn't play in the league. I didn't want to see half the clubs disenfranchised from the Welsh Premier League, so I proposed the idea of a second division with more lenient licensing rules.

The clubs voted in favour of the proposals as well as a further motion to grant the Football Association of Wales full control of the league, a move that resulted in the dissolution of Football League of Wales Limited, the legal entity that previously managed the division.

After the Welsh Premier League's member clubs had their say, Deakin's restructuring plans were circulated among the rest of the FAW's top brass for further review. Those plans, however, did not, get the seal of approval, and more than a year later, the league's clubs found themselves voting on alternative measures to reduce the division to just 12 teams. Deakin takes up the story:

> *I originally wanted to give the 10 clubs who could not secure a licence the chance to improve, and have a potential path to the top division afterwards, but the FAW Council came back and, after some discussion, told me it would be one division of 12 clubs.*

This was a contentious proposition, not least because it could have resulted in up to eight clubs being relegated in the 2009-10 season, depending on whether any teams from the Cymru Alliance and Welsh Football League's top flight were eligible for promotion. It was inevitable that some of the relegated teams would feel a massive sense of injustice come the end of that campaign, but these proposals were voted through nonetheless.

There was, however, an ongoing situation involving a club on the Welsh border that could have impacted the FAW's restructuring ambitions. Chester City of the English non-league had been expelled from the Blue Square Premier due to an unpaid tax bill, and their hierarchy reportedly lodged an application to join the Welsh Premier League in March 2010.

Chester's decision to seek refuge in the Welsh league system was not made at random. Not only had the club competed in the Welsh Cup on numerous occasions when the tournament hosted guest participants from along the border, but their home ground, the Deva Stadium, was actually located in Wales with just a part the car park and a small section of the structure located in England. In fact, the Deva had once been earmarked by TNS as a potential venue for their top flight and European fixtures before they moved ahead with Park Hall's development.

When quizzed on the reports of Chester seeking to join the division, Deakin was diplomatic, but he did, however, conclude that he would have welcomed the stricken English non-league outfit into the division and believes they would have been an asset to it:

> *I cannot recall the club making a formal application to join the league, but, if they had done the application would have had my support, given their geographical location, fan base and facilities. I can remember visiting the stadium as part of a study when we were trying to improve the overall standard of Welsh Premier club grounds. To achieve this we tried to get a substantial grant from the Welsh Government but, not surprisingly, to little avail.*

Ultimately, the FAW didn't have to spend much time mulling over how to incorporate Chester into their plans as the club was formally wound up the day after their application was purportedly submitted. They later reformed within the English pyramid as a phoenix club called Chester FC, a move the majority of their supporters were firmly behind.

Since its formation as the League of Wales in the early 1990s, the number of teams in the division had always fluctuated, with 18 being the average, but the new status quo would see it undergo a hard reboot with its lowest club count and a markedly different format.

2009-10

The FAW's overhaul came at a time when the Welsh Premier League was arguably at its most competitive. Ahead of the 2009-10 campaign, an unpredictable title race was anticipated between full-timers The New Saints and Llanelli, while Rhyl were expected to be no pushovers under Greg Strong, despite having their budget slashed that summer.

Then there was Neath, outsiders for a title challenge having gone fully professional off the back of their partnership with Swansea City. This agreement saw Swans players, including Kyle Graves, Dion Chambers and Kerry Morgan, join Neath to gain first-time experience.

Meanwhile, Bangor City supporters also had high hopes for the upcoming season following back-to-back success in the Welsh Cup. They were going from strength to strength under the management of Neville Powell and were expected to at least challenge for Europe.

Bangor City pay a visit to Bala Town early in 2009-10 campaign. (© Welsh Football Magazine)

On paper, it was TNS who had the strongest squad at the start of the season. Players like goalkeeper Paul Harrison, defender Chris Marriott and experienced midfielder Scott Ruscoe became integral parts of a team that went on to achieve total dominance of Welsh football. Manager Andy Cale recruited smartly in both transfer windows, bringing in Danny Holmes from Tranmere Rovers as well as top talent from rival Welsh clubs, including Bangor City duo Christian Seargeant and Chris Sharp, and Aeron Edwards from Caersws FC.

TNS had strengthened across the pitch, yet this wasn't enough to spark an upturn in their European fortunes. They were drawn against Iceland's Fram Reykjavík in Europa League qualifying and threw away early leads in both legs to lose 2-1 in each, and 4-2 on aggregate.

The home leg was the first continental fixture to take place at Park Hall, which meant that 1,000 extra seats had to be installed at the ground to satisfy UEFA's requirements. After the second leg in Oswestry, Andy Cale was upbeat about his team's performance and their prospects for the upcoming domestic season: "If we keep playing like that all season I'll be happy," he told BBC Sport. "We dominated and played fantastically well but they had two attacks and scored two - it was one of those ties. Their keeper was fantastic and people don't realise how much difference it makes [to Reykjavík] being in the middle of their season. We dominated the game but we were not match sharp. That will always be a problem for us, playing in Europe at this time of year."

Progression beyond the first round of a European competition was still a flight of fancy for the club at this stage, but TNS got their Welsh Premier League campaign off to the ideal start one month on from the Reykjavík defeat by mauling Prestatyn Town 5-0 at Park Hall.

The match was over as a contest by half time as goals from Jamie Wood and Matthew Berkeley, coupled with a Craig Jones double, saw The Saints head into the break 4-0 up. Sergeant added a fifth in the 49th minute to apply some extra gloss to the scoreline.

Europa League heartache soon became a distant memory as Cale's men won their next three games in a row - a run which included an impressive 2-0 victory at Bangor City - and kept clean sheets in three out of their first four Welsh Premier League fixtures, conceding for the first time in a 2-1 victory over Airbus Broughton at the end of August.

The Saints dropped their first points of the season several days later when they entertained Newtown. Neil Mitchell and Jamie Breese had given The Robins a two-goal lead with just over 20 minutes to play, but Steve Abbott's strike reduced the deficit before Marriott pounced in the final minute to ensure the spoils were shared and the hosts remained undefeated.

That unbeaten run came to an abrupt end in TNS' next match, an away day at Port Talbot. Managed by Mark Jones, The Steelmen were strong that season and they proved it by claiming a major scalp. Liam McCreesh, who went on to win Player of the Season for 2009-10, scored twice in a 2-0 win to condemn The Saints to their first reverse of the campaign.

"Little Liam did really well, but all in all, my side were smashing today," said Jones in a post-match statement published in the *Daily Post*. "I repeat what I said at the start of the season. My aim is to see us in the top 10 and qualify for the new super league. I believe there will be a major casualty in qualifying for the new league, a team that's been in the division for over eight years. To lose out would be devastating for any club and that's what we must focus on."

Carlos Castan (left) of Neath and Osian Jones (right) of Bala Town in action during the 2009-10 season. (© Shutterstock)

The loss at Port Talbot was only a minor setback for TNS as Cale's side quickly returned to winning ways. A 3-0 triumph over Connah's Quay Nomads in their next match was the start of a tremendous 22-game unbeaten run in all domestic competitions. It was those same opponents who ended that winning streak on 5 February 2010, with Mike Hayes' strike proving the difference in a surprise 1-0 success for The Nomads at Deeside Stadium.

Llanelli were locked in the two-horse title race with TNS throughout the campaign and the pair of frontrunners put serious distance between themselves and the chasing pack. It was an intense contest that essentially came down to the head-to-head fixtures between the teams. Both of them were edged by TNS, 2-0 and 1-0 respectively.

With five games remaining, however, it was Andy Leggs' Llanelli in pole position. They had a five-point lead over The New Saints, though this became two when TNS defeated their rivals at Park Hall, with former Bury defender Craig Jones scoring the only goal of the day.

TNS then leapfrogged The Reds the following weekend by seeing off defending champions Rhyl, while Leggs' men could only manage

Neath take on Bangor City in March 2010. (© Welsh Football Magazine)

a draw with Haverfordwest. The Saints were the ones with a two-point advantage now, and they weren't about to let that slip during the run-in.

Like all the best title races, the 2009-10 campaign came down to the final day. The New Saints were away to Aberystwyth Town with that two-point advantage still in place, and they endured a nervy and frustrating first half at Park Avenue. The deadlock remained at the interval but Cale's men pulled out all of the stops in the second period.

Chris Sharp, who had left Bangor to sign for TNS in January that year, opened the scoring in the 58th minute and was on target again in the 82nd. Sandwiched in between his brace was a goal from defender Steve Evans, one the The Saints' standout players all season. The 3-1 victory rendered Llanelli's 5-1 drubbing of Prestatyn moot, and crushed Aberystwyth's European dreams in the process. The Seasiders' defeat saw them surrender third place to Port Talbot, who drew 0-0 with Bala Town to book a Europa League ticket.

This was The New Saints' fifth Welsh league title, but their first in three years. Lifting the trophy on the final day of the season made it all the sweeter for the Oswestry-based club, as did the £250,000 revenue that came with Champions League qualification, no doubt: "The title is thoroughly deserved," BBC Sport quoted TNS assistant manager Mike Davies as saying after their title triumph. "It has been a fantastic season and one to remember. The Champions League is the league to be in and the competition all the lads are desperate to

135

play in - and there's the financial incentive as well which is brilliant for the club."

It certainly was a season to remember for TNS. Not only did they return to the top of the Welsh football pyramid, they also retained the League Cup several days later. On the way to the final, they knocked out Llanelli and Port Talbot to set up a crunch showdown with Rhyl.

The League Cup represented Rhyl's only hope of salvaging something from a season where increasing financial problems posed a serious threat to their future. A modest crowd of 375 turned up at The Airfield in Flintshire for the final, but those in attendance to cheer on TNS left happy, having watched their team pull off a 3-1 victory to complete a league-and-cup double.

Defeat in the final compounded a wretched campaign for Rhyl, who were relegated despite finishing sixth. Then, when the full extent of their financial situation came to light, the club was rendered ineligible for a licence to compete in the Welsh top flight.

The Lilywhites, however, weren't the only team who ended the campaign feeling deflated. Five other clubs fell through the trapdoor with them due to the FAW's restructure plans, with Connah's Quay, Porthmadog, Welshpool, Caersws and Cefn Druids all suffering the drop. A mass relegation just as Deakin had feared:

> I thought this was unfortunate. It was carnage that year when we had to relegate so many clubs, but in the long term, the restructuring of the division has benefited the league and Welsh football as a whole.

No teams from the divisions below met the criteria for promotion to the Welsh Premier League, which meant that Bala Town, Haverfordwest and Newtown - who finished 11th, 12th and 13th - were spared from relegation, having all been granted the necessary licences.

The final line-up for the revamped and streamlined Premier League had taken shape. The top 13, minus Rhyl, would compete in a division with a radically altered format in 2010-11, with TNS, Llanelli, Port Talbot, Aberystwyth, Bangor, Airbus, Prestatyn, Neath, Carmarthen, Bala, Haverfordwest and Newtown officially confirmed as the inaugural members of the new top flight. Each of the 12 clubs would play each other twice between August and January before the league split off into a Championship and Play-Off Conference, each hosting six teams.

*The New Saints celebrate John McKenna's goal at Neath in March 2010. (©
Shutterstock)*

To prevent stagnation around the middle of the table, the team who
finished top of the Play-Off Conference would join the Championship's
third, fourth, fifth and sixth team in an end-of-season play-off, the
winners of which would earn a place in the Europa League.

On paper, it was a shrewd way to encourage the teams to fire on
all cylinders until the end of the season. If a team wasn't battling
relegation or fighting for the title there would, in most cases, still be
the possibility of Europa League qualification to play for.

The clubs who qualified for the first edition of this revamped
Premier League were collectively christened the 'Super 12', and
together they'd begin writing a new chapter in the history of Welsh
domestic football, one that had the potential to help it grow and
evolve.

Looking back at the restructuring of the competition, Deakin
believes it was the right decision, though he admits that action
should perhaps have been taken sooner:

*I think it could maybe have happened sooner, but the catalyst for this
change was the introduction of the club licensing regulations. We were
ambling steadily along and then UEFA's new requirements landed. This*

concentrated minds and forced us to think about how we could help the teams in the Welsh Premier League meet the conditions. If we were unable to do that, the league would have died.

Over time, it has proved to be the right decision. I think, since I've retired, the league has continued to improve over the last 10 years. It has been well run and the competition has been given a lot more support than when I was overseeing it as a one-man band in 1992.

Such a dramatic shake-up was bound to have pros and cons over the years, and for Deakin, the biggest drawback of this format is exemplified when a team from one of the lower divisions wins their league, but cannot fulfil the off-the-pitch criteria for promotion:

Some teams end up disappointed when they can't meet the promotion requirements and my heart goes out to them. I live in Llantwit Major and our local team won the league in 2022 but couldn't meet the criteria for the Cymru Premier - they were a long way away from it. They're a good club, but they play on what is a recreation ground. To ever get promoted, they will probably have to move from where they're currently based.

It's disappointing for the club, and unfortunate that teams with ambitions to reach the top flight have to start planning years ahead or risk being rejected for a promotion they deserve.

Drew Fahiya (right) of Port Talbot and Martyn Beattie (left) of Welshpool in action during their Welsh Premier League match in February 2010. (© Shutterstock)

With the 'Super 12' line-up set in stone, Welsh Premier League enthusiasts shifted their attention to the Welsh Cup final, which was to be contested by holders Bangor City and Port Talbot Town, who had reached this stage of the competition for the first time in their history.

Port Talbot had a tougher route to the final than Bangor City, earning plaudits for overcoming The New Saints on penalties in the quarter-finals before beating Bala 1-0 in the semis. Bangor did, however, dump out an in-form Llanelli Town side in the last eight. The stage was set for a tantalising cup final at Parc y Scarlets between two teams who ended their league campaign just two points apart, and it did not disappoint.

Bangor started the match brightly and took the lead through Lee Hunt, who capitalised on an error from Port Talbot goalkeeper Lee Kendall to open the scoring in the sixth minute. The Citizens doubled their advantage less than 10 minutes later when Jamie Reed headed a second.

Port Talbot had proved their resilience all season, and it was on full display in this final. They took the game to their opponents in the second period and got one back just before the hour mark when Drew Fahiya's drive made the net ripple. They equalised with five minutes

Bangor City taking on Port Talbot in the 2010 Welsh Cup final at Parc y Scarlets, Llanelli. (© Welsh Football Magazine)

to go through Martin Rose, who combined well with McCreesh to peg Bangor back.

Extra time loomed, but Neville Powell's men dug deep at the death. As the match entered stoppage time, substitute Siôn Edwards swung in a free kick and Dave Morley rose highest in the box to head home and make it 3-2 to The Citizens. This capped off a hat-trick of Welsh Cups for Bangor to crown an astonishing run of 18 straight victories in the competition: "My players have guts and they've been fantastic all season," a triumphant Powell told reporters. "They deserve this reward. It looked as if Port Talbot could go on and win it but we showed our character and it means everything to the fans and the players to be back in Europe again."

Bangor were on cloud nine as their love affair with the Welsh Cup continued to bloom, and there were even greater things for them to come... in the short term, at least.

Welsh Premier League (2009-10)	P	W	D	L	For	Ag	Pts
1 The New Saints	34	25	7	2	69	13	82
2 Llanelli AFC	34	25	5	4	79	26	80
3 Port Talbot Town	34	19	8	7	56	23	65
4 Aberystwyth Town	34	19	7	8	54	41	64
5 Bangor City	34	19	6	9	75	45	63
6 Rhyl FC**	34	18	8	8	74	43	62
7 Airbus UK Broughton	34	12	13	9	49	37	49
8 Prestatyn Town	34	12	12	10	53	53	48
9 Neath FC	34	12	11	11	41	38	47
10 Carmarthen Town	34	12	9	13	45	38	45
11 Bala Town	34	12	9	13	39	47	45
12 Haverfordwest County	34	11	11	12	43	47	44
13 Newtown AFC	34	10	11	13	54	57	41
14 Gap Connah's Quay*	34	11	8	15	31	42	41
15 CPD Porthmadog*	34	6	6	22	23	66	24
16 Technogroup Welshpool*	34	6	5	23	30	70	23
17 Caersws FC*	34	3	4	27	26	94	13
18 Elements Cefn Druids*	34	1	6	27	16	77	9

* relegated due to reduction to 12 clubs

** relegated after to failing to meet licensing requirements

13

The Best of Bangor

Has there ever been a better cup team than the Bangor City side of the late noughties? Their triple Welsh Cup success under Neville Powell was a remarkable feat, a glorious winning streak that spanned 18 successive victories in the famous knockout competition.

If that wasn't impressive enough, The Citizens' run continued into the 2010-11 season. Re-entering the tournament as holders in round three, they saw off Bryntirion Athletic, Haverfordwest, Port Talbot Town and Connah's Quay Nomads on their way to a fourth successive final. The opposition tumbled like dominoes before the cup specialists.

Midfielder Craig Garside joined the club in the middle of this legendary cup run and has provided a valuable insight into what made this Bangor City side such formidable opponents in knockout competitions:

We had such a good group of players and cup competitions were perfect for us. Every time you play a cup tie, it's win or bust, but everyone in that team had each other's backs. We were always prepared to fight for each other and roll our sleeves up. I knew that if I knuckled down and did the work, the lad next to me would do the same. The team spirit was phenomenal and that helped us in our league campaigns as well.

Another reason we did so well on that cup run is because the team didn't change much during it. There was only the odd player who came in over that period, and I knew a lot of the lads before because a few of us were at Connah's Quay together. Even the ones who came in later knew each other from previous clubs, so that consistency helped us gel.

Bangor were the undisputed kings of the Welsh Cup during this period, but their crown had to slip at some point. That point turned out to be the very next game: the 2011 final against Llanelli, who had never won the tournament despite contesting two previous finals.

The match took place at Parc y Scarlets in front of 1,719 fans, and the outcome looked inevitable as half-time approached with Llanelli leading 2-0. Goal machine Rhys Griffiths had fired The Reds in front early on and Craig Moses did further damage in the 20th minute.

The end was in sight for The Citizens' cup odyssey, and while Alan Bull's consolation goal after the break gave them a glimmer of hope, a second Griffiths strike and a Chris Venables drive confirmed beyond doubt that Bangor's steely grip on the trophy had finally given, as Garside recalled:

> *It was inevitable that the run would come to an end, but that cup final was a bit of a double-edged sword for me anyway. I had a fitness test on the day of the final and failed it, so I was really down about that on a personal level. I think on the whole, losing a game like that is never nice, but looking back in hindsight, the club was proud to have won the cup three times and then reached a fourth final. There aren't many teams who can claim to have pulled off something like that. Four Welsh Cups on the bounce would have been unbelievable, but we can look back with our heads held high at what we did achieve.*

Bangor's incredible cup run - almost incomparable to any other in the competition's 145-year history – was over.

Back when the English Football League giants competed in the cup, Cardiff City lifted it a record five times on the bounce, but their formidable run in the 1960s and '70s did not include 22 consecutive wins. In those days, the tournament involved two-legged ties and replays, some of which The Bluebirds drew. Their biggest winning streak, though not unimpressive, was much shorter than Bangor City's, spanning 12 matches.

Being hammered 4-1 in a cup final would be a gut-punch for any team, let alone one that had likely forgotten what it feels like to lose a Welsh Cup tie, but Bangor fans had plenty to cheer about that season. The first Welsh Premier League campaign to sport the new 12-club line-up and retooled format was a memorable one indeed for Neville Powell's side.

2010-11

Rewind to the summer of 2010 and Bangor were entering this new age of Welsh domestic football as dark horses for a title challenge.

The New Saints and Llanelli were once again expected to jostle for the top spot, while relative newcomers to the world of full-time football, Neath, continued to build a squad that looked capable of challenging the elite and made local back-page headlines with a double transfer *coup*. Landing former Swans stars Kristian O'Leary and Lee Trundle was a clear statement of intent as their ongoing relationship with Swansea City continued to blossom.

The demise of 2009 champions Rhyl, however, created an opportunity for a team like Bangor, a club who were often contenders for Europe as 'the best of the rest'. Their cup heroics under Powell no doubt furthered their belief that they could compete with anyone.

The Citizens' 2010-11 campaign began with a superb result in the Europa League qualifiers. They overcame Finnish side Honka 3-2 on aggregate, and they did it the hard way. After a 1-1 draw in Finland, the Scandinavian outfit took the lead in the second leg - played at the Racecourse Ground - through Sampo Koskinen to edge ahead 2-1 on aggregate. That's the way it stayed until five minutes from time when David Morley levelled the match. His effort would have forced extra time, but Chris Jones popped up in the box in the 90th minute and scrambled the ball over the line to win it for Bangor at the death.

It was a scrappy goal, like last-minute winners often are, but the Bangor City faithful didn't care. This went down as one of the greatest European nights in the club's history, as Garside recounted:

For the first leg against Honka, I think I pulled my hamstring about halfway through the first period, and I played through it. I remember it being such hard work. Not because of the injury, just in general. They were so fit and passed the ball around really well.

We overcame them by doing what we did best. We banded together and battled for each other. I knew if I missed a tackle, one of my teammates would have my back. We were so good defensively - they even struggled to break us down in Finland.

I couldn't play in the second leg because of my hamstring injury, so I missed out on the whole atmosphere and the celebration of the win because I went away on holiday. It was a massive achievement to make it through to the next round in any case.

European results were clearly improving for Welsh Premier League sides. Elsewhere, The New Saints defeated Irish outfit Bohemians by

TNS head out onto the pitch to face Anderlecht in Belgium in the Champions League qualifiers. (© Phil Blagg)

the convincing aggregate scoreline of 4-1 in the Champions League qualifiers, overturning a 1-0 deficit from the first leg to do so.

Bangor and TNS were rewarded with glamour ties in the next rounds of their respective continental competitions, with The Citizens drawing Marítimo of Portugal and The Saints being pitted against Belgian giants Anderlecht. Neither of the Welsh sides were expected to trouble their opponents, yet they both bowed out with heads held high.

Powell's men suffered an 8-2 defeat in the first leg away from home, but regained some pride in the return fixture, once again played at the Racecourse. They took a shock lead in the 10th minute through Alan Bull before narrowly losing by two goals to one on the night. As Garside explains, the Bangor players were enjoying the European outings that success in Welsh domestic football brought them:

> *For the away leg, we went over to Portugal for the whole week and stayed in an all-inclusive resort. It was a great experience despite the result.*

Meanwhile, Anderlecht didn't have it all their own way over two legs against TNS, who gave the Belgians a minor scare during their first meeting in Wrexham despite losing 3-1. The away leg was more one-sided; a 3-0 victory for the Brussels behemoths, in which an up-and-coming Romelu Lukaku netted twice.

Europe was chalked up as a success for Bangor, and Powell in particular. That victory over Honka saw him become the first man to win a European fixture with The Citizens as both a player and as a manager, having been part of the team that beat Fredrikstad of Norway in 1985. He has more than earned his place in Citizens folklore over the years, and Garside was able to offer insight into what made him such a successful manager at Farrar Road:

> Nev used to play for Bangor so he always got what the club was about. What made him a good manager was his man-management. He knew his best eleven so he never had to juggle around a lot of players, which is difficult when you're part time.
> He always had a good assistant manager behind him too. Marc Limbert was a massive personality and was brilliant in his role. He often took control of tactics and Nev sorted the lads out, though sometimes it would be vice versa. They worked really well together.
> Without being one of the lads, Nev was one of the lads. He got involved with all the banter on the bus and the singing on the way to away trips. Everyone would have a drink in their hand on the journey home, would have to sing a song, and not taking part simply wasn't an option. The team spirit was unreal, and Neville was a big part of that.

No doubt there was an air of positivity around Farrar Road in the run-up to the new league campaign, and Bangor's opening day fixture was a tasty one: a home clash with Neath. Although The Eagles had finished in mid-table the season before, their standing in the Welsh game was rising all the time, and they were tipped for bigger things in 2010-11.

It was a close contest, and The Citizens edged it. David Morley netted their first goal of the season from the penalty spot in the 10th minute, but Liam Hancock equalised for moneybags Neath three minutes later. A stalemate appeared to be on the cards until six minutes from time when Bangor midfielder Eddie Jebb added his name to the scoresheet.

The evening before, TNS got their title defence off to an emphatic start with a 5-2 pummelling of Prestatyn, during which striker Chris Sharp scored a hat-trick. Competing with them would be a daunting

Bangor City defending a corner during their 1-0 victory, away to Carmarthen Town, in September 2010. (© grassrootsgroundswell)

proposition for a part-time outfit like Bangor, but under Neville Powell, The Citizens were gaining a reputation for punching above their weight.

Their opening-day victory was the beginning of a magnificent winning streak in the Welsh Premier League. They came out on top in *all* of their first 15 league matches, a flawless run that lasted until mid-December as Bangor marched on to set a modern-day British record.

The Citizens dropped points for the first time three days later when they travelled to Airbus UK and were held to a 1-1 draw, with Bull on target for the visitors. They did, however, stretch their unbeaten run to 17 games in the next fixture as goals from Jones and Morley downed Prestatyn Town 2-1 to ensure Powell's men ended 2010 on a high.

This exceptional run of form left Bangor sitting proud at the top of the table with a considerable 16-point lead. They looked like the safest of bets to bring home their first league title since the 1990s, but 2011 did not start brightly for the pacesetters. In the January transfer window, top goalscorer Jamie Reed signed for York City, then

Bangor City's official mascot, The Bangor Eye. (© Luke Tugwell)

of the English Conference, and cracks began to appear in Bangor's previously slate-smooth, peerless performances.

Reed scored his final goal for Bangor in their first loss of the campaign, a 4-2 reverse at Prestatyn on 2nd January and, three days later, it was back-to-back defeats as Llanelli Town hit them for two without reply at Stebonheath Park. Rhys Griffiths' penalty kick and a late strike from Chris Llewellyn was the difference between the two sides, and suddenly, Bangor City's advantage at the top of the Welsh Premier League was no longer the chasm it was at the turn of the year.

However, it wasn't long before the men from Farrar Road were firing on all cylinders again, romping to a 6-0 victory over Haverfordwest in their next league match before a lone Garside goal floored Newtown on the road. This set up a crunch clash with fellow title-chasers TNS in the final fixture before the Welsh Premier League's first mid-season split.

The showdown took place at Park Hall and TNS had an unbeaten home record to defend. Desperate to reopen the title race, The New Saints took the game to Bangor and twice led on the night, only for a pair of contentious refereeing decisions to peg them back.

With 50 minutes on the clock, TNS were 2-1 up and on course to reduce their rivals' advantage at the top of the table to single figures; but their stranglehold on the game began to slip when Danny Holmes was sent off for an alleged professional foul on Les Davies. From the resulting free kick, Aeron Edwards was adjudged to have handled in the box and Bangor were awarded a penalty kick that turned out to be crucial. Morley converted from 12 yards to rescue a point for The Citizens and maintain their 10-point advantage at the top of the league ahead of the Conferences phase.

After the game, New Saints manager Mike Davies - who had replaced Andy Cale in the Park Hall dugout in April 2010 - hit out at the refereeing decisions that cost his side so dearly, insisting that neither one should have gone against them: "Once again we've been affected by another poor performance from the man in the middle," the *Shropshire Star* quoted him as saying. "Danny was disappointed to go as he got a touch to the ball, while the handball decision was just farcical. We weren't happy, but I was really pleased with the attitude of the lads who battled really hard and even with 10 men we were still looking to win the game. Having been down to 10 men, it was important we didn't lose and we've still got to play Bangor twice more this season, so it is not the end of the world."

There was fierce competitiveness between The New Saints and Bangor as it became apparent that they were locked into a two-way title race. Garside, however, believes that every team had a rivalry with TNS to some extent as they were always the team to beat:

I think everyone had a rivalry with The New Saints. They were full-time and were the biggest scalp to claim. When we played them, we used quite a strange tactic. We would start off playing our usual 4-3-3 formation, but would quickly abandon it and go man-for-man all over the field. It was certainly unorthodox, but it worked.

I think the rivalry most clubs had with TNS is partly fuelled by jealousy because their players were all professional and a lot of the other clubs weren't. The fact we were their main rivals that season really helped spur us on as the title race gained momentum.

In mid-January, the Welsh Premier League split into two for the first time and returned the following month in a twin Conferences format. As the top two sides in the division, Bangor and TNS qualified for the Championship Conference, alongside Neath, Llanelli Town,

Prestatyn Town and Port Talbot Town, who occupied positions three through to six.

Despite storming the first phase, Bangor got off to a rocky start in the Championship Conference. Powell's men won only one of their first seven matches, a deeply concerning run of form that included a 3-2 defeat away to The New Saints on 19 March.

This result blew the title race wide open. Bangor, who were once sitting pretty at the summit with a 16-point lead, suddenly found their advantage reduced to just four points. With TNS holding a game in hand, The Citizens had to dig deep in their next two matches away at Port Talbot and Neath respectively, and they did just that, winning both games by two goals to one, to set up a fiery title showdown with The Saints on the final day of the season. Addressing his team's dip in form during the second phase of the competition, Garside insisted:

> *People on the outside might think some of the team were getting complacent after winning those 15 games on the bounce earlier in the season, but that wasn't the case. There were players in that squad who wouldn't let you do that. If anyone got above their station, there were lads there - like James Brewerton - who'd whip you back into shape.*
>
> *After Jamie Reed left, we changed formation and I don't think it was working. A few games after the split, we reverted back to what we knew and dug deep. After the split happens, you're obviously up against just the top teams in the division. Every game is difficult at that stage in the season, but we knew it was important to get back to basics with the formation.*
>
> *We were an old school team. We were tough, but we had players with ability as well. These were our strengths, and we had to get back to maximising them in those final games.*

By this point, The New Saints had edged one point ahead of Bangor and needed only a draw at Farrar Road on the final day to secure the league title, but overcoming The Citizens on their home turf was no mean feat in 2010-11. Farrar Road was a proverbial fortress, with Bangor having won 12 out of their 14 homes matches ahead of the title decider.

The ground was packed and in full voice while the action on the pitch was as tense and hard-fought as expected. Neither side could force a breakthrough in a goalless first period and that's the way it stayed until the 68th minute when Bangor won a throw-in deep in the

Bangor City's players celebrate their memorable title victory at Farrar Road.
(© Richard Birch)

TNS half. The ball was lofted into the area and a goalmouth scramble commenced.

Hearts were in mouths across the stands and panic ensued in the TNS box, but good instincts from Garside at the far post saw the hosts break the deadlock. The midfielder, who had netted both goals against Neath in the previous game, came sliding in to nudge the ball over the line and send Farrar Road into a frenzy. It proved to be the winning goal.

The final whistle sparked jubilant scenes as scores of fans decked in blue and white stormed onto the pitch. Bangor had done it! The part-timers from north Wales had overthrown the mighty TNS to win a league title for the first time in 16 years.

In the aftermath, an elated Powell hailed his players' spirit and fired a shot at their doubters: "We have come back from the dead as everyone wrote us off last week," the *Daily Post* quoted him as saying. "And we've come back and won our last three games so for those people who thought we were dead and buried, they don't know Bangor City. The spirit is worth 15 or 20 points to us this season. You've seen the determination against a good, professional TNS outfit and the league was theirs but we have come back and we've taken it off them. Seeing the supporters celebrate was something magical."

Looking back on the match, Garside added:

I can't put into words what it felt like scoring that winning goal. Bangor City have always been a massive team in Welsh football but they hadn't won the league for a while, so this meant so much to the club.

I was made up for the supporters as well. The fans were massive at Bangor and I think they have to take a lot of credit for that league title win. I'm an Everton supporter, and in the 1980s, the team's manager Howard Kendall used to tell his players that the Gwladys Street End was capable of sucking the ball into the net. It was the same at Bangor City.

I believe we were destined to win that league title and I think the fact it went down to the wire and was like a cup final in that last game really suited us.

Garside is unlikely to have had to pay for any drinks that evening, but from the way he described the post-game celebrations, it sounds like they weren't in short supply:

The celebrations afterwards were unbelievable. We went to a pub outside of Farrar Road and we were there until God knows what time. It was me, James Brewerton, Limbo, Nev, Nev's wife and Paul Smith. He only had a five-seater car but seven of us piled into it on the way home. We were in the back singing Adele songs.

The away trips and the European games were always amazing that season as well. We used to go out with the fans, so it felt like a proper community. It was the same when we won the league - everyone was there celebrating together.

April 2011 was a tough month to be a TNS fan. Not only did they lose a league title on the final day of the season, they were also knocked out of the Welsh Cup 1-0 by eventual winners Llanelli at the semi-final stage, going down to a Chris Venables strike six minutes from time.

There was, however, a consolation prize for The Saints, who didn't finish the campaign empty-handed. They got their revenge on Llanelli in the League Cup final, played at Park Avenue on 2 May. It was a goal fest in Aberystwyth that day, with the two teams ending the 90 minutes tied at 3-3. Two late goals in the space of as many minutes looked to have clinched the trophy for The Reds, only for Sharp to equalise for TNS with one minute to play.

Bangor City boss Neville Powell celebrates his side's title victory with his wife, players and supporters. (© Luke Tugwell)

Penalties looked inevitable as the last remaining minutes of extra time trickled away, but a hero emerged in the green and white of TNS. That hero was Scott Ruscoe, who found the net in the 120th minute to ensure his side won the League Cup for the third time in a row.

Meanwhile, in the Play-Off Conference, Haverfordwest County ended a 14-year stay in the top flight after finishing bottom of the table. Bala Town directly above them would also have been relegated had Cymru Alliance champions Connah's Quay or runners-up Rhyl managed to secure a licence for Welsh Premier League membership, but neither did.

The Play-Off Conference's top two teams - Aberystwyth Town and Airbus UK Broughton - qualified for the European play-offs, along with third-placed Neath, as well as Prestatyn Town and Port Talbot Town, who finished fifth and sixth in the Championship respectively. Fourth-placed Llanelli were already guaranteed Europa League football by virtue of winning the Welsh Cup.

The Welsh Premier League's inaugural European play-offs began on 10 May as Aberystwyth and Airbus contested their quarter-final at Park Avenue. Just over 400 fans showed up and watched the hosts triumph 2-1, with a late strike from Everton academy product James McCarten setting up a semi-final away to Neath.

McCarten scored another late goal at The Gnoll, though this time he finished on the losing side. Neath were 2-0 up before the defender struck and held on to book their ticket to the final, in which they would face Prestatyn, the conquerors of Port Talbot in the other semi.

Neath had home advantage for the play-off final and almost 1,000 supporters descended on The Gnoll for this one. The Eagles took the game by the scruff of the neck and broke the deadlock in the first minute through former Welsh youth international Chad Bond.

Prestatyn put up a fight against their big-spending hosts and equalised in the first period through Lee Hunt. It was a tactical change, however, that swung the match in Neath's favour. With the hour mark fast approaching, Andy Hill - the club's longest-serving player - came off the subs bench to bag a brace and knock the wind out of The Seasiders' sails.

Jon Fisher-Cooke hit a last-minute consolation for Prestatyn, but the match finished 3-2 to the home side, propelling them into Europe and going some way towards justifying the amount of money that had been pumped into the club over the previous two seasons.

Andy Hill scoring the winning goal as Neath beat Prestatyn in the play-off final at The Gnoll. (© Welsh Football Magazine)

There were many talking points from the first season of the Welsh Premier League's new format. Some hailed it as a step in the right direction for several reasons, chief among them a record average gate increase of 25% to 343, the highest average ever recorded for the division. Granted, this sounds like a diminutive figure, and only the Estonian top flight had a smaller average in Europe at the time; but it was something to build on and would likely have been higher if the teams like Barry Town and Rhyl had remained in the division.

The first season with the revamped format and mid-season split was considered a success, although the main headline-grabber was Bangor City's final-day title triumph at the expense of The New Saints. When the dust from this thriller at Farrar Road had settled, Neville Powell proclaimed that it would be a long time before another part-time side would beat TNS to the league title.

This turned out to be a very accurate prediction.

Welsh Premier League (2010-11)	P	W	D	L	For	Ag	Pts
Championship Conference							
1 Bangor City	32	22	4	6	80	44	70
2 The New Saints	32	20	8	4	87	34	68
3 Neath	32	16	10	6	62	41	58
4 Llanelli	32	18	8	9	58	41	53
5 Prestatyn Town	32	10	10	12	44	46	40
6 Port Talbot Town	32	8	12	12	37	48	36
Play-Off Conference							
7 Aberystwyth Town	32	11	9	12	42	54	42
8 Airbus UK Broughton	32	11	8	13	53	53	41
9 Newtown	32	8	11	13	40	55	35
10 Carmarthen Town	32	10	5	17	39	64	35
11 Bala Town	32	10	3	19	41	57	33
12 Haverfordwest County	32	5	4	23	30	77	19

Play-off winners: Neath

14

The (New) Saints March On

2011-12

The New Saints have attracted more than their fair share of critics over the years. That tends to happen when you're as successful as they are, yet many of these detractors will tell you their distaste for the Oswestry-based outfit is about more than just trophy cabinet envy.

There are fans of the original Oswestry Town and Llansantffraid FC clubs who felt alienated when the teams merged and, despite the club's outreach efforts with both camps, have been unable to warm to TNS. Moreover, there are rival supporters who believe that The Saints are English cuckoos in the Welsh football nest and should pursue a future within the English system.

While many of the arguments against their footballing presence on the Welsh side of the border fall down under scrutiny, others are worthy of constructive debate. Yet whether you love them or loathe them, there's one thing that cannot be taken away from The New Saints: they've always been a *very* well run football club.

Since telecoms magnate Mike Harris brought Oswestry Town and Llansantffraid FC together in a cross-border union, the fully-professional club that was born out of the merger has grown into an absolute powerhouse that towers over Welsh domestic football.

Obviously, the boatload of cash that Harris has pumped into TNS over the years has helped them achieve this status, but these funds have been invested the *right* way. Big money has been spent on infrastructure, with Park Hall's £3 million redevelopment giving them a 3G pitch and a state-of-the-art community hub, among other impressive facilities. The Saints have also ploughed funding into youth development and became the first Welsh Premier League side to be awarded with official academy accreditation in 2002.

A steady flow of prize money, smart investment and European revenue helped TNS thrive over the years and it wasn't long before they achieved total domination of the Welsh game. Their journey to this point hit the straight and narrow in the 2011-12 season.

Losing a league title to part-timers Bangor City the previous season was a heavy blow for The Saints, but strong performances in Europe and a Welsh League Cup to add to the trophy collection was enough to keep manager Mike Davies in a job. He moved into a different role with The Saints in April 2011, though, and became their new director of football, with Carl Darlington taking over head coaching responsibilities ahead of the new campaign.

The 2011-12 season began positively when they claimed a European scalp, knocking Irish side Cliftonville out of the Europa League qualifiers. Phil Baker's fourth-minute goal in the second leg in Belfast was decisive, giving TNS a 2-1 aggregate lead following a 1-1 draw at Park Hall, and they held firm to set up a tie with FC Midtjylland of Denmark in the next round.

The Danes, however, thumped TNS 8-3 on aggregate, but an Alex Darlington brace in the away leg helped the club snatch a sliver of pride. In any case, that Cliftonville result in the previous round was a milestone for the club, as it was their first Europa League triumph.

This was a *strong* TNS squad and many of the players it comprised became integral to the decade of staggering success that lay ahead. Up front, they had free-scoring Greg Draper - an English-born New Zealander with one full international cap to his name - and a host of other quality attacking options in Darlington, Scott Quigley and Chris Sharp.

In midfield, Scott Ruscoe brought experience and a goal threat, while Aeron Edwards ran the engine room. Chris Marriot and Simon Spender became great servants to the club in the full-back positions while goalkeeper Paul Harrison claimed the number one jersey for a decade and a half, and eventually set a record for most consecutive appearances in the Welsh top flight.

Along with Llanelli and Neath, The New Saints were one of three full-time clubs in the Welsh Premier League and were favourites for the title; but they didn't stroll to the top domestic prize that season. Once again, part-timers Bangor City provided fierce competition and looked determined to cling onto their crown following their heroics of 2010-11.

TNS were the division's early pacesetters, though they hit a few speed bumps in November and relinquished top spot after picking up just one point out of nine. Back-to-back defeats to Bangor and

Afan Lido were unexpected, yet the real shock came after that: Davies suddenly resigned from his post with The Saints trailing leaders Bangor by two points.

Although the outgoing director of football's exit was abrupt, he insisted that it was not connected to recent results and defended his record at the helm: "I think I can go with my head held high," he told the official Welsh Premier League's website. "I have led the club to runners-up spot in the Welsh Premier [League], the first-ever European victories against Bohemians and Cliftonville, and two League Cups."

One month later, TNS installed a new head honcho to work alongside Darlington. The man charged with bringing the title back to Park Hall was former Middlesbrough and Crystal Palace defender Craig Harrison, and this turned out to be an inspired appointment.

Harrison appeared on the club's radar while he was managing Airbus Broughton. He exceeded expectations at The Wingmakers, guiding them to a top-half finish in 2009-10 to secure a place in the inaugural 'Super 12' division, despite having a miniscule budget. Before that, he had been out of football for many years. Injury had brought his playing career to a premature end and his love for the sport soon dwindled but, as the coach himself explained, he had rediscovered his passion for the beautiful game at Airbus:

On my 30th birthday, my wife organised a surprise party for me, and Gareth Owen was in a band she had booked to perform. Gareth was the manager of Airbus at the time, and not long before that, Alan Bickerstaff had left his post as his assistant manager.

So, I got talking to Gareth and we arranged to meet for a coffee. The rest after that is history. I went in as his assistant, Gareth left after six months and Airbus offered me the job. I had to do my coaching badges first, but within a few years, I'd done my pro licence as well.

I had no intentions of getting back into football, but that chance meeting with Gareth changed that. My love for football came flooding back at Airbus and I was as determined as ever to be successful in the game. I wanted to use the disappointment I still felt as a result of my playing career ending prematurely as a driving force to push me forward.

Harrison joined TNS for the Championship Conference phase of the 2011-12 season with everything to play for. He ushered in a technical passing game that was as easy on the eye as it was effective.

80p SOUVENIR PROGRAMME No. 0111

CLWB PELDROED DINAS BANGOR

BANGOR CITY F.C.

Ground: Farrar Road, Bangor

ATHLETICO MADRID
EUROPEAN CUP WINNERS CUP † 2nd ROUND 1st LEG.
Wednesday, 23rd October, 1985
Kick off 6.00 p.m.   ALL TICKET

The official matchday programme from Bangor City's famous Cup Winners' Cup clash with Atlético Madrid. (© Owain Hughes)

Having fallen behind Bangor as winter was setting in, The New Saints barely faltered after that and went into the final day of the season as league leaders.

The Citizens, meanwhile, moved grounds as the title race was heating up, leaving their famous Farrar Road stadium behind in December 2011. The council-owned site was sold off and the ground eventually demolished to make way for a new retail development. A supermarket now occupies this location, with no obvious evidence that there was ever a football ground there, let alone one that played host to three league title-winning campaigns and European fixtures against the likes of Atlético Madrid.

Bangor City gave the ground a good send-off, thumping rivals Prestatyn 5-3 in the final match there, a game which ended with a mass pitch invasion. Their form was, however, shaky after they moved to their new home at Nantporth on the Menai Strait the following February.

TNS went into the season's final weekend just two points ahead of the second-placed Citizens, who they were due to host at Park Hall in the concluding fixture, but Harrison was confident his team could deliver the goods in a crunch game:

TNS had lost that title to Bangor the season before I came in. To give ourselves the best chance of winning it back, I introduced more professionalism and greater accountability. On the pitch, I wanted us to play with more pace and be more dynamic. We continued to play possession-based football, but with more forward momentum.

I recruited players who were fitter, stronger and more dimensional. TNS were already playing beautiful, attractive football but teams were starting to use different strategies to stop that. Anything from a high press, so we couldn't play out, to a low block. Some would go man-for-man and others would try every formation under the sun. We needed to be more dynamic and multi-dimensional to stay one step ahead of the opposition.

Incredibly, the match was almost a like-for-like repeat of the previous season's final-day firecracker, except it was Bangor who were on the road this time. The New Saints were hungry for revenge, and executed their task with lethal efficiency. Draper opened the scoring early on after racing clean through on goal. One-on-one with Bangor keeper Lee Idzi, he kept his cool and guided the ball into the net to make it 1-0.

Christian Seargeant extended The Saints' advantage with a direct strike from a free kick, and Draper struck again before the break to leave Bangor all but defeated. TNS continued to maul the wounded Citizens in the second half, with Ryan Fraughan rifling home a fourth just after the hour mark, and Draper completing a sensational hat-trick from the penalty spot. It was an unforgettable afternoon for the hosts, who emerged 5-0 winners and were presented with the Welsh Premier League trophy in front of a home crowd of 1,468, as Harrison fondly recalled:

The players were really up for that game and it was a special one for me too. When you win a big trophy for the first time, it's never the same doing it again.

It was very tight that year. We had to win something like nine out of the last 11 games to reverse the points deficit. Neath and Bangor were in front of us and Llanelli were a strength then too. I remember we lost at home to Neath and then won nine and drew two. We needed to go on that run to give ourselves any chance of winning the title.

One of my biggest strengths as a manager is demanding high standards from my squad and backroom staff, coming from a background of professional football. The demands I placed on the players were higher than what they had been before. That was purely because of my single-minded desire to get back to as high a level as possible in football.

The New Saints kicked on from that point and went from strength to strength, starting with victory in the Welsh Cup final on 5 May. That year's instalment of the cup was its 125th anniversary and, to mark the significance of the occasion, the FAW extended a one-off invitation to the exiled clubs playing in England. However, only Wrexham, Newport and Merthyr Town accepted the offer.

Despite being absent from the tournament since the mid-1990s, Wrexham had still won more Welsh Cups than any other team, so they were quite the scalp for Airbus UK Broughton. Then of the Conference National league, Wrexham had fielded a youthful side for the third-round tie against The Wingmakers and it was a close contest that went to extra time. Airbus' notable 2-1 victory was ultimately decided by a late winner from veteran defender Mark Allen.

Barry Town had dumped out Merthyr Town in the first round before losing 3-2 at Newport County, who were then hammered 4-0 in round four by The New Saints, who laid down a statement of intent on their way to the final.

The much anticipated return of the exiled clubs turned out to be an anti-climax of sorts, with Cardiff City, Swansea City and Colwyn Bay declining to take part, and the three returning clubs largely treating it as an opportunity to give fringe and youth players a runout. This was likely due to the FA of Wales being unable to offer a European spot to an English-based side in the event of them winning the trophy, as UEFA regulations prevented this.

The 2011-12 Welsh Cup final took place at Bangor City's new home of Nantporth and TNS' opponents were one of the oldest teams in Wales, Cefn Druids.

The Druids were a second-tier outfit back then, though they had knocked out three Welsh Premier League sides on their way to their first final in 108 years, claiming the scalps of Prestatyn Town, Aberystwyth Town and Airbus UK Broughton.

TNS didn't take their lower-league opponents lightly and were quick out of the starting blocks, taking an early lead when Fraughan's cross was nodded over the line by the ever-prolific Draper. The Druids' goalkeeper Chris Mullock was a busy man that afternoon, and he found himself picking the ball out of the net again, moments later, when Darlington smashed home.

Those two quick-fire goals in the opening stages were their undoing, and despite Mullock having to make a string of crucial saves after this point, Cefn Druids more than held their own against the champions of Wales and made them work for this 2-0 victory right up to the final whistle.

The Welsh Cup triumph saw The New Saints complete a league-and-cup double for the first time since 2005. After the match,

Harrison jokingly claimed that he was relieved his side didn't bag the League Cup too, as that would have left little scope to build on their success the following season. He also made a point of praising The Druids for providing such stern opposition.

The Saints hopes of bringing home a treble in 2011-12 had been dashed in early April when Newtown put them out of the League Cup at the semi-final stage on away goals. TNS won the first leg at Park Hall 3-2, but a late strike by Luke Boundford in the second leg proved decisive and helped The Robins set up a final against two-time winners Afan Lido.

In the final, played at Aberystwyth Town's Park Avenue, Lido goalkeeper Craig Morris was the hero, pulling off three crucial saves in a tense penalty shootout, after the two finalists had played out a 1-1 stalemate, to help his side lift the trophy for the third time in their history.

The League Cup final was a squandered opportunity for Newtown. They finished rock bottom of the Play-Off Conference and the Aberystwyth showpiece was a chance for their players to redeem themselves for a poor campaign. The *Daily Post* did, however, praise The Robins' performance in the final and described the outcome as "harsh" on them.

There was one positive to come out of the season for Newtown, though, and that was being spared from relegation by virtue of only one second-tier club qualifying for a top-flight licence. That club was Connah's Quay, who brought to an end their absence from the Welsh Premier League by winning the Cymru Alliance for the second time in a row.

The decisive factor in Newtown's survival was, however, Neath suffering a painfully familiar plight for fully professional Welsh Premier League clubs. Despite relative success on the pitch, the Gnoll outfit hit choppy financial waters and struggled to meet the full list of requirements set out by the FAW and UEFA for clubs taking part in their competitions. They were denied a domestic and continental licence for the coming season and, following an unsuccessful appeal, were later wound up at the High Court.

This meant that The New Saints and Llanelli - who returned to the Europa League that season thanks to a 2-1 win over Bala in the play-off final - were the only full-time clubs remaining in the Welsh Premier League, but The Reds' professional days were numbered too.

Welsh Premier League (2011-12)	P	W	D	L	For	Ag	Pts
Championship Conference							
1 The New Saints	32	23	5	4	75	31	74
2 Bangor City	32	22	3	7	72	45	69
3 Neath	32	18	8	6	60	36	62
4 Llanelli	32	18	5	9	63	37	59
5 Bala Town	32	14	7	11	48	41	49
6 Prestatyn Town	32	8	4	20	41	63	28
Play-Off Conference							
7 Airbus UK Broughton	32	10	9	13	48	50	39
8 Aberystwyth Town*	32	8	10	14	47	59	33
9 Port Talbot Town	32	8	9	15	39	51	33
10 Afan Lido FC	32	7	11	14	40	55	32
11 Carmarthen Town	32	10	2	20	33	67	32
12 Newtown AFC**	32	7	5	20	44	82	23

*1pt deducted; ** 3pts deducted

Play-off winners: Llanelli

2012-13

The two clubs' fortunes in 2012-13 were worlds apart. TNS continued to thrive under Harrison and Darlington's watch and strolled to the league title that season, finishing 22 points ahead of their closest challengers, Airbus UK Broughton. Llanelli, meanwhile, were swallowed up by debt, liquidated and relegated to Welsh League Division Three.

The men in green and white wrapped up the league in March with five games to spare, defeating Carmarthen Town 3-0 at Park Hall to complete their successful title defence. It was a freezing afternoon in Oswestry, with mounds of snow piled high behind the touchlines, but The Saints were in red-hot form. Scott Ruscoe broke the deadlock and a double from Michael Wilde - who had rejoined TNS from Chester in July 2012 - put the game beyond the visitors.

Re-signing Wilde was a shrewd move on Harrison's part. He was the Welsh Premier League's top goalscorer that season with a total of 25 strikes, and those goals were instrumental in helping The Saints equal Barry Town's record of seven league titles.

With Barry, and the other clubs who had dabbled in full-time professionalism, now out of the picture, the way was paved for

The Saints to march on to even greater glory. As the only full-time club in the division, The New Saints had a bigger budget than their competitors, could attract better players and had superior resources - but does this mean they had an unfair advantage? Harrison wouldn't strictly disagree with anyone who claimed that:

I do think we had an unfair advantage, but as it's been proven in recent years, it hasn't always been the team with the most resources who has won the league - you can go all the way back to Leicester City in the Premier League as an example of that.

I'd say, a lot of the time, it is the team with the most resources who have the biggest and best chance to be successful - but it's not down to that alone. For our opponents, most games were like cup finals and the expectation levels for us to win every time were huge. If we drew a match, it was like we had been beaten. We didn't lose many in that period, mind.

Although The New Saints have been consistently successful, I think it will be a long time before another team dominates the way we did during my first spell in charge.

TNS may have dominated the league, but it was their only silverware that term. In January, they had lost the League Cup final to Carmarthen Town on penalties following a 3-3 draw at Latham Park, and one week after sealing the league title against the same opponents, they were up against Bangor City in the semi-finals of the Welsh Cup, with The Citizens - who had finished third in the league - eager to reignite their love affair with the trophy.

They were well on course to do exactly that, as Bangor edged a close contest against the league champions. After TNS had lost Fraughan to a red card, The Citizens made their numerical advantage count and won it late on through a spectacular lob from Chris Jones.

Bangor marched on to the final a month later, but lost to local rivals Prestatyn Town at the Racecourse Ground. The Seasiders got their hands on the trophy for the one and only time to date thanks to a superb showing in Wrexham, where goalkeeper Jonathan Hill-Dunt put in a man-of-the-match performance, saving a Dave Morley penalty with the scoreline at 1-1, and producing a string of further stops to keep Bangor at bay until the full-time whistle.

Prestatyn came out swinging in extra time, during which goals from Andy Parkinson and Jason Price in rapid succession were

Bangor's bane. It finished 3-1 and The Seasiders made history against the odds, booking their first European adventure in the process.

There was further disappointment for Bangor that month as they also lost a European play-off semi-final to eventual winners, Bala Town, the league's surprise package of 2012-13. The Lakesiders went on to go the distance and reach the continent courtesy of a 1-0 win over Port Talbot in the final.

Welsh Premier League (2012-13)	P	W	D	L	For	Ag	Pts
Championship Conference							
1 The New Saints	32	24	4	4	86	22	76
2 Airbus UK Broughton	32	17	3	12	76	42	54
3 Bangor City	32	14	9	9	64	52	51
4 Port Talbot Town	32	13	8	11	51	52	47
5 Prestatyn Town	32	11	7	14	62	79	40
6 Carmarthen Town	32	10	7	15	36	50	37
Play-Off Conference							
7 Bala Town	32	17	5	10	62	41	56
8 Gap Connah's Quay*	32	12	5	15	62	69	40
9 Newtown	32	10	7	15	44	54	37
10 Aberystwyth Town	32	9	10	13	40	59	37
11 Llanelli	32	10	6	16	41	69	36
12 Afan Lido	32	8	3	22	43	79	27

* 1pt deducted

Play-off winners: Bala Town

2013-14

Surprises were few and far between in the Welsh Premier League the following season, especially in the upper reaches of the table. The New Saints ran another one-horse title race, losing just three times all season and wrapping up the title after 29 games. Airbus UK Broughton were their closest challenges for the second campaign running, although The Wingmakers were 14 points off the pace and never looked like serious title contenders.

This was a double-winning season for the all-powerful Oswestry-based side. As well as surpassing Barry Town's record title haul, TNS went the distance in the Welsh Cup too. In the final they faced a tenacious Aberystwyth side - who had finished top of the Play-

Off Conference - at the Racecourse Ground, and had to produce a stunning comeback to land the trophy.

A double from Chris Venables, the second of which came from the penalty spot, had given Aberystwyth a two-goal lead at the interval, but with a strike force as potent as the Draper-Wilde double act tearing up the final third, this TNS team could not simply be written off. They found a foothold in the contest in the 72nd minute when Draper struck home a penalty kick, and the in-form Kiwi drew his side level five minutes later with a close-range header.

Aberystwyth were looking for their first Welsh Cup triumph since the 1899-1900 season, and their wait for another taste of glory in the competition was further extended in the 84th minute when The Saints' top goalscorer, Wilde, struck a sweet volley that turned out to be the winning goal.

Breaking records and leaving milestones behind in their dust were things this Saints side did for fun, though at this point, a domestic treble continued to elude them. Their chances of achieving one in 2013-14 went up in smoke in October when Harrison's former employers Airbus beat them by two goals to one in the third round of the League Cup.

The Wingmakers were later knocked out at the semi-final stage by Bala Town, who went on to contest the final against the holders, Carmarthen Town, on 11 January.

The match, which marked Bala's first major cup final, took place in front of S4C's cameras, but the network didn't get to broadcast any goals in normal time, or the extra time that followed. A hat-trick of saves from Carmarthen goalkeeper, Steve Cann, in the resulting penalty shootout was, however, worth tuning in for as the South African-born shot-stopper kept cool under pressure to help The Old Gold lift the trophy for a second year on the bounce.

Trophy success for teams like Prestatyn and Carmarthen made good - 'underdog beats favourite' - headlines but upsets like these became few and far between in the years to come.

TNS' power continued to grow, with Mike Harris running a tight ship off the pitch while Harrison and Darlington ensured the team flourished on it and recruited well. New signings such as winger Ryan Brobbel - formerly of Middlesbrough's youth academy, York City and Hartlepool United - and Polish forward Adrian Cieślewicz added flair and raw talent to their ranks.

The New Saints also held onto many of their key players, including Paul Harrison between the sticks, Marriott, Edwards and Draper, and now boasted a squad that was head and shoulders above any other in the Welsh Premier League; on paper, at the very least.

While the addition of Craig Harrison to their dugout was a major factor behind the team's rapid improvement and sustained success, the TNS boss believes that credit should also go to owner Mike Harris, whom he believes is not just dedicated to helping his own club develop, but raise the standards of Welsh domestic football as a whole:

> *A huge amount of praise has to go to Mike Harris. One thing you can never question about Mike is his commitment to the football club - it's always 100%. It's part of him and there was always lots of communication between myself and him on a daily basis.*
>
> *It's his baby and he spends a lot of his own time at the club. He's always pushing, not just for TNS, but for the league as well. He wants to make the entire league better. Mike Harris will always look after himself and TNS - we all look after our own to some extent as that is human nature - but he will also stand up for the league out of a desire to improve it.*

Although TNS were stealing the spotlight in Welsh football, it's important to note that they weren't the only club who made history during this period. Prestatyn Town, for instance, won a two-legged Europa League match against Liepajas Metālurgs of Latvia on penalties following a 3-3 draw on aggregate, marking their continental debut in style and building on the Welsh Cup success of the previous campaign.

The Seasiders, however, had a poor domestic campaign and finished second-bottom ahead only of Afan Lido. They survived the drop due to only one team being demoted that season, but a growing player exodus saw the club finish rock bottom one year later and drop out of the Welsh Premier League.

Welsh Premier League (2013-14)	P	W	D	L	For	Ag	Pts
Championship Conference							
1 The New Saints	32	22	7	3	87	20	73
2 Airbus UK Broughton*	32	17	9	6	56	34	59
3 Carmarthen Town	32	14	6	12	54	51	48
4 Bangor City	32	14	6	12	47	50	48
5 Newtown AFC	32	12	6	14	46	58	42
6 Rhyl FC	32	11	5	16	43	49	38

Welsh Premier League (2013-14)	P	W	D	L	For	Ag	Pts
Play-Off Conference							
7 Aberystwyth Town**	32	15	9	8	72	48	51
8 Bala Town	32	13	6	13	61	45	45
9 Port Talbot Town	32	10	8	14	47	65	38
10 Gap Connah's Quay	32	10	8	14	47	65	38
11 Prestatyn Town	32	9	8	15	42	47	35
12 Afan Lido	32	3	6	23	21	100	15

*1pt deducted; ** 3pts deducted

Play-off winners: Bangor City

2014-15

It's difficult for Saints fans to choose a highlight from the 2014-15 season as there were so many. Among them was a staggering 30-game unbeaten run in the league, with TNS' one and only league defeat that season coming in the third round of fixtures, away to Airbus, who claimed a 1-0 victory and maximum points courtesy of a goal from Glenn Rule.

Harrison's men didn't lose again from that point, in any domestic competition, winning the Welsh Premier League with 77 points on the board - 17 more than second-placed Bala Town - and four more than they had racked up during the previous campaign.

Draper and Wilde continued to run riot in the final third, both finishing in the top goalscorers' chart at the end of term with 33 strikes between them. That combined haul, however, was only a handful more than the total that the league's top marksman, Chris Venables of Aberystwyth, managed on his own. The Shrewsbury-born forward had a stellar campaign, bagging 28 goals to land the Golden Boot, and has since become one of the Welsh Premier League's all-time leading scorers.

TNS boss Craig Harrison with the Welsh Cup. (© FAW)

As for TNS, they just kept on winning, obliterating all that stood before them until that elusive domestic treble was within touching distance. A brace from Quigley, with a Seargeant effort sandwiched in between, saw them overcome Bala Town 3-0 in the League Cup final in January, and their splendid form continued through the winter months and into spring.

No Welsh team had pulled off a domestic treble since Rhyl's unlikely heroics in 2003-04, but The New Saints earned themselves the chance to win a silverware hat-trick of their own when they lined up against Newtown in the Welsh Cup final on 2 May 2015.

There was little between the two sides in the first half, but TNS were quick off the mark in the second and drew first blood when Matty Williams latched onto a through-ball and got the better of Newtown goalkeeper Dave Jones in a one-on-one situation.

The Robins, who went on to win that season's European play-off, fought valiantly for an equaliser, though half-chances were all they could muster, and the contest was decided five minutes from time. Shane Sutton brought down Quigley in the area and the referee pointed to the spot, paving the way for Williams to step up, score his second of the afternoon and confirm it would be TNS' name etched into the trophy.

This was The Saints' fifth Welsh Cup, but more significantly, it was their first domestic treble. Four league titles in a row and a clean sweep of the domestic trophies in 2014-15 was impressive, yet perhaps the most astonishing thing about this New Saints side is that they accomplished even greater things from here. No team in the history of the Welsh top flight had won back-to-back treble-double at the height of their success - but that would change just 12 months on from TNS' 2-0 cup final victory over Newtown.

Welsh Premier League (2014-15)	P	W	D	L	For	Ag	Pts
Championship Conference							
1 The New Saints	32	23	8	1	90	24	77
2 Bala Town	32	18	5	9	67	42	59
3 Airbus UK Broughton	32	18	4	10	62	34	58
4 Aberystwyth Town	32	14	10	8	69	61	52
5 Port Talbot Town	32	13	4	15	54	59	43
6 Newtown AFC	32	10	8	14	52	65	38

Welsh Premier League (2014-15)	P	W	D	L	For	Ag	Pts
Play-Off Conference							
7 Gap Connahs Quay	32	11	10	11	44	43	43
8 Rhyl FC	32	11	9	12	41	42	42
9 Carmarthen Town	32	12	6	14	48	42	42
10 Bangor City	32	9	8	15	48	62	35
11 Cefn Druids	32	7	6	19	38	64	27
12 Prestatyn Town	32	4	6	22	43	86	18

Play-off winners: Newtown

2015-16

There was actually a title race of sorts in 2015-16 as Bala Town were fast becoming a force in Welsh football. They ran The Saints close that season, and still had an outside chance of catching them at the summit with little more than a month of the campaign remaining.

Bala's brave title challenge finally crumbled at Park Hall on 9 April. The New Saints needed a win over their nearest rivals to wrap up their 10th league title and goals from Ryan Brobbel and Aeron Edwards helped see them home and dry. It finished 2-0 to the hosts, though Bala spent significant spells of the game on the front foot, and fought hard to stay in the title race.

The Lakesiders finished just seven points behind TNS, but they weren't the only team in the upper reaches of the division who exceeded expectations.

Newly-promoted Llandudno FC enjoyed a remarkable debut season in the top flight, finishing third, only five points worse off than Bala, who they would join in the qualifying rounds of the 2016-17 Europa League.

A scoreboard showing TNS going 1-0 up against Hungary's Videoton. (© Phil Blagg)

169

The playing surface at Llandudno FC's ground, now known as the OPS Wind Arena. (© Llandudno FC)

The Seasiders were thriving during this period. A couple of years earlier, then-Wales manager Chris Coleman visited their ground, Maesdu Park, to officially open a £420,000 3G pitch. This was followed by the launch of a strategic partnership with local firm MBi Consulting Ltd, resulting in the club becoming known as MBi Llandudno Football Club for a spell and their home ground being renamed Parc MBi Maesdu.

Meanwhile, The New Saints had an historic double-treble firmly in their crosshairs, having overcome underdogs Denbigh Town to lift the League Cup in January 2016. A 5-0 hammering of Connah's Quay Nomads in the semi-finals of the Welsh Cup on 2 April brought it within touching distance, and their opponents in the final were a high-flying Airbus UK side who consistently challenged for trophies during this period, only to fall marginally short each time.

Airbus had hammered Port Talbot Town 7-0 in the semi-finals, which was no doubt a difficult result to stomach for The Steelmen, but it paled in comparison to what hit them several weeks later. Despite finishing in 10th spot in the league table, they were relegated from the top flight as the FAW denied them a domestic licence on financial grounds.

TNS fans watching their team in European action in Hungary. (© Phil Blagg)

Played at the Racecourse Ground, the 129th edition of the Welsh Cup final was a familiar story for both TNS and Airbus. The defending champions took the lead not long after the half-hour mark when Brobbel fired home from an acute angle. They took a one-goal advantage into the break but doubled that in the second half through Scott Quigley, who scrambled home from close range after Adrian Cieślewicz's deflected shot fell kindly for him.

TNS were not at their best, though they prevailed in Wrexham. A dramatic hail storm descended on the Racecourse Ground as their trophy presentation commenced, almost as if Mother Nature had intentionally chosen to punctuate The Saints' double-treble celebrations. For Harrison, it was a career defining milestone:

I think winning the second one and making it back-to-back trebles felt like a greater achievement than the first. I'm not saying it's easy to win a treble in any league, but doing it again was the harder part because the expectations were higher after we did it the first time. People perhaps thought that the first one was a one-off, but we proved them wrong by doing it all over again.

With a double-treble now adorning their honours board, you might be wondering how The New Saints could possibly top their success of

2015-16, but winning was an addiction for Harrison and his squad of hungry professionals, and they weren't done making history.

During this period of dominance, TNS' European fortunes continued to improve. They produced strong performances against much bigger clubs, including Helsingborgs, Legia Warsaw and Slovan Bratislava, and won a continental tie for the first time in four years when they knocked B36 Tórshavn out of the Champions League qualifiers in the summer of 2015.

Harrison's side built on this the following season by seeing off Tre Penne of San Marino 5-1 on aggregate in the first qualifying round of the same competition, before bowing out to APOEL - the most successful team of all time in Cyprus - 3-0 overall, with all of the goals coming in the second leg away from home following a goalless draw at Park Hall:

I think there were signs that we were improving in Europe during this period. Those wins in San Marino and the Faroe Islands were significant because they were the only occasions that a TNS team has beaten a European opponent home and away.

Obviously they are games we should be winning. I got that and I did understand the expectations. We drew some tough opposition in the next rounds, the likes of Legia Warsaw, APOEL Nicosia, Helsingborgs and Slovan Bratislava. These were big teams and we usually gave a decent account of ourselves against them. I remember we were once minutes away from going through against Videoton, who are called Fehérvár FC now.

The next step for us was always to go that bit further in Europe, but you need the luck of the draw. I do think group stage football is a realistic target for the top Welsh clubs now, since we've got the Europa Conference League. When you look at Southern and Northern Irish teams aiming for that, from a Welsh point of view, it should always be the aim too.

The New Saints may have missed out on further European outings that summer, but they would make headlines across the continent - and indeed, the world – the following season.

Welsh Premier League (2015-16)	P	W	D	L	For	Ag	Pts
Championship Conference							
1 The New Saints	32	18	10	4	72	24	64
2 Bala Town	32	15	12	5	48	27	57

Welsh Premier League (2015-16)		P	W	D	L	For	Ag	Pts
3	MBi Llandudno	32	15	7	10	53	46	52
4	Gap Connah's Quay	32	15	3	14	50	42	48
5	Newtown AFC	32	11	9	12	46	54	42
6	Airbus UK Broughton	32	12	6	14	46	55	42
Play-Off Conference								
7	Carmarthen Town	32	14	5	13	45	52	47
8	Aberystwyth Town	32	13	7	12	51	47	46
9	Bangor City	32	13	6	13	49	52	45
10	Port Talbot Town	32	10	9	13	39	56	39
11	Rhyl FC	32	5	12	15	36	50	27
12	Haverfordwest County	32	5	6	21	27	57	21

Play-off winners: Connah's Quay

2016-17

There were positives to draw from the Welsh clubs' European adventures in the summer as TNS and Connah's Quay registered qualifying wins to put coefficient points on the board. Bala and Llandudno were handed difficult ties against Swedish opposition and fell at the first hurdles, but for the latter club, the two-legged continental tie they took part in still holds a special place in their history.

Llandudno were embarking on their first ever European campaign, and only one to date. Standing before them in the first qualifying round of the Europa League was none other than Scandinavian giants IFK Göteborg, arguably one of the biggest clubs a Welsh domestic side has fought on the continent.

Göteborg eased to a 5-0 win in the first leg in Sweden, but it was a grand occasion for the Llandudno contingent involved. Flying to Scandinavia to play a competitive match against a famous European club showed how far they had come in a few short years.

The second leg took place at Nantporth Stadium where the brave Seasiders put up quite the fight, losing 2-1 to the Swedes. Danny Hughes' consolation strike in the 72nd minute still makes him the only Llandudno player to have scored in Europe to this day.

The following month, TNS' domestic campaign began with a victory, though an unremarkable one. Goals from Brobbel and Cieślewicz helped them to a 2-1 win at home to Aberystwyth Town,

The Llandudno team that faced IFK Göteborg in the Europa League qualifiers. (© Llandudno FC)

who threatened a late fightback when Chris Jones found the net with 10 minutes to go.

Little did anyone know, but these three points were the beginning of a phenomenal winning streak which broke a world record that had stood for 44 years.

The great Ajax Amsterdam side of the 1970s, renowned for its 'Total Football' philosophy, originally set the record for most consecutive wins by a top-flight club in the 1971-72 season. Boasting a team of world class players including Johan Cruyff, Arie Haan and Johan Neeskens, the Dutch giants won an eye-watering 26 straight games across all competitions.

On 30 December 2016, The New Saints went one better than this. Goals from Aeron Edwards and Jon Routledge gave them a 2-0 win over Cefn Druids and a 27th consecutive victory overall - this was, as Harrison noted, enough to rewrite footballing history on a global scale:

Ajax were very humble about it. I think they acknowledged it on social media and sent a letter to the football club, which is very commendable. Obviously there's no way in the world that we can compare ourselves to that Ajax team - it's a different stratosphere, but there's always something that connects us now.

That record comes up every few years. A couple of years ago, Manchester City were closing in on it as they had won, I think it was 24 or 25 in a row, but they didn't get over the line. Whenever a team goes on a run like that, they realise our record is the one to break.

It's nice being part of that and being spoken of in the same breath as the likes of Johan Cruyff's Ajax and Pep Guardiola's Manchester City. I understand that we are not comparable with those teams, but our record is now the one for sides like that to beat.

While some might downplay the scale of this accomplishment, given that The New Saints were a fully-professional team picking off one part-time opponent after another, it's worth noting that it wasn't just Welsh teams that they overcame on this formidable spree.

For the 2016-17 season, The Scottish FA revamped the Scottish Challenge Cup after entering a sponsorship agreement with Irn-Bru. The new and expanded version of the competition was a cross-border tournament that teams from Northern Ireland's NIFL Premiership and the Welsh Premier League were invited to compete in.

TNS, along with Bala Town, entered the cup in the fourth round. Bala didn't make it any further than that, losing 4-2 to Alloa Athletic on their tournament debut, but The Saints pulled off impressive wins over Forfar Athletic and Scottish Championship side Livingston on their way to the semi-finals. These two victories were a small part of their world record-setting run.

St. Mirren were runners-up in the Challenge Cup that year, and it was them who ended Welsh interest in the tournament by defeating TNS 4-1 in the semis on 19 February. As Harrison noted, this result meant that The Buddies - who later lost the final 2-1 to Dundee United - were one of only a handful of teams to get the better of TNS in *any* competition in 2016-17:

I think we gave a good account of ourselves in those matches and came up against a really good St. Mirren team after beating Livingston. We had three away games in that competition, starting with Forfar, who Greg Draper scored a hat-trick against.

That St Mirren side had John McGinn playing for them and we found him difficult to handle. We actually went 1-0 up through a great Ryan Brobbel goal, but they were the better team overall and deservedly won the match.

I think we can be proud of our performances in that competition. We represented Wales well, as did Connah's Quay when they made it all the way to the final in 2019.

Although St. Mirren made short work of the Welsh champions, TNS earned praise for their performance in the Scottish Challenge Cup. The question now was who, if anyone, in Welsh football could stop the green and white juggernaut from rolling onto yet another treble?

For much of the season, the answer to that question looked like a resounding 'nobody'. A resurgent Barry Town side, who had overcome years of adversity to win promotion from the second tier in 2017, proved no match for TNS in the Welsh League Cup final in January, with Harrison's men romping to a 4-0 victory to claim the first silverware of the season.

In the league, TNS' record-breaking run left them out of sight in the title race. It finally came to an end with a 3-3 draw against relegation-battling Newtown in their first outing of 2017, but it wasn't long before they reclaimed their crown. A 4-0 dismantling of Bangor City in early March - in which Jamie Mullan scored a brace, and Adrian Cieślewicz and Steve Saunders one each - got The Saints over the line and wrapped up their sixth consecutive title.

A hat-trick of trebles looked more than inevitable one month later when TNS clinically dispatched Connah's Quay Nomads in the semi-finals of the Welsh Cup. Goals from Cieślewicz, Edwards and Mullen helped them to a comfortable 3-0 win and set up a showpiece against Bala Town, who had overcome Caernarfon in the last four.

All signs pointed to a New Saints victory in the final. The two sides had met on 29 previous occasions and The Lakesiders had come out on top in a grand total of zero of them. In all competitions they had locked horns six times in 2016-17 and TNS had won every time, including a memorable 6-4 victory in the league just a week earlier.

Despite TNS' record-breaking feats and insatiable appetite for silverware, this Bala Town side had been making history of their own under manager Colin Caton. The former Colwyn Bay defender had racked up an impressive trophy haul since taking charge at Maes Tegid in 2003, including three Huws Gray Alliance League Cups, one Huws Gray League title and the Europa League Play-Off trophy at the end of the 2012-13 campaign.

The New Saints weren't the only ones in the midst of the most successful period in their history, but they went into the 130th Welsh Cup final as red-hot favourites.

The match took place at Bangor City's Nantporth stadium and an upset was looking unlikely when, after the interval, Draper broke the deadlock for the holders with a close-range tap-in. Bala, however,

Bala Town celebrating their Welsh Cup win in 2017. (© Bala Town FC)

refused to be swept aside by TNS, like so many other teams had been before them.

The Lakesiders' goalkeeper Ashley Morris produced key saves to prevent The Saints from killing off the contest, and 13 minutes from time, their tenacity was rewarded when a deflected strike from sub Jordan Evans found its way beyond Paul Harrison to make it one apiece.

That unprecedented treble-treble was slipping from The Saints' grasp and it soon became apparent that this was going to be Bala's afternoon; their time to enjoy the greatest day in their history. With five minutes remaining, Kieran Smith met Chris Venables' cross with a thumping header to put Bala 2-1 up and whip their supporters into a frenzy.

That was the way it finished. Plucky Bala Town had done it! They lifted their first Welsh Cup and derailed The New Saints' trophy-winning spree against all the odds: "It means everything, winning it for the first time," Caton told BBC Wales. "It's difficult to challenge TNS because they're so good, but [on] a one-off occasion it's gone our way."

For Bala Town, it was a day of glory that would never be forgotten, but how does Harrison feel about it? Surely winning eight out of the last nine domestic trophies was some consolation for this cup final defeat? According to the man himself, this isn't exactly the case:

I was devastated by that result. At the time, I didn't realise it was going to be my last game in charge of TNS. A lot of people said "Well done, you did the double" at the end of that season, but when you're the type of person I am, that isn't good enough. I think setting these standards was a key part of our success, because nothing was ever enough.

We always wanted to be better in every way we could. On the pitch, off the pitch, training sessions, recruitment, professionalism - everything you could think of I wanted to improve. A different person might have been happy with eight trophies out of nine, but it took a lot of getting over for me because a treble-treble would have been very special.

After winning six Welsh Premier League titles, four Welsh Cups and three Welsh League Cups, Harrison left Park Hall to try his hand at management in the English National League with Hartlepool. He departed as a club legend, but this wasn't the last TNS would see of him.

Welsh Premier League (2016-17)	P	W	D	L	For	Ag	Pts
Championship Conference							
1 The New Saints	32	26	1	3	101	26	85
2 Gap Connah's Quay	32	16	10	6	45	24	58
3 Bala Town	32	16	9	7	61	46	57
4 Bangor City	32	16	4	12	53	53	52
5 Carmarthen Town	32	10	9	13	40	46	39
6 Cardiff Metropolitan University	32	10	6	16	41	41	36
Play-Off Conference							
7 Newtown AFC	32	12	9	11	59	41	45
8 Cefn Druids	32	9	12	11	40	48	39
9 Llandudno FC	32	7	14	11	31	45	35
10 Aberystwyth Town	32	10	4	18	41	63	34
11 Rhyl FC	32	8	6	18	38	76	30
12 Airbus UK	32	5	6	21	37	78	21

Play-off winners: Bangor City

15

Dragons Reborn

While The New Saints and Bala Town were busy making history and headlines in 2017, Welsh football's sleeping giant was quietly awakening from its slumber.

Barry Town and their fans had been on a long arduous journey - full of twists, turns, hurdles and fiery resistance - since their relegation more than a decade earlier, but on 18 April 2017, they completed the kind of comeback you'd usually only read about in fairytales.

That date will forever be etched into the hearts of their supporters, as this was the day The Dragons' return from oblivion was finally completed. A superb showing at home to Goytre United in Welsh League Division One was the result that did it. Ahead of the match, they knew three points would secure a return to the top division with two games to spare, and they got the job done, clinically and unstoppably, in front of just over 600 home fans.

Luke Cooper, Tyrell Webbe and Drew Fahiya were all on target as the hosts - who were now competing under the moniker of Barry Town United - thundered to a 3-0 victory. There's a special place in Linnets history reserved for this trio and their manager, Gavin Chesterfield, yet the club's resurgence was a group effort involving heroes on and off the pitch.

Chesterfield, who is an undisputed legend at Jenner Park, was quick to acknowledge the collaborative nature of the club's revival:

That Goytre United game I remember so well. The whole journey up to that point was a rollercoaster and I was on edge during that match. But before me, I could see players coming of age, the club thriving again and smiles back on the fans' faces.

We were back dining at the top table of Welsh football once again. People give me a lot of credit as the manager who delivered that, but a manager is only as good as the people he has around him and the players on the field. We all came together as one to achieve this and we couldn't have done it if everyone wasn't pulling in the right direction.

Barry Town United celebrating their Welsh League Division Two success under Gavin Chesterfield in 2014-15. (© Welsh Football Magazine)

Winning promotion to the Welsh Premier League after a 13-year absence would be hugely significant for any club, but for Barry fans, this was extra special. After all they had endured, they were back where they belonged, albeit with part-time status and a new name.

To truly understand what Barry Town supporters went through over the years, we have to flip the calendar back to the end of 2003-04. Relegation and administration were only the beginning for a stricken club that was put through the meat grinder time and time again.

Local businessman and ex-barrister Stuart Lovering bought Barry Town in December 2003. Before he arrived on the scene, they were at serious risk of going under, just one season after they had won three league and cup doubles in a row at the peak of their power.

Although Lovering's acquisition had kept The Dragons afloat in the short term, it wasn't long before the club's supporters began questioning his status as their knight in shining armour.

Relegation from the top flight may have looked inevitable before the new ownership arrived, but everyone at Barry must have been wondering what they had got themselves into with Lovering, several months into his rein, when reports claimed he was planning to build a new 40,000-seater stadium for the team and grow their stature to rival Real Sociedad's.

Having ambition is one thing, but when you're averaging just 500 fans per match and bound for the drop, there's a clear dividing line between this virtue and delusion. Assuming Lovering wasn't misquoted about his plans, how many away fans did he think the likes of Maesteg Park and Briton Ferry would bring to games?

Not long after The Dragons' relegation to the second tier was confirmed, Lovering announced that he was increasing ticket prices at Jenner Park, making them the most expensive in all of Welsh domestic football. It was, in fact, only a few pounds more to watch neighbours Cardiff City play in the English Championship at the time.

With decisions such as this, it was little wonder that Barry Town were still in financial difficulty. To help keep the team's neck above water, the official supporters club rallied to raise £4,000 as a cash injection. This, however, didn't stop Lovering from falling out with them - labelling the group "part of the old regime that brought [the] club to the edge of extinction" - banning them from fundraising at Jenner Park and removing their 'official' status.

The ever-unpredictable owner then ran the risk of a full-scale mutiny from the fanbase when he sacked popular manager Colin Addison - who was brought in to firefight during the 2003-04 season - on the eve of the new campaign and dubbed him a "prima donna".

Addison's deputy David Hughes replaced him at the helm and, based on their early form, The Dragons actually began the season well, looking like they could be in the mix for promotion. Hughes, however, quit several months later when his budget was slashed: "The playing budget has been cut and I am not prepared to go back to what was happening last season when we were relegated," *WalesOnline* quoted the outgoing boss as saying. "I want to stay, but I have made commitments to my players which are now not possible. I am not prepared to ask players to take a wage cut."

Further off-field chaos derailed any hopes of a swift on-field return to the Premier League. Lovering's hopes of winning any popularity contests among Barry fans had long since faded, but when he announced plans to move the team more than 20 miles from its Jenner Park home, battlelines for all-out war were drawn.

The club's majority owner added Vale of Glamorgan Council to his ever-growing enemies list when he became embroiled in a spat with the local authority over the rent at Jenner Park. An independent district valuer had declared that the club should pay £42,000 for each season until the end of their lease, a figure that Lovering argued was too high for a part-time team.

Rather than pay the bill or attempt to settle the dispute, Lovering uprooted Barry Town's senior side and moved them more than 20 miles away to the White Tips Stadium in Trefforest, where they played their home matches between January 2005 and May 2006.

Watching their beloved football club being uprooted and relocated at the whim of the owner struck Barry fans like a knife to the heart. Few Linnets supporters were willing to make the trek, most likely because a fair number of them no longer recognised their beloved club after its new owner had moulded it into something else entirely. Crowds at their new Trefforest home dwindled, eventually dipping to less than 30. Soon afterwards, Lovering slashed the playing budget to zero. The chaos had now become an utter shambles.

Just a few short years on from trophies galore and European away days at the likes of Porto and Dynamo Kyiv, Barry Town were now an amateur club. Although The Linnets were able to return to Jenner Park for the 2006-07 season after the council dispute was resolved, that campaign was another unmitigated disaster which ended in relegation. A 6-1 defeat against Afan Lido, for which Barry had a squad of just 12 players to pick from, sealed their fate.

These were dark days for the beleaguered club and they left them at their lowest ever position on the domestic football pyramid, Welsh League Division Two.

The proverbial black clouds over Jenner Park showed no signs of shifting, though a few rays of light crept through during this turbulent period. Barry's Supporters Club drew up plans to launch their own team dubbed 'Barri Linnets', and later 'Barry FC', to act as the custodians of The Dragons' proud legacy, a legacy the current ownership continued to disregard.

Lovering was unimpressed by this and threatened legal action against the budding team, accusing them of passing themselves off as the official Barry Town FC. Word that the ex-barrister was willing to sell the club just two years after acquiring it came shortly after this. No doubt most Barry fans will have welcomed this news, until they heard his asking price: a whopping £400,000, almost four times what he originally paid for it.

As if things couldn't get any more farcical, the manager Lovering selected to lead the team into their new campaign in the third tier, Phil Clay, resigned just days after taking on the role, presumably after the reality of managing amid the club's current predicament set in.

At the time, this went down as yet another debacle for the fallen giants of Welsh football, yet in hindsight, it worked in their favour since it paved the way for Gavin Chesterfield to take up the Jenner Park hotseat. The highly respected coach was a catalyst for change at Barry Town and the green shoots of recovery rapidly began to sprout under his watch. Chesterfield was a young manager eager for a chance to show what he could do, as he himself explained:

> *My first involvement with Barry Town was when I applied for the vacant manager's job. When I initially applied for the position, I missed out to a more experienced manager. I was 27 or 28 at the time and I was just desperate for an opportunity. When it didn't work out with the other manager and they got back in touch with me, it felt like fate.*
>
> *I wasn't aware of the full extent of the situation there at the time. I didn't know much about the issues between the chairman and fans. The main challenge I was made aware of is that I would have no budget to work with, but as a new manager, I was eager to prove myself.*

Despite the challenges of working with the team's erratic owner, Chesterfield led The Linnets to promotion from Welsh League Division Two in 2008. Results changed almost overnight, to such an extent that Barry went on to mount a challenge for back-to-back promotions under their new manager:

> *During my first season there, when we got promoted, I have to say, I was largely left to my own devices and allowed to crack on. I got a good group of young players together who really cared for the football club and we did well from the off.*

Chesterfield was a breath of fresh air, but to say Barry Town's newfound vigour was entirely down to him sells their dedicated fanbase short. After plans to form a breakaway club were met with resistance from the ownership, a band of diehard Linnets loyalists formed the Barry Town Supporters Committee and agreed a deal with Lovering to handle footballing matters at Jenner Park on a non-profit basis, free of interference from above.

Fuelled by fan power, The Dragons looked in good shape on the pitch in 2008-09 and boosted their hopes of a return to the top flight with a 21-game unbeaten run towards the end of the campaign. However, as Chesterfield admitted, a three-point deduction for failing to play a league fixture against Pontardawe Town earlier in the season proved costly and saw them finish third:

> *That felt like a huge setback, if I'm being honest, and it was all down to an administration error. Having said that, although the team was competing well near the top of tier two, I don't think we were anywhere near ready to play in the Premier League at that time. We didn't have the structure in place and there were still difficulties off the pitch.*

Another promotion so soon into Chesterfield's tenure wasn't to be, but Barry Town commanded respect once again and dared to dream of better days to come.

Yet those dreams quickly dissipated when more Lovering controversy reminded everyone that The Linnets were still a shambles off the field. Although the owner remained intent on offloading the club and gradually lowered his asking price to more realistic figures, it was clear he was growing frustrated with the search for a buyer. Threats to pull the playing budget once again or withdraw Barry Town from the Welsh football system were seemingly ever present.

Barry fans can be forgiven for thinking the nightmare was almost over in 2010 when Shamrock Coaches owner Clayton Jones - who had previously attempted to acquire the club in 2003 - re-emerged with a credible takeover bid and bold plans to appoint Wales legend John Hartson as his director of football. The agreement crumbled at the eleventh hour.

Fearing that Lovering would eventually come through on his threat to pull Barry out of the league if an alternative buyer wasn't found, Linnets fans mobilised once again and launched the 'Stand Up For Barry' campaign, an initiative to raise awareness of the team's plight and fight for its future, using *Facebook*, *Twitter* and other social media platforms to spread the word.

The campaign attracted an outpouring of support and even found engagement among celebrities, including Joe Calzaghe, Alistair Campbell and broadcaster Kirsty Gallagher. Barry-born Australian prime minister Julia Gillard also sent a message of solidarity to the Supporters Committee as the search for a new owner grew increasingly desperate. Chesterfield was in awe of what the fans had achieved:

That campaign was absolutely life-changing for this club. Stand Up for Barry and the Barry Town Supporters Committee, particularly their presence on social media and their relentless desire to fight back, changed the face of everything that was happening.

It really opened my eyes to the power of social media and its potential to help people stand up for what they believe in. The campaign to raise awareness of our plight and the Barry Town Supporters Committee are the bedrock upon which this football club survived.

In 2012, Barry Town celebrated their 100th anniversary, though they did so as an amateur outfit living each day under the threat of extinction. However, the fan-run Linnets did enjoy some good times on the pitch amid all of this uncertainty, reaching the third round of the Welsh Cup in 2011-12 and going all the way to the semi-finals the following season.

The match in which they booked their place in the last four of the coveted competition is an undisputed highlight of Barry's days as an amateur club. Their opponents in the quarter-finals were Flint Town United, and The Dragons - who were backed by a vociferous travelling support - made a real statement of intent with a surprise 2-0 victory.

Goals from Ryan Evans and Ryan Jenkins either side of half time sealed the victory and propelled the ascending Linnets into the semis, making them the only amateur side left in the cup. Elated Barry fans spilled onto the pitch upon the final whistle to revel in the win with the players and Chesterfield, who led the celebrations draped in a huge Welsh flag.

Friction with Lovering, however, continued to cast a shadow over this period, and during the cup run, he controversially sacked Chesterfield only to later reinstate him. It was typical of the chairman's unpredictability and he soon announced fresh intentions to withdraw Barry Town from all Welsh football competitions unless a viable takeover bid materialised.

The fans fought desperately against this scenario and the wider footballing community rallied behind them, but Lovering finally delivered on his repeated threat in May 2013. Barry Town were

The Barry Town United team ahead of their cup showdown with TNS in January 2017. (© John Smith)

pulled from the Welsh football system with two league fixtures still to play.

Despite the club's staff, players and members of the Barry Town Supporters Committee expressing their determination to keep the club alive and complete the season under the new moniker of Barry Town United, all of the club's results in 2012-13 were expunged.

During a meeting of the Football Association of Wales Council the following month, The Dragons were denied a licence to play Welsh League football and were told they could only continue as a "recreational football" outfit. This might have been the end for Welsh domestic football's faded star, but those who hold the club dear vowed to fight on, as Chesterfield explained:

> *I believed we could come back from this after the great work the Barry Town Supporters Committee and Stand Up for Barry Town campaign had done. I was a young manager at the time, but I knew I was working for a fantastic football club. I'd seen Barry at their best when they had something to fight for, and this was the biggest battle yet.*
>
> *Clubs like us are the fabric of Welsh football. They are in the hearts and minds of the community and will always survive in some form while there's someone fighting for them.*

A drawn-out dispute ensued and the fight for The Dragons' future found its way to the High Court. Since their establishment in 1912

Barry Town boss Gavin Chesterfield leaving the court following the team's landmark legal victory over the FAW.

Barry Town had been involved in some historic showdowns, from domestic cup finals to high profile European adventures, but some, including Chesterfield, would argue that their day in court was far more significant than any of their on-field escapades.

> It was huge. We managed to secure the services of a magnificent barrister called Jonathan Crystal. He taught me so much about how to structure an argument. When he was fighting our corner, I've never seen anything like it in my life.
> We were against the tide and against the odds, but he showed me the importance of stepping up and standing your ground. I was in awe of the way he argued our case.
> Jonathan more or less took the case on an expenses-only basis, despite having represented big celebrities in the past. He came to Barry because his parents were refugees there. I don't know the exact details, but he wanted to give something back to the town.

At the High Court, the fan-led resistance got the result they so craved. The FAW Council's decision to deny them a domestic football licence

A commemorative bottle of champagne to mark Barry Town United's long-awaited promotion to the Welsh top flight. (© Jeff McInery)

was declared unlawful and the way was paved for the fan-run Dragons to spread their wings in competitive football once again.

This was the dawning of a new age for the reborn Barry Town United, one full of promise and free of Lovering's reviled ownership. Having to start again in the fourth tier must have seemed like a minor inconvenience when the alternative was fading out of existence.

From here, The Dragons remembered how to breathe fire again. Under Chesterfield, they won consecutive league titles to claw their way back into the second tier and were beaten finalists against TNS in the League Cup the following year. This comeback trail, years in the making, eventually led to that fateful evening in April 2017, fondly remembered by Chesterfield, when Barry beat Goytre United to complete their return to the Welsh Premier League's promised land:

> Going back way before this game, we won division three at the first attempt, division two at the first attempt and were runners-up in the second tier the year Cardiff Metropolitan University got promoted. We then won it the year after.
>
> The players that had stuck with us from the start still made up around 90% of the squad at this point. The idea was to bring in younger players who could grow with the club over time. Those lads were 19 or 20 when we were in the third division, so they were around 25 by the time we reached the Welsh Premier League and were in their prime.

The Linnets had amassed a squad that was capable of not just surviving in the top division, but being competitive in it. The likes of Curtis Watkins and Luke Cooper added solidity at the back, Jordan Cotterill brought creativity to the midfield, and they had plenty of

Barry Town's Callum Sainty celebrates with the travelling fans after the 1-0 away win at TNS. (© Ian Johnson)

options up front with Jonathan Hood, James Dimitriou and former Southampton striker Kayne McLaggon on their books.

2017-18

Barry Town United wasted no time establishing themselves as a side to be respected in the top flight. Almost a thousand fans showed up for their first match back in the big time, a home clash with Aberystwyth Town. They led at the interval through Ryan Newman's goal in the 27th minute, only for Jonny Spittle to strike late on and ensure the spoils were shared.

Chesterfield's men secured their first Welsh Premier League win in over a decade on 9 September 2017 when a brace from athletic centre-forward McLaggon inspired them to a 2-0 victory at home to Newtown, this time with just over 500 fans in attendance.

For the first half of the campaign, The Dragons' form was erratic, though they did pull off some surprise results, including an away victory at high-flying Bangor City later that month, and a shock win over The New Saints at Park Hall. Both games finished 1-0 to The Linnets, and a McLaggon goal was the difference on each occasion.

Although Barry were capable of giving anyone a game on their day, a run of three straight defeats at the end of the Welsh Premier League's first phase left them in the bottom half of the table and, the previous month, the club had made an early exit from the Welsh Cup at the hands of Caernarfon Town, who went on to win the 2017-18 Cymru Alliance.

Having also dropped out of the League Cup at the quarter-final stage in the autumn - losing 2-0 to eventual finalists Cardiff Met - Barry's entire season hinged on a good showing in the Play-Off Conference, in which they started in ninth place.

Chesterfield's men were, however, hugely impressive from this point until the end of the season and didn't lose any of their remaining league fixtures. The conferences phase began with a 3-1 win over Aberystwyth, with goals from Hood, Cotterill and McLaggon, and Barry enjoyed a 10-match unbeaten run, concluding with a 1-0 victory against Carmarthen.

During that mighty unbeaten streak, Barry dropped points only twice, drawing with Prestatyn and Newtown, and ended up topping their conference section. This meant, as Chesterfield outlined, that they joined Cardiff Met and Cefn Druids in the European play-offs at the end of the season:

I didn't expect us to challenge for Europe that season but I was really proud of what we were achieving around then. The season before, we reached the final of the Welsh League Cup, where we narrowly lost to The New Saints.

We were a group of lads who had come through the leagues together and I was delighted with how we handled the step up. The fact that we held onto those players for so long really says a lot for the club. In that conference phase, I think we had adapted well to the challenges of the top flight. We knew what to expect from teams and had grown up a bit by then.

A fourth team should have made the play-offs, but in a development that shook Welsh football to its foundations, second-placed Bangor City were denied the Tier 1 Licence required to compete in the Welsh Premier League and European tournaments the following season. Bala Town, who had finished fourth, took their place in the Europa League qualifiers. As a result of this, Cefn Druids received a bye to the play-off final, leaving Barry Town United and Cardiff Met to fight it out in the only semi-final.

The contest took place over one leg, played at Cardiff Met's Cyncoed Campus on 12 May, and for The Dragons, it was the biggest match they had played in since returning to the top flight.

Despite giving a great account of themselves by challenging for Europe in their first season back in the Welsh Premier League, The Dragons were brushed aside by a strong Cardiff Met side. Striker Adam Roscrow, who went on to play for Wales C and compete in the English Football League with AFC Wimbledon, scored a brace as The Archers eased to a 4-1 victory. Chesterfield acknowledged that Barry were no match for the university side on the day:

> *It was difficult to take because of the significance of the occasion, but in all fairness we were a distant second against Cardiff Met. They taught us a lesson about the differences between playing in the bottom six over a fair period of time and playing in the top six, although that hasn't always rang true over the years in the European play-offs.*

A late consolation goal from Ryan Newman was all The Linnets had to show for their play-off campaign, but their opponents didn't make it to Europe either. One week later, a James Davies goal was their undoing during a 1-0 loss to The Druids in the final.

Barry's return and unlikely bid for European football was one of the big talking points in Welsh domestic football during 2017-18, but it wasn't the only one. The downfall of three-time champions Bangor City made national headlines, and there was also a shock result in the Welsh Cup at the quarter-final stage.

Now managed by former Saints player Scott Ruscoe, The New Saints were still the strongest team in the league and won it by 14 points. Along the way, they also retained the League Cup by seeing off Cardiff Met in the final to make it double honours, and were hotly-tipped to go the distance in the 2018 Welsh Cup too.

TNS' hopes for another treble were dashed on 6 March when they travelled to Connah's Quay in the quarter-finals to face a fired-up Nomads side at Deeside Stadium, and unexpectedly crashed out, despite taking an early lead through Aeron Edwards. The hosts hit back when Michael Bakare buried a free kick from 23 yards, and completed a memorable win via Callum Morris, who fired home a crucial penalty in the 49th minute.

The Nomads then swept aside a beleaguered Bangor in the semis, dumping more misery on their crisis-hit opponents by thumping them 6-1 to set up a showpiece against Aberystwyth Town, the conquerors of Newtown in the last four.

The final took place at Latham Park in front of 1,455 fans, and it was a one-sided affair. Under the management of former Manchester City skipper Andy Morrison, The Nomads were fast becoming a force to rival TNS, and they made a statement of intent that day.

Veteran striker Michael Wilde netted twice, with Bakare and substitute Andy Owens also amongst the goals as Connah's Quay turned their opponents over. Ryan Wade notched a consolation for Aberystwyth with The Nomads three up, but Morrison's men were too strong and totally worthy of their 4-1 win, which saw them lift the trophy for the first time in their history.

Amid the champagne-soaked celebrations, Morrison threw down the gauntlet to The New Saints and spoke of his determination to one day steal their long-retained crown: "We don't want to stand still," said the Nomads manager in a statement published by the *Daily Post*. "We want to go after TNS, somebody's got to go and challenge them and I just feel there's a lot of really good stuff at this club at the moment."

Within a few short years, Morrison and Connah's Quay would realise their ambitions.

Welsh Premier League (2017-18)	P	W	D	L	For	Ag	Pts
Championship Conference							
1 The New Saints	32	23	5	4	83	32	74
2 Bangor City	32	19	3	10	49	32	60
3 Connah's Quay Nomads	32	17	6	9	46	29	57
4 Bala Town	32	15	4	13	37	48	49
5 Cefn Druids	32	12	8	12	38	41	44
6 Cardiff Metropolitan University	32	12	7	13	46	41	43
Play-Off Conference							
7 Barry Town United	32	16	5	11	39	31	53
8 Newtown AFC	32	12	4	16	52	55	40
9 Aberystwyth Town	32	10	7	15	47	56	37
10 Llandudno FC	32	9	9	14	40	44	36
11 Carmarthen Town	32	8	5	19	35	62	29
12 Prestatyn Town	32	4	7	21	27	68	19

Play-off winners: Cefn Druids

16

Shattered Dreams

2018-19

The Welsh Premier League's 2018-19 season was an eventful one, with more than a few surprises in store. While nobody was shocked to see The New Saints reclaim their crown once again, there were signs that the division was gradually becoming more competitive, at least among the chasing pack.

Connah's Quay Nomads continued to establish themselves as credible rivals to TNS, though the eventual runners-up were 12 points off the pace come the end of term.

Directly below them was a side nobody expected to fly so high: Barry Town United. Under Gavin Chesterfield, the revitalised Linnets built on a solid 2017-18 campaign and stormed to third place, securing Europa League qualification after just two seasons back in the top flight.

An impressive 5-2 victory away to Bala Town on 6 April 2019 was the result that brought European football back to Jenner Park after a 15-year absence, as The New Saints' 6-0 drubbing of Newtown during that round of fixtures guaranteed third spot for The Dragons.

Barry were not the only team who defied the odds to reach the promised land of the Europa League. Cardiff Met, who finished top of the Play-Off Conference, beat Bala on penalties in the European play-offs to secure a continental tour for the first time in their history; a result that made international headlines as The Archers became the first university football team to qualify for Europe. In truth, Cardiff Met developed into something more than your average university team when they merged with Inter Cardiff in 2000, but their accomplishments under manager Christian Edwards were monumental nonetheless.

The Cardiff Met manager and his scholarly charges enjoyed double celebrations in 2019 as they also brought home the League Cup for the first time. A double from Adam Roscrow helped them to a 2-0 victory in the final against surprise package from the Rhondda, Cambrian & Clydach Vale Boys & Girls Club, who had produced a giant killing against The New Saints in the previous round.

Headlines were made at both ends of the league table as newly-promoted Llanelli Town, the reborn incarnation of former champions Llanelli AFC, lasted only one season in the top division. They won just five league games all season, finished rock bottom with 16 points and were relegated to the second tier, along with 11th-placed Llandudno.

The Seasiders' relegation came only a few years on from the most successful period in their history, during which they won the 2014-15 Cymru Alliance, finished third in the Welsh Premier League and represented the nation in a Europa League qualifier against IFK Göteborg.

As has been the case for many Welsh teams before them, success sadly wasn't sustainable for The Seasiders, and they have since joined a disconcertingly long list of domestic clubs in serious financial peril.

At the time of writing, the Cymru North outfit recently lost their entire team and had their ground condemned after the FAW and UEFA dubbed its playing surface a "health and safety hazard". The will to save them among the team's staff, supporters and local community is strong, though, and they are amassing the capital needed to install a new pitch through fundraising initiatives, while accepting refugee status at Conwy Borough FC.

There's no denying that there were major developments during the 2018-19 Premier League season that echoed across the years; but they were ultimately overshadowed by an even bigger story that was playing out in the second tier of Welsh football.

The downfall of Bangor City the season before, following the FAW's decision to deny them a Tier 1 Licence, sent seismic shockwaves through Welsh football. The three-time champions were one of the jewels in The Welsh Premier League's crown, with a storied history behind them, an enviable collection of domestic silverware and a diehard fanbase. Although the licensing body's ruling in April 2018 was a stake through Bangor City's heart, The Citizens' demise can be traced back much further than this.

Cardiff Met celebrating winning the 2019 Welsh League Cup. (© FAW)

Bangor's success on the pitch began to dwindle several years earlier as the glorious Neville Powell era came to an end. The long-serving manager enjoyed nine years at the helm, adding triple Welsh Cup success and one league title to the trophy cabinet during his tenure. Under Powell and other managers before him, The Citizens regularly challenged for silverware and were almost ever present in the qualifying rounds of European competitions, but it was a continental result that seemed to trigger a downturn in the club's fortunes. In 2014-15, they were pummelled 8-0 on aggregate by Icelandic side Stjarnan in the qualifying rounds of the Europa League, and a difficult domestic campaign followed. Powell's men flirted with relegation all season but ultimately avoided the drop in 10th place.

The Citizens were unable to arrest this decline in 2015-16 and could only muster a 9th-place finish. That summer, a Cheshire-based consortium with ties to former Chester City owner Stephen Vaughan acquired the club from a hierarchy that was becoming increasingly desperate to offload it. The new regime, which arrived amid promises of heavy investment and ground improvements, removed Powell from the dugout within a month: "Bangor City FC have today announced that they have relieved manager Neville Powell of his duties," read a club statement issued in July 2016. "The club would like to thank Neville for all the hard work he has done over the years and wish him well in the future."

One man with a unique perspective on Bangor's downward spiral is Chris O'Neal. As well as being a lifelong Citizens fan, the former Gwynedd councillor worked with the club's management group during what is arguably the most turbulent period in its history. According to O'Neal, leaving Farrar Road for Nantporth in 2012 was the catalyst that triggered the decline in Bangor City's fortunes both on and off the pitch:

> *The downfall of the whole club came when we moved from Farrar Road to Nantporth. This took the club out of the heart of the city. The Bangor City experience was Farrar Road. On match days you'd get on the local bus, get a bag of chips and head to the ground. Most of the home fans were from the surrounding estates. The atmosphere at Farrar Road was second to none in the Welsh Premier League and when we made the move to Nantporth, it just wasn't the same.*

Under new owners Vaughan Sports Management (VSM), a period of off-the-field turmoil set in and the managerial merry-go-round spun at pace in the wake of Powell's departure. Andy Legg was initially named as his successor, but the former Wales international lasted just three months in the role as he was unable to commit to a full-time contract. His successor, Ian Dawes, also proved to be a short-term addition to the dugout.

Dawes fell foul of Welsh Premier League licensing regulations which state that all top flight managers must hold, or be in the process of obtaining, a UEFA Pro Coaching Licence. Journeyman Gary Taylor-Fletcher, who had joined Bangor off the back of a short-lived stint with Accrington Stanley, became player-manager for the rest of the season, and guided Bangor City back into Europe after a three-year absence via the 2016-17 play-offs, in which they defeated Cardiff Met 1-0 in the final. Dean Rittenberg scored the only goal of the game and Taylor-Fletcher himself was the provider: "We had to dig in at the end and we were hanging in but I can't ask for anything more. We're in Europe, it's all we wanted," BBC Sport quoted the player-manager as saying. "We knew we had the quality and that was the edge. They had the fitness but we had the final quality."

Although Taylor-Fletcher brought Europa League football back to Bangor, he took a step down to the position of assistant manager in May 2017 to allow Kevin Nicholson, the youngest-ever Englishman to hold the UEFA Pro Licence, to take over the top job.

Stability seemed to have returned for Bangor on the pitch, but for some, red flags around VSM's ownership were there from the start. While at Chester, Stephen Vaughan became the first football club owner to fail the English FA's fit and proper persons' test due to a VAT fraud conviction dating back to his time with rugby league club Widnes Vikings.

Gary Taylor-Fletcher in action for Bangor City. (© Andre Pepper)

Eyebrows were raised when Vaughan was present at the official launch of VSM's takeover, but new chairman Ivor Jenkins was quick to state for the record that the businessman - who, at the time, was banned from serving as a company director in the United Kingdom - would not be involved in the running of the Welsh Premier League outfit. His son, former Chester City and Boston United player Stephen Vaughan Jr, was later installed as Bangor City's director of football and would also take on coaching duties with the club.

Vaughan Sports Management arrived on the scene promising big investment to make Bangor City a force in Welsh football once again, but less than two years on from their acquisition, The Citizens found themselves under scrutiny for financial irregularities. This led to that fateful moment when they were refused a Tier 1 and UEFA Licence for the 2018-19 season. Despite finishing second in the league, Bangor were prohibited from taking part in Europa League qualifying or the domestic top flight the following season.

Looking back at this dark day for the three-time Welsh champions, O'Neal was critical of the FAW for clamping down so hard on Bangor. He suggested that bad blood between the governing body and the club may have played a part in the decision to deny them a licence and even accused some individuals within the organisation of letting Bangor down.

With their future plunged into uncertainty, the club launched an appeal against its expulsion, only for the FAW's Licensing Appeals Body to uphold the original ruling: "The Appeals Body were not satisfied that Bangor City has rectified the original concerns of the First Instance Body," read an FAW statement issued in April 2018.

Bangor City's hierarchy responded with a strongly-worded statement of their own, in which they questioned the validity of their exclusion but vowed to "work with the relevant parties at the FAW to ensure [they would] never [be] in this position in the future." Two months later, they had a winding up petition from Her Majesty's Revenue and Customs to ward off, due to unpaid taxes. Although this was a credible threat to the team's existence, they survived it by settling the debt, albeit after the original deadline had passed.

Bangor lived to fight another day and their battlefield for the 2018-19 season was the Cymru Alliance. Despite their monetary woes, The Citizens were able to retain and attract quality players by Welsh second-tier standards and began the campaign as promotion favourites.

Boasting one of the strongest squads in the division, with defender Phil Baker and goalkeeper Andy Coughlin adding experience to their ranks, and promising youngsters such as Jacob Farleigh and Sameron Dool on the rise, Bangor also packed international talent in the shape of Guinean midfielder Yalany Baio and Italian striker Francesco Serafino.

In the context of the Welsh game, Bangor were a big fish in a small pond and were earmarked as the team to beat. It was a competitive Cymru Alliance that season, and The Citizens found stern opposition in Airbus UK Broughton, Flint Town United, Porthmadog, and their bitter rivals Rhyl, for whom financial difficulties were also looming.

Bangor won just over half of their league games, but were miles off the pace set by eventual winners Airbus. They lost 11 times on the way to a fourth-placed finish, level on points with Rhyl directly below them, but a whopping 25 behind the champions. In the Welsh Cup, they made it as far as the fourth round before going down 2-1 at home to Caernarfon Town, who were then eliminated by Connah's Quay Nomads in the quarters.

The Nomads made it to the final where they met TNS, having knocked the Welsh champions out of the previous season's competition at the quarter-final stage. The outcome this time, however, did not defy the form book as The Saints ran out comfortable 3-0 winners.

As was usually the case with Bangor City during this troubled period, off-field issues eclipsed footballing matters throughout their Cymru Alliance campaign.

Claims of shady business practises on Vaughan Sports Management's part appeared in the press in October 2018 when the club's auditors, Salisbury, resigned after claiming to have uncovered 11 points of concern about the club's financial management. Among the allegations were unexplained gaps in accounts, missing financial documents and inadequate paperwork for a transaction which saw £258,000's worth of club shares transferred to VSM.

Stephen Vaughan Jr. took on the role of chairman in March 2019, and within three months, Bangor were accused of violating a

Bangor City taking on Prestatyn in the final competitive match at Farrar Road. (© Christopher Williams)

string of FAW and league regulations. The proposed punishment was about as severe as they come: a heavy fine and a 42-point deduction which would have relegated them to the third tier of Welsh domestic football. On top of this, The Citizens were facing a transfer embargo and another tax dispute with HMRC.

An appeal was lodged, though Bangor were unable to contest the transfer embargo as they missed the deadline to challenge this sanction. As a result, the stricken club were unable to sign any professional players or renew any contracts for the rest of the calendar year. They were, however, successful in overturning their points deduction and staving off the resulting relegation after several rounds of appeal - during which they were represented by Chris O'Neal - and repelled another HMRC winding-up order with a late tax bill payment.

Vaughan Sports Management's Bangor legacy is not a proud one. The firm's record there is marred by allegations of underhanded dealings, relegation and instability. Many Citizens fans were eager to see the back of them, and in September 2019, they got their wish.

One month earlier, the *North Wales Chronicle* reported that an "unnamed Italian" was in advanced talks to buy Bangor City from VSM. The newspaper went on to claim that the new owners were planning to keep Stephen Vaughan Jr. at the club, in the position of manager.

The report was right on the money in some respects. A consortium of investors acquired Bangor from Vaughan Sports Management, and Italian musician and producer Domenico Serafino - the father of Citizens striker Francesco - was appointed as chairman.

Vaughan Jr., however, didn't stick around but the club's new hierarchy landed an unbelievably high-profile manager in his place. Argentinian World Cup winner Pedro Pasculli, who once played alongside Diego Maradona at international level, became the new Bangor boss in October and was charged with getting the club back into the top flight.

Reflecting on the VSM era, O'Neal was quick to defend Stephen Vaughan Jr. and insist that Bangor were heading in the right direction under his regime until financial issues arose:

We played some of our best football for years during the Vaughan Sports era and got back into Europe. The troubles off the pitch are well documented, but there was a plan in place before the financial problems took hold. Stephen Vaughan Jr., who I associated with, came into the club with nothing but good intentions, but he just ran out of money.

O'Neal's views on VSM's ownership were not unanimously supported by the club's fans, many of whom welcomed the latest takeover bid with open arms. However, for the first time in years, Bangor fans had cause to be optimistic. A seemingly rich new owner had liberated them from a period of turmoil, there was a big name in the dugout, players from around the world were flocking to the club, and heavy investment was pledged.

Serafino and Pasculli assembled a squad comprised almost entirely of overseas players, with new recruits flooding in from continental Europe, South America and Africa. Among them was former Auxerre and Barnsley midfielder Hugo Colace, who played alongside Carlos Tevez, Javier Mascherano and Pablo Zabaleta as an Argentine youth international.

Ahead of the 2019-20 season, the Football Association of Wales carried out an in-depth review of the Welsh football pyramid and revamped it based on the results. The top flight was rebranded as the Cymru Premier but retained its 12-team roster and conferences format. There were, however, bigger changes in store for the second-tier leagues.

For the first time, the governing body would own and administer the two regionalised divisions directly below the top flight, and they were renamed Cymru North and Cymru South. JD Sports, who were already sponsoring the Cymru Premier and the Welsh Cup, extended their commitment to Welsh football by lending their name to the second-tier leagues too.

Bangor were raring to go ahead of the inaugural Cymru North campaign, but if their situation going into the new season sounds like it was too good to be true, that's because it was.

The first season of the Serafino era saw little improvement on the pitch, despite positive results here and there. They were unbeaten in their first five matches in all competitions and put The New Saints out of the League Cup on penalties in September, before narrowly losing to Bala in the next round. From this point on, their form was largely inconsistent.

With a new hierarchy and team in place, hopes were high that City would improve on the previous season's fourth-placed finish, though by the turn of the year, this looked unlikely. Whether they'd have arrested their erratic form and pushed for promotion is unclear as the 2019-20 Cymru North campaign was halted prematurely by the Covid-19 pandemic.

The Citizens' final match of the season was a 2-0 win at Llandudno in February, with Esteban Goicoechea and Facundo Placeres among the goals. This left the club in fifth place in the division since the final standings were determined on a points-per-game basis.

Although the season was curtailed by the coronavirus outbreak, fifth place was seen as an underperformance and the club parted company with Pasculli. Colace replaced him in the dugout, but the chaos and instability that marred Bangor during the Vaughan Sports Management era would rear its ugly head again, exacerbated by the pandemic.

The 2020-21 Cymru North season was initially postponed and ultimately cancelled, falling victim to the Welsh Government's measures to tackle the spread of the virus. During Covid, however, it became clear that Bangor fans were right to be concerned about who was running the club.

Supporters must have felt a disconcerting sense of *déjà vu* in April 2021 when Bangor were denied a Tier 1 Licence for failing to declare financial accounts with their application and not providing evidence that the necessary coaching qualifications were in place.

At the time, O'Neal publicly expressed his frustration towards the club's hierarchy for apparent inertia on the matter of filing the necessary accounts: "I've clearly made my opinion known on this case now to the directors [and] financial backers, and unless they pull the strings to get the accounts in then unfortunately I'm going to be cutting all ties, as this has gone on too long," he said in a statement issued at the time. "To come to this stage where everything should by now be a walk in the park and we get a kick in the teeth instead."

This was the beginning of another farcical downward spiral for the three-time champions of Wales. Colace didn't last long into the 2021-22 season and was relieved of his duties by Serafino after the team won only four of their first 12 Cymru North matches. Poor form, however, wasn't the only reason behind the Argentinian coach's dismissal.

Earlier that week, Bangor were hauled before an FAW disciplinary panel over allegations of unpaid wages. These claims were echoed by an investigative documentary aired by BBC Wales, in which players and staff claimed that Serafino did not pass on any of the furlough money he claimed during the coronavirus pandemic to his employees.

Players who had joined Bangor City from overseas and relied on their footballing income to support their families allegedly went up to six months without being paid. The documentary also found alarming parallels between Bangor and Italian club A.S. Sambenedettese which, under the ownership of Serafino, stopped paying its players and eventually went bust.

An image of Colace pledging solidarity with his unpaid playing staff was circulated on social media in the weeks preceding his sacking, incurring the ownership's wrath. The group was pictured brandishing a banner reading "Even without wages our integrity is not broken".

While Serafino vehemently denied any foul play regarding the club's furlough funds, the Football Association of Wales was unwilling to dismiss the matter of unpaid wages during Bangor's disciplinary hearing. The panel ruled that all "all outstanding monies" had to be paid within 31 days of 29 October, leaving the club with a bill of almost £53,000 to foot.

Failure to settle this debt would result in Bangor City being suspended from "all football-related activity", and this was no hollow threat. The FAW made good on their promise when the payment deadline came and went with the club's staff still out of pocket.

As The Citizens were frozen out of Cymru North, this led to all of their subsequent fixtures being postponed, and as a result, they began racking up fines and points deductions, a snowball effect that was only halted when all competitive football in Wales was paused for the festive period due to the Welsh Government's latest package of Covid-19 sanctions.

There may have been a way back for Bangor at this point, had Serafino somehow managed to pay all of his outstanding debts, including the mountain of fines that had built up following their suspension from Cymru North, but that was never likely to happen. Instead, the club informed the FAW that it was withdrawing from Cymru North for the 2021-22 campaign, but vowed to return for the following season. The governing body accepted their resignation and their record for the current season was expunged.

The plans for a comeback have never materialised. In fact, Bangor City have since surrendered their lease on their Nantporth stadium

Nantporth Stadium, Bangor City's home from 2012 to 2022. (© Welsh Football Magazine)

and, at the time of writing, are in the process of being formally removed from the Companies House register.

This is how a town lost its football club, and not just any football club. Bangor City were a wonderful asset to the Welsh top flight, a team whose fans had witnessed countless trophy celebrations and joined them on unforgettable European adventures over the years. A generation of youngsters grew up with ambitions to one day play for Bangor City and now, thanks to dire mismanagement, those dreams had been shattered.

Many will tell you that the club falling into the wrong hands was the reason behind their downfall, but the BBC investigation into Bangor's collapse also highlighted the absence of a fit and proper persons test for Welsh football club owners as a potential contributing factor. Could such a test have saved The Citizens from being run into the ground? It was, after all, the failure to meet these requirements in English football that prevented Stephen Vaughan Snr. from retaining control of Chester City, due to his prior history of involvement in fraud. Chris O'Neal remained undecided:

I'm not sure it would have saved us. Who gets to define what a fit and proper person is? If someone who has had issues of violence in the past turns up with a massive amount of money to invest, are they fit and proper? Who should make that call?

It's also worth highlighting that the desperation of the club's previous ownership to sell up was always going to increase the risk of it ending up in less-than-ideal hands, regardless of whether Vaughan's acquisition bid fell foul of background checks. Bangor City's fate is one that should never have been allowed to happen to any football club, but sadly for the Welsh game, something alarmingly similar happened to another of its teams around the same time.

Port Talbot Town were originally relegated from the top flight in 2015-16 after failing to meet the licensing criteria and, ahead of the 2019-20 campaign, The Steelmen were bumped further down the pyramid to Welsh Football League Division One when they were denied the Tier 2 Licence required to compete in the newly-formed Cymru South.

A bright light went out in the town of Bangor when The Citizens fell, but embers of hope remain. In April 2019, amid the chaos of VSM's ownership, the Bangor City Football Club Supporters' Association voted overwhelmingly in favour of starting a breakaway club, Bangor 1876, a phoenix outfit that proudly shoulders the responsibility of safeguarding the town's footballing memories and traditions: "We want fans to reconnect with each other and restore the pride and feeling of being a supporter of our historic club," the group said in a statement. "The new club is a creative and positive solution for an ever-changing and precarious situation. We are not disowning Bangor City FC or its history, the club is OURS, it belongs to the fans and local community. 'Owners' will come and go but the people remain. Keep the faith."

O'Neal, who remained with the original Bangor City until the summer of 2020, did not back the phoenix club initially as he was convinced the team was salvageable. He has since admitted that he "made a bad choice" in standing by the club's hierarchy. Today, the former county councillor views Bangor 1876 in a more positive light:

I wouldn't say I'm fully behind the phoenix club but I have no negativity towards it. I was against it at first because, at the time, I didn't think the reasons it was originally set up were right. But I can see now that there were good intentions behind it and we wouldn't have any senior football in the town of Bangor without it.

Now managed by former Citizens player Michael Johnston, Bangor 1876 have become a beacon of hope for City supporters, many of whom firmly believe that their town might one day have a team competing in the Welsh top flight again.

Just four seasons into their existence, the phoenix club have fought their way up to the second-tier Cymru North division, having won promotion via the Ardal Northern play-off final in 2022-23. Could they make it all the way to the top and replace their famous predecessors in the upper echelons of Welsh domestic football?

Given what fan power has done for Welsh football clubs in the past, don't even think about writing them off.

Welsh Premier League (2018-19)	P	W	D	L	For	Ag	Pts
Championship Conference							
1 The New Saints	32	23	5	4	99	16	74
2 Connah's Quay Nomads	32	19	5	8	76	33	62
3 Barry Town United FC	32	17	5	10	54	51	56
4 Caernarfon Town	32	13	7	12	45	47	46
5 Newtown	32	13	7	12	53	56	46
6 Bala Town FC	32	13	5	14	55	63	44
Play-Off Conference							
7 Cardiff Metropolitan University	32	16	3	13	53	51	51
8 Aberystwyth Town	32	13	5	14	44	44	44
9 Carmarthen Town AFC*	32	12	6	14	49	53	39
10 Cefn Druids	32	10	9	13	43	49	39
11 Llandudno FC	32	5	7	20	33	65	22
12 Llanelli Town AFC	32	4	4	24	31	101	16

*3 points deducted

Play-off winners: Cardiff Metropolitan University

17

The Rise of the Nomads

When The New Saints strolled to their eighth consecutive league title in 2019, the Welsh top flight looked in danger of becoming an indefinite one-horse race. How could anyone stop the mighty TNS when they had such a distinct advantage over their rivals on and off the pitch?

The Saints were, as usual, the team to beat ahead of the 2019-20 season, the first league campaign to be contested under the Cymru Premier banner. Although the FAW's restructuring of the Welsh football pyramid meant minimal changes for the division at its pinnacle, this new era brought a shift in the balance of power that caught everyone off guard.

Connah's Quay Nomads have been a part of Welsh football since just after the Second World War, but their fans had to wait a lifetime to enjoy the kind of success TNS supporters can almost take for granted. The modern day incarnation of the club started out in 1946, founded by Everton and Wales defender TG Jones as Connah's Quay Juniors. As the name suggests, they were a youth football outfit, and enjoyed great success at this level, which put them in good stead to add a senior team to their roster two years later, starting out in the Flintshire League.

The 'Nomads' suffix was introduced ahead of the 1952-53 season, by which point the Deeside outfit were plying their trade in the regionalised Welsh League, North. Over the decades, they became journeymen in the Welsh system, dabbling in everything from local football to the Clwyd League; a cross-district championship that began in the mid-1970s.

There was minor trophy success for The Nomads, with silverware coming their way in competitions including the Welsh Intermediate Cup and North Wales Amateur Cup, which were added to the honours list alongside an impressive collection of regional league titles. Although many of their accomplishments at this stage were relatively low key, The Nomads had a part to play in shaping Welsh

Deeside Stadium, the home of Connah's Quay Nomads. (© Welsh Football Magazine)

football at a pivotal point in its history. They were founder members of the Cymru Alliance in 1990 and then the League of Wales two years later.

One man who witnessed the gradual rise of The Nomads firsthand is club historian Dave Rapson, who also served as their vice chairman and treasurer until 2012. He has great insight into how the club became a force in Welsh football:

> *Despite being one of the founder members of the League of Wales in 1992, Connah's Quay Nomads were expected to struggle in the top flight. It took two decades for the club to stamp its name on the league, largely through top ten finishes in half of those seasons and a Welsh Cup semi-final appearance in 1993. Slipping out of the league when it was reduced by six teams was a bitter pill; but successive Cymru Alliance titles followed immediately, resulting in a return to the top division in 2012.*

Connah's Quay were mainstays in the top flight for years and they brought major silverware back to Deeside in 1996 by defeating Ebbw Vale in the League Cup final. Despite that short stay in the Cymru Alliance between 2010 and 2012, The Nomads made gradual progress over the years and eventually became one of the strongest teams in the Cymru Premier.

Their meteoric rise in stature began with the appointment of Manchester City legend Andy Morrison as first team manager and director of football in November 2015. The change in the club's fortunes was almost instantaneous as the Scottish coach guided them to fourth place in the league in his first season in charge; a best-ever finish for The Nomads.

Things only got better from there as Connah's Quay went on to win the 2016 European play-offs, beating Airbus Broughton in the final via Wes Baynes' late goal. This result, as Rapson outlined, saw the Deeside club qualify for Europe for the first time and pocket £150,000 along the way:

> *Andy Morrison's arrival in the autumn of 2015 was the catalyst for six years of success. His initial objective was to achieve a shot at European competition and this he pulled off in that first season by winning the play-off game against Airbus.*

Morrison, who was a firebrand on the pitch during his playing days, continued to inspire his Connah's Quay charges and challenge them to set yet more club records. They were a well organised outfit that didn't play the most attractive brand of football, yet it proved effective.

Milestones were passed throughout his time in charge. At the start of the following season, they claimed their first European scalp thanks to a 1-0 aggregate triumph over Norwegian side Stabæk Fotball. They held their Scandinavian opponents to a goalless draw in Rhyl before stunning them in the away leg, Callum Morris scoring the only goal of the tie early on.

Not only was this a first continental win for The Nomads, the results over the two legs marked the only occasion in 24 years and 214 games that a Welsh domestic side had kept clean sheets both home and away in a European fixture, commented the club historian:

> *The victory over Stabaek in The Nomads' first European tie was probably the most significant moment in the club's history at that time and led to nine other lucrative ties over the following five campaigns against some notable opponents. Results like this one could hardly have been foreseen just a few years earlier.*

As success on the pitch continued, Connah's Quay set their sights on full-time status. This has proved a gradual and ongoing process under the ownership of Gap Personnel Group founder Gary Dewhurst, but the club took a major step towards achieving it in the summer of 2017 when they signed four players - Jake Phillips, Declan Poole, Rhys Williams and former Manchester United youth defender Joe Heath - on full-time contracts.

The Nomads hierarchy had lofty ambitions and it wasn't long before those plans began to bear fruit in the shape of silverware. Their 4-1 victory over Aberystwyth Town in the 2017-18 Welsh Cup final saw the Deesiders get their hands on the famous trophy for the first time, adding extra gloss to an already successful campaign in which they finished third in the league.

Morrison shared the club's ambitions and next turned his attention to knocking the all-conquering TNS off their perch, a perch they'd been securely and comfortably at home on for almost a decade. He would get there eventually, but first, there was still time to make history on another front.

The club made a bold statement of intent in October 2018 by appointing former New Saints manager Craig Harrison as a first-team coach. Harrison was a proven winner at Welsh top-flight level, and his presence at the club helped attract yet more quality players.

Among them was ex-Hibernian forward Jamie Insall. The Englishman looked set for a promising career up in Scotland, having impressed during back-to-back loan spells with East Fife, but his progression was stalled by a positive doping test in 2017. This kept him out of football for well over a year, until Connah's Quay offered him the chance to get his career back on track. Despite having a number of suitors, Insall explained why he chose to join the Welsh outfit over offers from clubs in the English system:

> I had a few options in England at the time, but the thought of playing in Europe was massive for me. I had a good relationship with Craig Harrison at the time, and he got me to come up to Deeside to see what the club was about. Once I sat down with Andy Morrison and spoke to him, there was no going back. I decided to join The Nomads there and then.

A highlight of their 2018-19 campaign came in the Scottish Challenge Cup. A string of good performances earned them a place in the semi-finals where Edinburgh City lay in wait. Connah's Quay had home advantage and the two teams looked evenly matched over

90 minutes, with Michael Wilde netting with 18 minutes on the clock to cancel out Josh Walker's opener.

One-all was how it stayed after extra time and a tense penalty shootout followed. George Horan, who was in top form for The Nomads all game, buried his side's sixth spot-kick before goalkeeper John Danby denied Ciaran Diver to hand the hosts a memorable 5-4 shootout victory. This made them the first non-Scottish side to reach the final, another unforgettable moment for club historian Rapson, and for Welsh football:

> *We were being hailed as the scourge of Scottish football in one newspaper because of these results. Scottish and Irish opponents were an unknown quantity and thus the victories probably outweighed the Welsh Cup win over Aberystwyth in 2018.*

In the final, they faced a much-favoured Ross County side. The Staggies were the leaders of the Scottish Championship, and when they met The Nomads at the Caledonian Stadium in Inverness in late March, it was easy to see why. Morrison's men put up a fight and led early in the first half through Michael Bakare, yet ultimately found themselves outgunned and went down 3-1.

2019-20

While Connah's Quay earned plaudits for their performances against Scottish teams in 2018-19, the following season, they outdid themselves against Tartan opposition.

Their 2019-20 campaign began with a two-legged Europa League qualifier against Kilmarnock, who had finished third in the Scottish Premiership behind the Old Firm the season before. Killie were widely expected to sweep the part-time Nomads aside, despite making tough work of the first leg in Rhyl, which they edged by two goals to one. With home advantage on Killie's side in the return fixture, nobody gave the Welsh minnows a prayer, but there was a shock result for the ages on the cards at Rugby Park that night.

Although Killie dominated play, they were left stunned five minutes into the second half when Ryan Wignall opened the scoring for Connah's Quay, levelling the tie on aggregate. The hosts still had a slender advantage via the away goals rule, but that was obliterated in the 79th minute as Callum Morris converted from the penalty spot

to make it 2-0 on the night. The small band of Nomads fans who made the long journey North to Rugby Park went wild when the final whistle sounded with the scoreline unchanged. The Kilmarnock supporters, however, hit their team with a chorus of boos, clearly livid at the outcome of the tie.

BBC Sport described the defeat as an "embarrassment" for Kille, while *The Guardian* dubbed it a "nightmare" start for new Rugby Park boss Angelo Alessio, who was making his home debut in the dugout. For The Nomads, however, it was the greatest result in their history and arguably the biggest scalp a Welsh domestic club has claimed in Europe to date.

Although he was among the substitutes for both legs, the result holds a special place in Jamie Insall's heart, since it was against a team from a division he was once banished from:

> *That second leg against Kilmarnock at Rugby Park was a special night. I had a lot of stick from their supporters in both legs for my time in Scotland and the unfortunate events that happened to me up there, but it was amazing in the end.*
>
> *I have to admit, that was one of the most special nights in my football career. To go up there and knock out a team who came third in the Scottish Premiership in the manner we did. It makes the hairs stand up on the back of my neck just thinking about it.*

There were mixed fortunes for the other Cymru Premier sides on the continent that summer. TNS won a Champions League qualifier at the expense of Kosovan side Feronikeli, beating them 3-2 on aggregate, before losing 3-0 over two legs to Danish giants Copenhagen. Their European campaign then came to an abrupt end in the Europa League qualifiers, in which they suffered heavy defeats home and away to Bulgaria's Ludogorets Razgrad, losing 9-0 overall.

More than 2,000 fans showed up in Cardiff to watch Barry Town return to European action against Irish outfit Cliftonville, but they didn't see any goals on the night. The Linnets then endured a disappointing evening in the away leg, going down 4-0 in Belfast and bowing out.

Meanwhile, Cardiff Met's European debut was also a short-lived one. They took on Progrès Niederkorn of Luxembourg in the Europa League, a team who had produced a sensational giant killing against Rangers in the same competition two years earlier. The students claimed some pride with a 2-1 win in the second leg at home, with Jordan Lam and Dylan Rees on target, but conceding in the second half proved costly. Mayron de Almeida's strike made it 2-2 on aggregate and sent the visitors through on away goals.

Although Connah's Quay were eliminated in the next round by FK Partizan, their famous victory over Kilmarnock helped spur them on to even greater things that season. They started their Cymru Premier campaign with three draws on the bounce, though this would be the beginning of a long unbeaten run. Their first win of the campaign came on 30 August when they travelled to Bala Town for a Friday night showdown. Michael Wilde scored the only goal of a tight contest to bag maximum points for The Nomads.

Morrison's side then went 16 league matches without defeat, and there were some memorable results along the way, including a 4-1 win over Aberystwyth in mid-September and a 4-0 dismantling of Barry Town United in November, with Wilde and Insall scoring two each in the latter fixture.

Insall had made a flying start to his Nomads career, and at the end of October was rewarded with a Cymru Premier 'Player of the Month' award. It was clear he had forged a strong working relationship with Morrison, who was October's 'Manager of the Month', as he later acknowledged:

You always knew where you stood with Andy, if you were in his good books or his bad. His main strength was refusing to be beaten and he had that will to win at any cost. We always had a very good working relationship. I think he saw me as someone with the same values as him, both on and off the pitch.

At this point of the season, Connah's Quay were clearly emerging as worthy contenders to The New Saints' long-held throne. The two sides met at Deeside Stadium on 1 November and proved to be each other's equals. In an eventful second half, Dean Ebbe opened the scoring for the visitors, but former TNS forward Wilde came back to haunt his old club with a late equaliser. The 1-1 draw ensured that The Nomads held onto top spot in the Cymru Premier, although Scott Ruscoe's defending champions were poised, only one point behind.

Connah's Quay's undefeated run spanned another three matches, finally ending on 13 December with a surprise defeat at Cefn Druids.

Cody Ruberto opened the scoring for The Ancients on the stroke of half time before Joe Faux's last-minute strike sealed the points.

Ever resilient, The Nomads bounced back with four wins in a row, setting up a crunch clash with TNS in the final match before the split. It played out at Park Hall and, once again, there was little between the two title favourites as Morrison's men took the game to their hosts and landed the first blow, with Wilde heading Connah's Quay in front early on. They went into the break level pegging, though, as Callum Morris put through his own net.

TNS had key players missing through suspension but proved their strength in depth, digging deep to grind out a 2-1 win. Veteran defender Simon Spender scored the winner in the second half to give TNS a four-point advantage at the top of the league going into the split.

This was a setback for The Nomads and it double underlined just how tough it would be to end The Saints' dominance over Welsh football. The Nomads were up for the challenge with 30 points still to play for in the second phase of the Cymru Premier - or so everyone thought - and a League Cup showpiece to look forward to, having reached the final in that competition.

Connah's Quay contested the trophy against plucky Cymru South outfit STM Sports - who had knocked out Newtown and Aberystwyth *en route* to the final - and the top-flight side put in a dominant display. A first-half brace from Michael Wilde saw them plant one hand firmly on the trophy before a spectacular volley from Jamie Insall put the outcome beyond doubt.

With the first silverware of the season heading to Deeside, it was back to business in the league, but only four rounds of fixtures took place in the 2019-20 Championship Conference as the coronavirus pandemic reared its ugly head, forcing the FAW to curtail the season.

Before the campaign came to a premature end, The Nomads won their first two Championship Conference matches, beating Barry Town United and Caernarfon Town to set up an intense showdown with title rivals The New Saints at Deeside Stadium. TNS had started the post-split phase with a wobble, losing 2-1 to Newtown and dropping two further points in a 1-1 draw at Bala Town. This allowed Connah's Quay to overtake them at the summit, holding a one-point lead before the duo locked horns on 21 February.

Gale-force winds battered the pitch at Deeside Stadium that night and made play difficult for both sides. Neither team gave the other an inch before the interval, but the home side managed to force a breakthrough deep into first-half stoppage time. Saints defender Joash Nembhard's misplaced header fell invitingly for Craig Curran, who guided the ball beyond visiting goalkeeper Paul Harrison to open the scoring for the hosts.

It proved to be the winning goal and the result gave Morrison's side a four-point advantage at the top of the Cymru Premier, with seven matches scheduled to play. However, due to a Covid-blighted twist of fate, just one more round of fixtures took place.

Connah's Quay maintained their unbeaten run in the Conference Championship with a 2-2 draw against Bala, in which Wilde and Insall were the goalscorers, while The Saints were held 2-2 at home by Barry Town United.

The season fell victim to the pandemic little more than a week later. The restrictions that were coming in around the world to curb the spread of the virus made domestic football in Wales unviable and the Cymru Premier was halted on 13 March.

On 19 March, the FAW announced how the title race would be decided. The governing body used an unweighted points-per-game system to determine the final standings in the league, and this ranked Connah's Quay in top spot due to TNS' poor form post-split.

The Nomads were celebrating as jubilantly as lockdown restrictions allowed, but The New Saints were incensed. The dethroned champions were adamant that an alternative format - such as a behind-closed-doors play-off between the top two teams - should have been adopted to complete the season, and they took their argument to the High Court.

The FAW insisted that other formats for completing the season were carefully considered, but ultimately not feasible. The governing body also stated that its decision was in accordance with UEFA guidelines on football during the pandemic, and the court agreed.

Insall recalled being at home with his family when news of his side's title triumph broke. He later celebrated with his teammates in traditional Covid-era fashion, over a Zoom call:

> I was just chilling at home with my mum and son when the FAW confirmed that we were champions. As we were in the middle of a pandemic, we couldn't really celebrate it the way we would have wanted, but I did have a bit of a Zoom call with the lads.

Bala Town's Chris Venables, the five-times Cymru Premier top scorer. (© Andrew Page)

The New Saints lost their bid to have the decision overturned on appeal, but owner Mike Harris later said that he had no regrets about mounting the challenge and claimed Connah's Quay Nomads would likely have done the same had the situation been reversed: "I am naturally disappointed the judge has failed to give sporting merit its chance. But we hope football never gets blighted by a virus again in the future," Harris told BBC Sport. "I would have absolutely thought Connah's Quay would have done the same thing if we had been awarded the title under a numerical system."

Bala Town's points-per-game haul was enough to propel them into the first qualifying round of the Europa League and the Golden Boot ended up at Maes Tegid too, with veteran forward Chris Venables topping the scoring chart with 15 strikes to his name.

Since there would be no end-of-season play-offs or Welsh Cup football beyond the quarter-final stage, fourth-placed Barry Town United were granted the final European spot and would enter the 2020-21 Europa League in the preliminary round.

Spare a thought, though, for Carmarthen Town in 11th place, who were relegated with a final points ratio that was just three short of survival. Bottom club Airbus UK Broughton, who were only one point worse off, dropped into Cymru North while The Old Gold fell into Cymru South.

Connah's Quay had ended The New Saints' stranglehold on the Welsh top flight, but their critics - a few of them garbed in the green and white of TNS - were quick to speculate that the outcome of the title race might have been different had Covid-19 not intervened.

Cymru Premier (2019-20)	P	W	D	L	For	Ag	Pts
Championship Conference							
1 Connah's Quay Nomads	32	16	8	2	47	19	56
2 The New Saints	32	16	4	6	69	27	52
3 Bala Town	32	15	4	7	53	23	49
4 Barry Town United	32	12	6	7	35	29	42
5 Caernarfon Town	32	11	5	10	36	38	38
6 Newtown	32	10	5	10	25	30	35
Play-Off Conference							
7 Cardiff Metropolitan University	32	9	8	8	30	29	35
8 Cefn Druids	32	10	5	10	37	39	35
9 Aberystwyth Town	32	7	6	13	36	55	27
10 Penybont	32	5	6	14	25	48	21
11 Carmarthen Town	32	4	6	15	28	45	18
12 Airbus UK Broughton	32	4	5	17	28	67	17

Final standings determined by points per game (PPG)

Play-off winners: N/A

2020-21

With this in mind, the 2020-21 season marked an opportunity to silence those critics, and silence them they did. Their campaign began with an early Champions League exit following a 2-0 defeat to FK Sarajevo in the first qualifying round, which was played over a single leg, behind closed doors at the Cardiff City Stadium while Covid-19 restrictions remained in place.

The Nomads dropped into the Europa League and were drawn against Georgian outfit Dinamo Tbilisi. The Welsh club went into the match under-strength, with three players testing positive for Covid and another two having to join them in self-isolation after displaying symptoms.

If Dinamo approached the game expecting an easy ride, they were given a rude awakening at the Racecourse Ground, where the depleted Welsh champions fought them with fire and brimstone. The Nomads were moments from taking the match into extra time, only for Callum Roberts to concede a penalty at the death. Giorgi Gabedava fired home from the spot to score the only goal of the night and hand a galling defeat to Morrison's side.

Elsewhere, there were European qualifying wins for Bala and TNS, with The Lakesiders dispatching Valletta of Malta 1-0 via a Venables strike, and The Saints winning 3-1 against Slovak side MŠK Žilina after extra time. Despite these hugely commendable results, a heavy defeat for Barry Town against Faroese outfit Runavík in the next round proved damaging for Welsh football.

The Dragons were pasted 5-1 by a team they will no doubt have fancied their chances against, given that the Faroe Islands' league is not considered vastly superior to the Cymru Premier. As a result, Wales dropped to 51st place on the UEFA coefficient ranking table and its top division lost one of its European spots for the 2022-23 season.

TNS and Bala were eliminated in the next round by B36 Tórshavn and Standard Liège respectively. The New Saints' exit was regarded as a disappointment, though Bala were lavished with praise for their performance in a 2-0 loss to the Belgians.

Back on the domestic front, Connah's Quay headed into the new Cymru Premier campaign with confidence following their laudable European efforts and won six from their opening seven matches. They were, however, lucky to avoid defeat on the opening day. The Nomads were trailing 1-0 at home to Bala Town heading into stoppage time before Sameron Dool rescued a point in the 94th minute with a sublime effort from 25 yards.

Off the back of those six consecutive wins, Morrison's side travelled to Park Hall to face the previous season's runners-up The New Saints. The visitors were on top for spells of the match but ultimately went down to a Louis Robles strike following a corner. As a result of that defeat, The Nomads fell to second in the league and dropped further points in their next fixture, a goalless draw at Barry Town United in front of S4C's cameras. Their fans, however, quickly realised that there was no major cause for concern as Connah's Quay went on a club record nine-match winning streak on the back of that Jenner Park stalemate.

It began with a 2-1 win at Caernarfon Town on 13 November and ended with a goalless draw at Penybont on 13 March. During this run, the goals were flying in for the Deesiders and Michael Wilde in particular, with the former TNS striker bagging nine along the way.

Observers may wonder why it took four months to play just nine games of football, and the answer is, of course, the coronavirus pandemic. Covid-19 was still a long way from fading into the background of everyday life and a spike in cases during the winter period forced the FAW to suspend the Cymru Premier campaign in the middle of December.

The season resumed in early March and upon its return came a shock announcement. Although they were very much in the mix for the title, TNS made a change in the dugout and replaced managerial duo Scott Ruscoe and Steve Evans with Australian coach Anthony Limbrick, who had previously managed Woking, and Grimsby Town on an interim basis.

Limbrick got his tenure underway with a 4-1 demolition of Caernarfon in the final match of Phase 1 of the Cymru Premier, but Connah's Quay's devastating form saw them head into the post-split stage in pole position, with a three-point lead over TNS.

Four days before Christmas, the Welsh Government announced that all sporting events in the country had to be played behind closed doors from Boxing Day to help suppress Covid-19's Omicron variant. This cast doubt on the possibility of getting crowds into Cymru Premier grounds before the end of the season, but public health had to be prioritised.

The Championship Conference phase started poorly for the defending champions as Penybont handed the Nomads their first home league defeat in over two years. A first-half penalty from Kane Owen and Kostya Georgievsky's strike secured maximum points for the visitors, but the Deesiders were made of resilient stuff and would bounce back spectacularly. They romped to a 6-1 victory at Caernarfon Town three days later before a lone Michael Wilde strike downed Barry Town United on 17 April. A 2-0 win over Bala Town came next, and this set up another tense grudge match with The New Saints at Park Hall.

The two contenders went into the game level on points, and what followed was the defining moment in the title race. The Nomads were unstoppable in Shropshire. Wilde once again gave former club TNS nightmares as he bagged a hattrick in a memorable 4-1 win.

Nomads striker Michael Wilde scored three in a 4-1 win away at TNS in April 2021. (© John Smith/FAW)

Early signs suggested that this title showdown would be closer than the final scoreline suggests as Ryan Brobbel cancelled out Wilde's opener to make it 1-1 with 24 minutes on the clock. The Nomads, however, dominated from that moment onwards as the former Saints striker helped himself to another two before the interval and Jamie Insall completed the rout in the second half.

Despite the titanic clashes between TNS and Connah's Quay over the course of those two seasons, Insall downplayed the notion of a rivalry between the two clubs and claimed he only saw them as a team standing in the way of what he wanted to achieve. He did, however, admit that he enjoyed silencing Saints chairman Mike Harris' social media musings:

I don't think it was a big rivalry between the two clubs, to be honest. I came to Connah's Quay wanting to make history and win the league, which they never had done before, and they were nothing more than an obstacle in the way of what I wanted to achieve.

Given the quality of the opposition, to win it two seasons out of three was amazing... and, of course, Mike Harris' "banter" on Twitter made it a hell of a lot sweeter.

The result left Morrison's men three points better off than TNS at the summit of the Cymru Premier, but a 2-1 reverse for The Nomads in their next fixture - a home clash with Bala Town - gave The Saints the chance to climb back to the top of the pile. Limbrick's side were, however, unable to break down a stubborn Caernarfon side the night after, drawing 0-0 with The Canaries, despite their opponents finishing the game with nine men.

The two title chasers went head-to-head again on 1 May and battled to a goalless stalemate. They both won their next two fixtures to send the race to the wire, but it was The Nomads' crown to lose given that they started the day two points ahead.

On the final day, they were away to Penybont while The Saints were at home to Bala Town. The two matches were shown live simultaneously by S4C as the broadcaster gave fans the chance to follow both at once, with supporters of each team no doubt nervously darting between two different devices to stay abreast of where the title was heading.

Although TNS made short work of The Lakesiders, beating them 2-0 via goals from Ben Clark and Adrian Cieślewicz, Connah's Quay held their nerve and matched their result. They dispatched Penybont clinically and professionally, with George Horan and Aeron Edwards heading a goal each to ensure that the dragon-adorned trophy remained in Deeside.

The Nomads had silenced the detractors who claimed that the points-per-game system was the decisive factor behind their first league title. They had stood up to The New Saints over the course of a long, coronavirus-impacted season and, as Insall insists, reflecting on his team's accomplishments over the two seasons, proved superior to them:

> We definitely made up for not being able to celebrate our first title win in person that second year. For me, that side we had was amazing. We had a bit of everything and what we achieved has to go down as one of the best stories to happen in the Welsh system for many years.

Amid their on-pitch celebrations, Morrison gave a post-match interview to reporters and described how much it meant to him to retain the top prize in Welsh football: "We were the best team last year and this year we've cemented that, so we've won two titles today, not just one and that's what means a lot to me," he said. "People might say you've got to let these things go but I can't. I had to make sure we gave an account of ourselves this year and it reflected what we did last year and we've done it. We worked so hard last year. I was in the kitchen, on my own last year, when we were awarded the title and I wasn't with the players that I've got a bond with and grown to love over the years," the Nomads boss added. "We just didn't get the celebrations and it was special today because we were all together and it was right."

TNS ensured that Connah's Quay Nomads were pushed as hard as any Welsh champion since the top flight took on its 12-team format, but a place in the Europa Conference League play-offs was ultimately their only consolation. Third-placed Bala Town joined them in the same competition, as would the winners of the end-of-season play-offs between Newtown and Caernarfon Town, following their respective victories over Penybont and Barry Town United in the play-off semi-finals.

Ahead of the final, there were repeated calls to the Welsh Government to allow supporters to attend the showpiece, which would be held at Caernarfon's home ground, The Oval, due to The Cofis finishing sixth in the league compared to Newtown's seventh.

Connah's Quay Nomads celebrate their 2020/21 Cymru Premier success. (© John Smith/FAW)

There was a strong argument to approve this, given that fans got the green light to watch Swansea City contest the EFL Championship play-off final against Brentford at Wembley Stadium on the same day, but the powers that be didn't budge on their position.

Although the showpiece was supposed to be played behind closed doors, plenty of fans showed up at the ground, most of them Caernarfon-supporting locals. They climbed onto vantage points to peer over the fence at the action, and this certainly gave the match an atmosphere.

It was a shame the stands weren't packed out for this one because those 90 minutes that followed were some of the most entertaining the play-offs have ever seen. Newtown, who found themselves trailing 3-2 at one point, won the match 5-3 thanks to a double from substitute James Davies and a late strike by fellow sub, Jamie Breese.

In 2020-21, there was no relegation from the Cymru Premier. Top flight matches were only able to go ahead because they were granted "elite" sporting status during the pandemic. Wales' lower divisions did not qualify for this exemption, which meant that Cymru North and South did not take place, and therefore no second-tier teams

Nomads manager Andy Morrison proudly wears a #RealChampions hoodie after his team clinched the 2020/21 league title. (© John Smith/FAW)

could be promoted. This was a relief for the division's bottom two, Flint Town and Cefn Druids, especially the latter who only managed to rack up four wins and 16 points all season.

The lack of any lower league football also meant that the Welsh Cup and Welsh League Cup could not be completed in 2020-21, although the first round of the latter competition did take place, only to be wound up when December's coronavirus restrictions were announced.

While the vast majority of competitions on the Welsh football calendar could not go ahead, the completion of the Cymru Premier campaign in its entirety that year has to go down as a resounding success for everyone involved. The top-flight clubs faced such adversity throughout the pandemic - losing players to positive Covid tests on a regular basis and missing out on gate revenue every week - but they pulled it off, and each and every one of those 12 teams lived to fight another day.

Cymru Premier (2020-21)	P	W	D	L	For	Ag	Pts
Championship Conference							
1 Connah's Quay Nomads	32	25	4	3	70	20	79
2 The New Saints	32	24	5	3	84	17	77
3 Bala Town	32	18	6	8	67	42	60
4 Penybont	32	13	7	12	42	40	46
5 Barry Town United	32	13	4	15	42	53	43
6 Caernarfon Town	32	10	7	15	43	67	37
Play-Off Conference							
7 Newtown	32	12	6	14	57	53	42
8 Cardiff Metropolitan University	32	11	7	14	47	46	40
9 Haverfordwest County	32	10	7	15	38	56	37
10 Aberystwyth Town	32	8	9	15	47	53	33
11 Flint Town United	32	10	2	20	38	58	32
12 Cefn Druids	32	4	4	24	25	95	16

Play-off winners: Newtown

18

The State of Play

2021-22

Three decades ago, some believed that a Welsh national football championship was nothing more than a pipedream - and even when the concept became a reality with the inception of the League of Wales in 1992, the naysayers were certain it wouldn't stand the test of time - but on 13 August 2021, the Cymru Premier's latest campaign kicked off with two fixtures beneath the Friday night lights, and the competition's 30th season was underway.

The Welsh top flight has come a long way over the last three decades. There have been format changes and rebrandings, clubs have come and gone, and records have tumbled. Needless to say, the league is very different to the one which debuted on the same day as the English Premier League, but in 2021-22, there was a familiarity about the final standings.

After losing their crown to Connah's Quay for two Covid-affected seasons, The New Saints achieved total dominance once again and romped to a record 14th league title, only pausing their momentum when more coronavirus restrictions hit between Christmas and New Year.

Manager Anthony Limbrick had far superior resources at his disposal than his counterparts, but nobody can deny that his team did it in style that season. TNS ran almost unopposed, losing just twice all campaign and finishing 21 points clear of second-placed Bala Town.

The Australian coach got the best out of the squad he inherited, inspiring creativity in the likes of Chris Marriott, Adrian Cieślewicz and Ryan Brobbel, while adding serious firepower to his ranks with the summer capture of striker Declan McManus from Dunfermline Athletic. The former Scotland youth international was a shrewd signing who has thrived in Wales. McManus scored 24 times during

TNS' title-winning campaign, and bagged the Golden Boot along with a Cymru Premier 'player of the season' award.

Limbrick's Saints didn't just claim silverware in the Cymru Premier, as the Welsh Cup came roaring back after a two-year absence and was a resounding success in 2022. TNS narrowly avoided a banana skin at second-tier Carmarthen in the quarter-finals, with The Old Gold holding them to a 0-0 draw, before bowing out bravely on penalties.

This set up a semi-final clash with a rapidly-ascending Colwyn Bay side. One of the original 'Irate Eight', The Seagulls had joined the Welsh football pyramid two seasons earlier and were fast becoming one of the most exciting domestic sides in the country, backed by a fiercely loyal fanbase.

Now thriving in the Welsh domestic league structure, Colwyn Bay might one day compete with the best in the top flight, but in this cup tie they couldn't quite get the better of the TNS. More than 1,000 fans flocked to Rhyl to watch the two teams battle it out, and Colwyn Bay pushed The Saints all the way. An early Daniel Davies goal, however, proved their undoing in a match that was a credit to the domestic game.

In the other semi-final, an ambitious Penybont side led by player-manager Rhys Griffiths dumped out Bala Town on penalties to book their place in the final for the first time.

The showpiece took place at the Cardiff City Stadium, which made it a grand occasion for everyone involved. From the stands, 2,417 supporters watched the action unfold, ensuring that this was the highest-attended Welsh Cup final since 1995-96.

Incidentally, TNS - or to put it more accurately, their predecessors Llansantffraid FC - won that 1996 final to get their hands on the coveted trophy for the first time, and this one went their way as well. A brace from Jordan Williams in the first period and a Declan McManus strike after the interval put them 3-0 up with less than an hour on the clock.

Penybont, however, had fight in them in the second half and they didn't throw in the towel until the final whistle sounded. Shaun MacDonald pulled a goal back for them in the 85th minute before a thumping header from Daniel Jefferies made it 3-2 in stoppage time. That was how it stayed, but Griffiths' side were highly commended for their spirited performance, as were their fans for the atmosphere they brought to the ground.

One woman who's highly qualified to judge the success of the 2021-22 Welsh Cup is S4C's Nicky John. As a *Sgorio* presenter since 2006, she's covered the cup extensively and offered her thoughts on the first edition of the competition after the global pandemic:

> *I'm a big Welsh Cup fan as it's a great opportunity for clubs that might not usually meet to come up against each other. It's been so good to have Colwyn Bay back involved in the Welsh system, and I think you can see from their form since then that they are going from strength to strength. I've seen Welsh Cup finals played all over the country, and while each occasion brings its own bit of magic, playing at the Cardiff City Stadium - which has played such an important role in the story of the success of our national side over recent years - it will have been a great experience for both The New Saints and Penybont to contest their showpiece there.*

For TNS, this double-winning campaign marked their best season for several years. The only blemish was an early exit from the League Cup at the hands of Cymru North side Penrhyncoch. The Saints had made 11 changes for the match having been in Europa Conference League action in midweek, and were beaten 2-1 by the second-tier Roosters.

The season also marked one of their best showings in Europe to date. They began their continental tour with a two-legged clash against Northern Ireland's Glentoran in the first qualifying round of the Europa Conference League, winning 3-1 on aggregate. In the next round, TNS were paired with Kauno Žalgiris of Lithuania and were ruthless in both legs, winning 5-0 away and 5-1 at home - a club-record aggregate victory.

Limbrick's men looked destined to go further in Europe than any Welsh domestic club before them when they beat the Czechia outfit Viktoria Plzeň by four goals to two in the first leg of the third qualifying round. Declan McManus struck a hat-trick at Cardiff City Stadium as The Saints planted one foot in the play-off round of the competition.

Despite taking a two-goal advantage to eastern Europe, their opponents put in a strong performance in the return leg and defeated The Saints 3-1 - despite falling further behind on aggregate to Louis Robles' early opener - to force extra time and penalties.

It was a thrilling tie over the two legs, but it ended in shootout agony for TNS. Leo Smith and skipper Chris Marriott missed their spot-kicks while the Czechs were clinical, burying all of their

The New Saints lift the 2021-22 league trophy after regaining the title. (© John Smith/FAW)

penalties to progress 4-1 and end Cymru Premier interest in Europe for another year: "Of course we're disappointed but I'm proud of the players and staff," an upbeat Anthony Limbrick told BBC Sport following his side's painful Euro exit. "It was a huge effort considering the opposition, to take them to penalties was quite the achievement. When you play these top teams there's fine margins, we conceded late in both games and the players were dead on their feet by the end because they couldn't have done any more."

Meanwhile, it was a rollercoaster campaign for defending champions Connah's Quay. The Nomads made a slow start to the season and Andy Morrison stepped down as manager on 28 September, with his side lying in sixth place in the table having lost two consecutive games.

The Nomads' hierarchy "reluctantly accepted" Morrison's resignation and former TNS boss Craig Harrison, who was already coaching at the club, was named as his successor. Form was steady under him for the remainder of the first phase, but their season was dealt a crippling blow ahead of the Championship Conference when they found themselves in hot water with the FAW.

The Nomads were found guilty of fielding an ineligible player for six matches. The charge was related to the signings, as free agents, of Portuguese midfielder Paulo Mendes in September, and ex-Wales international Neal Eardley in October. Since Cymru Premier clubs can only sign one free agent between the summer and winter transfer windows, they were penalised for recruiting Eardley, having already brought in Mendes the month before.

Connah's Quay protested and claimed that Mendes' transfer was completed on 31 August, within the confines of the summer window, but the matter was referred to an arbitration panel which ruled against the club, stating that "both charges have been proved".

The Nomads paid a heavy price. They were docked 18 points, a penalty that ejected them from the Championship Conference and put their future in the Cymru Premier in serious jeopardy. Caernarfon Town took the defending champions' place in the top six.

Harrison's men began the Play-Off Conference phase six points above the drop zone and were drawn into a relegation scrap with the likes of Barry Town, who, after clawing their way back into the top flight and enjoying newfound success there, were treading water again.

Bottom club Cefn Druids were already dead and buried, having failed to win a single game in the first phase of the league, but it was otherwise tight in this conference; and ultimately, there were only 11 points between the second relegation spot and the play-offs.

Despite the adversity they had suffered, Connah's Quay proved surprisingly resilient in the second half of the season and survived the drop by seven points. In addition, they also won the League Cup in early February, beating Cardiff Met in the final on penalties.

The Nomads really turned it around and can look back on a chaotic season as a successful one - but the same cannot be said of Barry Town United. Gavin Chesterfield's side couldn't dig themselves out of trouble, ending up in 11th spot and back in Cymru South. The magic was sapped out of their fairy tale, but don't worry about them - The Dragons have bounced back from much worse and won't be disappearing into the ether this time.

In the end-of-season play-offs, the prize up for grabs was less prestigious than in previous campaigns as Wales' decline in the UEFA coefficients meant that the winner would qualify for the Scottish Challenge Cup, rather than the Europa Conference League.

Resigned to the fact that this was better than nothing, Caernarfon took on Flint Town in the final, having edged out Cardiff Met and Penybont in the semis respectively. The match took place at The Oval

Caernarfon Town celebrate winning the 2021-22 play-offs. (© John Smith/FAW)

and was tense and hard-fought, despite the lesser prize at stake. After 90 minutes, the teams were deadlocked and goalless, but extra time proved more eventful. Midfielder Danny Gossett put the hosts in front with a vicious strike on the turn, but Ben Nash hooked home just six minutes later to draw Flint Town level.

The fans were bracing themselves for penalties, but it never came to that. In the final minute of extra time, Laurie Bell headed in at the far post to win it for Caernarfon, seal their first play-off triumph and book them a ticket for the 2022-23 Scottish Challenge Cup.

Nicky John, who has been a Caernarfon resident for the last 15 years and a keen supporter of her local club, believes that The Cofis were somewhat hard done by to be denied a European tour, but was quick to point out what a successful season it was for them:

> Caernarfon Town were possibly unlucky to win the play-offs at the end of the season and miss out on the chance of playing in Europe as they would have done in previous years due to only three European spots being awarded to Wales last season. However, for The Cofis to finish fourth was great progress in itself for the club and to be rewarded with a tie in the Scottish Challenge Cup was something to relish.

Cymru Premier (2021-22)	P	W	D	L	For	Ag	Pts
Championship Conference							
1 The New Saints	32	25	5	2	86	26	80
2 Bala Town	32	16	11	5	67	37	59
3 Newtown	32	15	6	11	50	35	51
4 Caernarfon Town	32	13	4	15	46	53	43
5 Flint Town United	32	12	6	14	51	53	42
6 Penybont	32	10	10	12	49	57	40
Play-Off Conference							
7 Cardiff Metropolitan University	32	10	10	10	35	38	42
8 Aberystwyth Town	32	11	14	14	38	45	40
9 Connah's Quay Nomads*	32	15	6	6	44	18	38
10 Haverfordwest County	32	10	8	14	45	46	38
11 Barry Town United	32	8	7	17	31	47	31
12 Cefn Druids	32	2	3	27	22	109	9

*18 points deducted, ineligible players

Play-off winners: Caernarfon Town

2022-23

You didn't need to have the powers of Paul the Octopus to have correctly predicted which club would win the 2022-23 Cymru Premier title.

Since reclaiming their crown from a beleaguered Connah's Quay Nomads side the season before, The New Saints have been unstoppable in the domestic arena. For almost the duration of its latest campaign, the Welsh top flight was a one-horse race as the division's only full-time club thunderously galloped to their 15th league title.

After a difficult year, The Nomads re-established themselves as TNS' closest rivals. Managed by former Prestatyn and Flint boss Neil Gibson, the League Cup holders were solid for most of the campaign, but to truly compete with The Saints over the course of the season, they would need to have been Welsh football's answer to Arsenal's 'Invincibles' class of 2004.

That's because the defending champions lost just one league match all season, their sole defeat coming in February at Cardiff Met's Cyncoed Campus, where The Saints let a two-goal lead slip and lost 3-2. Christian Edwards' ever-impressive Archers, who finished fourth, struck back in the second period with a double from Chris Baker, either side of an Elliott Evans strike.

Gibson's Nomads experienced defeat just five times in the league, yet with TNS enjoying a 22-match unbeaten streak before that shock result in the capital, they were a distant second to the runaway champions by the time the campaign entered its final stretch.

It was during a visit to Connah's Quay in March that TNS had the chance to wrap up the title, needing a point to get themselves over the line. The Nomads' form was ropey in the run-up to the match, but they made things difficult for their opponents and held them to a goalless draw, though this obviously wasn't enough to prevent the title from returning to Park Hall.

One man who knows just how difficult The Saints will prove to dethrone is Bala Town goalkeeper Alex Ramsay. As The Lakesiders' first-choice keeper since 2020, the shot-stopper has come up against the champions of Wales on numerous occasions, and he believes that there are pros and cons to having one fully professional club in the top flight.

It's difficult to say whether TNS' dominance is a good thing because, at the start of the season, every club in the division should ideally be able to hold title ambitions. Unfortunately, with the position we're in, all of the part-time clubs can only, realistically, compete for second.

The biggest downside of having one full-time team is that we already know who is likely to win the league before a ball is even kicked. But having a fully professional team raises the profile of the competition, and in recent years, they've had decent European results, which helps too.

Looking at it from the inside, I can say it would be nice if the Cymru Premier was a bit more competitive and the title race wasn't over by February or March time.

There was a gulf of 22 points between the top two come the end of the season. The Saints' total dominance was also emphasised with a whopping +95 goal difference, thanks, in no small measure, to the Cymru Premier's top marksman, Declan McManus, who contributed 26 of them, while Ryan Brobbel and Ben Clark chipped in with 14 and 13 respectively to join the Scot on the top scorers' chart.

Although Connah's Quay were no match for The Saints in the league, they did dump TNS out of the League Cup in early August. Michael Wilde opened the scoring for the hosts at Deeside Stadium, but McManus levelled the tie at 1-1 late in the second period to send the match to penalties. Both sides missed spot-kicks but it was the holders who edged the shootout, booking their place in round three when Ryan Harrington's decisive effort made it 5-4.

The result put a minor downer on Craig Harrison's return to the TNS hotseat, with the former Crystal Palace and Middlesbrough player having left a coaching role at Connah's Quay to replace Anthony Limbrick at the helm of the Welsh champions. Despite delivering a league-and-cup double the previous season, the Aussie coach had paid the price for a poor European campaign, in which Northern Ireland's Linfield knocked The Saints out of the Champions League qualifiers 2-1 on aggregate, overturning a 1-0 deficit from the first leg at Park Hall to do so.

TNS dropped into the Europa League qualifiers where they met Icelandic outfit Víkingur Reykjavík, but Welsh sides have not fared well against opposition from the volcanic nation in the past, and so it proved on this occasion too. Kristall Máni Ingason struck two penalties for the Scandinavians in the away leg as they won 2-0, followed by a goalless draw at Park Hall.

The previous season's runners-up, Bala Town, also made an early exit from the Europa Conference League. The Lakesiders came up against Irish opponents in the shape of Sligo Rovers, who defeated them 2-1 at home, with Lassana Mendes opening the scoring for the Welsh side, before strikes from Aidan Keena and Max Mata left them with work to do in Ireland.

Sligo, who went on to shock Motherwell in the next round, were given a game by Bala on their home turf, and needed penalties to overcome The Lakesiders as former Wales midfielder Dave Edwards - a major transfer *coup* for Bala in the summer of 2021 - found the net to give them a 1-0 win on the night. Edwards was among those on target for the visitors in the shootout, but misses from Luke Wall and Jonny Spittle condemned them to an early Euro exit.

Alex Ramsay believes his side were unlucky to bow out, based on that second leg performance.

We were actually quite disappointed when we were drawn against Sligo Rovers because we knew they were a fit team and were in-season. It was clear that they would be difficult games but we were really pleased to go into the second leg at only 2-1 down, and were quite optimistic when we got to the ground and saw it was quite a tight pitch. We fancied our chances and were unlucky to lose the tie, on aggregate, from the way we played in that second leg. Although we won on the night, we missed big chances over the 120 minutes in Ireland and were bitterly disappointed to go out on penalties.

Of the Cymru Premier's continental representatives in 2022-23, only Newtown won a European tie over two legs, putting in a convincing and energetic display against Faroese team HB Tórshavn at TNS' Park Hall ground to overturn a 1-0 reverse from the away leg.

The Robins came flying out of the traps and hit their opponents for two in the first period, with Henry Cowans and Lifumpa Mwandwe on target. The visitors bit back in the 48th minute through Paetur Petersen to force extra time, but it was Newtown who had the final say. Chris Hughes' side triumphed 4-2 on penalties, with Mwandwe burying the winning spot kick.

Newtown exited the competition in the second qualifying round, their conquerors being Spartak Trnava of Slovakia, who beat them 2-1 and 4-1 to progress 6-2 on aggregate. The Robins went on to finish sixth in the league to keep their hopes of a return to Europe alive, via the play-offs.

The following month, Wales' representatives in the Scottish Challenge Cup failed to register any wins. Entering the competition in round three, TNS lost 3-0 at home to a strong Dundee side who went on to win promotion to the Scottish Premiership, while Caernarfon Town were undone by a last-minute goal in a 1-0 away reverse to Clyde. BBC Sport commended the 2022 play-off winners for putting in a "brave defensive display" against their Scottish League One opponents.

The first silverware of the season was up for grabs in late January when Connah's Quay lined up against Bala Town in the League Cup final. Bala had seen off Cardiff Met 2-0 in the last four, while The Nomads had defeated second-tier Taff's Well by the same scoreline.

Played at The Rock, this was the 30th edition of the Welsh League Cup final and it finished with a new name on the trophy. The two sides played out a heated goalless draw over 90 minutes, during which plenty of chances were created and each lost a player to a red card. It took penalties to separate them, and it was Bala who came out on top.

Ramsay was impressive all game between the Lakesiders' sticks, and it was his crucial save from Michael Wilde's spot-kick that helped

*Bala Town following their victory in the 2022-23 Welsh League Cup final. (©
Clwb Pêl-Droed/Lewis Mitchell)*

his team secure the trophy for the first time in their history. The shot-
stopper explained that this cup win was hugely significant for himself
and the club:

> Winning the League Cup was massive for us. People from the outside
> looking in might not think it's a big trophy to get your hands on, but it was
> a really special moment for the club and me personally, given that it was
> the first time Bala had won it. I was so happy for the club, the community,
> the volunteers and staff that work tirelessly for us and the chairman.
> The players know how hard these people work, and that's why winning
> that final was so important to us. It came at a good time as well. Last
> season wasn't a particularly good one for us, but winning that trophy gave
> us a highlight to look back on.

At the wrong end of the table, it was a nightmare season for Airbus
UK Broughton, who not only finished bottom, but ended up with a
-4 points total too. The Wingmakers, who were docked points for
fielding ineligible players against Caernarfon and Pontypridd United,
drew just twice during a winless campaign that goes down as the
worst since the Welsh top flight began.

The second relegation place was closely contested during the
Play-Off Conference phase, with Aberystwyth Town flirting with the
drop until they picked up form in the final stretch. It was ultimately

TNS taking on Bala Town in the 2022-23 Welsh Cup final. (© M Langshaw)

between them, Pontypridd, Caernarfon Town and Flint Town United, with the latter falling through the trapdoor on a dramatic final day thanks to a 3-2 defeat at Ponty.

Meanwhile, Bala are still making history on a regular basis under manager Colin Caton and almost made it to three finals in 2023, entering May with a Welsh Cup showpiece against The New Saints to contest and a play-off semi-final with Newtown hot on the heels of that.

There would, however, be no European football at Maes Tegid the following season as the hotly-favoured TNS romped to a 6-0 win at Nantporth Stadium in Bangor in front of 1,231 supporters, the majority of whom were disappointed Bala fans. The Lakesiders were competitive right up to half time, only trailing 1-0 to a McManus goal at the break, but Bala's hopes of repeating their Welsh Cup heroics for 2017 were laid to rest 11 minutes into the second period as quick-fire strikes from Danny Redmond and Ryan Brobbel put TNS out of sight.

Further goals from substitutes Jordan Williams and Adrian Cieślewicz added to Bala Town's misery before a second from Brobbel completed the rout and helped The Saints secure the biggest Welsh Cup final victory since 1931, as well as a league-and-cup double.

Although Bala had claimed silverware earlier in the season via the League Cup, Ramsay admits that this heavy defeat proved difficult for the team to bounce back from and ultimately affected the squad's play-off push, which ended with a 4-2 defeat to Newtown in that semi-final.

Personally, I shouldn't have played in the cup final because I was carrying an injury and could barely kick the ball. We were under no illusions about how difficult it was going to be against TNS. When you play them, the aim is to get to half time still in the game, and we were, but they got another goal early in the second half, and it's really difficult once they have you at 2-0.

We had gone through a really tough period in the run-up to that game. I don't think we'd won a match in 10 attempts. I'll be honest, it was really difficult to pick ourselves up after that cup final defeat and go into the play-offs. It was a long season anyway, due to playing in Europe earlier in the campaign, but that defeat against TNS wasn't the ideal preparation for a semi-final.

With TNS having already secured Champions League qualification via the Cymru Premier, the result catapulted third-placed Penybont into Europe for the first time. Rhys Griffiths' side, who ended the season with 52 points, had made no secret of their ambition and desire to improve, and this was a significant milestone for them, one year on from losing the 2022 Welsh Cup final to TNS.

Penybont were ultimately joined in the Europa Conference League qualifiers by another of the Cymru Premier's rapidly improving sides, Haverfordwest County. The Bluebirds finished top of the Play-Off Conference and, after defeating Cardiff Met on penalties following a goalless draw in the European play-off semi-finals, only Newtown blocked their path to the continent.

It was a memorable final between these two sides, thanks in no small part to an agreement between the clubs to allow supporters free entry. This wonderful gesture resulted in a big crowd of 1,826 at Latham Park, and they enjoyed an action-packed first half in which Newtown's top goalscorer Aaron Williams cancelled out an opener from Jordan Davies.

The scoreline remained 1-1 after 90 minutes and the extra time that followed failed to separate the pair. For the second time in a week, Haverfordwest held their nerve in a penalty shootout to send their fans into raptures. Bluebirds goalkeeper Zac Jones, who hails from New Zealand, is fast gaining a reputation as a penalty-stopping specialist, and he was the hero for them on the day, denying Williams early in the shootout to set his team up for a 4-3 victory.

The result brought another eventful Cymru Premier campaign to its conclusion. While it was refreshing to see a new name on the

Rhys Griffiths, the Welsh Premier League's top scorer for seven consecutive years (2005-06 to 2011-12) and now manager of Penybont FC (© Lewis Mitchell/ FAW)

League Cup and four clubs back in Europe, shadows continue to loom large over Welsh domestic football. There's no escaping the fact that low attendances and a seemingly indefinite, one-sided title race are problematic for all involved.

Although there are no quick fixes for either issue, some improvement appears to be forthcoming. Cream naturally rises to the top and there are some great clubs from the lower reaches of the Welsh football pyramid who did some significant climbing in 2022-23.

Former exiles Colwyn Bay stormed Cymru North to claim a place in the Cymru Premier for the first time since rejoining the Welsh system, while Barry Town United were Cymru South champions. Both clubs have a real buzz about them and are among the best supported on the domestic pyramid, with 2022-23 average gates of 720 and 575 respectively.

The potential that Barry and Colwyn Bay bring to the Cymru Premier is enormous. Not only will their presence almost certainly drive up average attendances across the country, they could grow and thrive in the top division, and eventually make it more competitive.

Further down the rankings, Bangor 1876 won promotion to Cymru North while rivals Rhyl 1879 established themselves as one of the favourites to follow them in 2022-23. If the reborn versions of these great rivals can make it all the way to the top flight, they'd be a credit to it.

Then there are the existing top flight clubs who are showing great ambition and tangible signs of progression on and off the pitch, such as Haverfordwest and Penybont. Both teams deservedly made it to Europe last season and are dreaming of bigger things on the horizon.

The potential is there for the Cymru Premier to improve organically, but to truly fulfil its potential, it needs more support from above. The Football Association of Wales has pledged to increase its promotion of the league and explore ways to revolutionise and revitalise it.

While the governing body has talked a good game on this front, the clubs, their supporters and the countless staff and volunteers who empower them believe now is the time for action, not words, and they wait with bated breath for a new dawn for Welsh league football.

Cymru Premier (2022-23)		P	W	D	L	For	Ag	Pts
Championship Conference								
1	The New Saints	32	26	5	1	112	17	83
2	Connah's Quay Nomads	32	17	10	5	45	23	61
3	Penybont*	32	16	10	6	51	32	52
4	Cardiff Metropolitan University	32	16	4	12	41	59	52
5	Bala Town	32	12	8	12	51	37	44
6	Newtown	32	12	5	15	49	56	41
Play-Off Conference								
7	Haverfordwest County	32	14	5	13	49	44	47
8	Pontypridd United	32	12	5	15	41	52	41
9	Caernarfon Town	32	12	3	17	51	54	39
10	Aberystwyth Town	32	11	5	16	41	73	38
11	Flint Town United	32	9	8	15	41	53	35
12	Airbus UK Broughton**	32	0	2	30	18	100	-4

*6pts deducted **6pts deducted

Play-off winners: Haverfordwest County

Epilogue

The Welsh top flight celebrated its official 30th anniversary in August 2022, so what better time to assess how far the competition has come in those three decades, consider its successes and failures, and mull over where it might be heading in the years to come?

Much has changed since those 20 inaugural member clubs ushered in the League of Wales' debut season. The number of teams in the division has risen and fallen, the format has been tinkered with and professional clubs have come and gone, yet some things remain constant.

Newtown and Aberystwyth Town can't claim to be among the most successful teams in the history of the top flight - despite qualifying for Europe more than a handful of times between them - but they have proven to be the most enduring. Now that Bangor City have capitulated, this duo are the only clubs who boast unbroken membership of the league.

Aberystwyth Town unveil a plaque celebrating their 1000th JD Cymru Premier game in February 20222, becoming the first club to reach the milestone. (© John Smith/FAW)

Aberystwyth became the first team to reach the milestone of 1,000 top-flight matches when they took on Haverfordwest County in February 2022, and Newtown joined them in this exclusive club later that month when they lined up against Cardiff Met.

On the subject of records and milestones, one player who long held the honour of making the most appearances in the league is a man who turned out for both of these clubs over the course of three decades. Defender Colin Reynolds began his career with Newtown as a teenager in the 1980s and enjoyed over 300 senior appearances for the club between 1992 and 2002.

Reynolds firmly established himself as a Robins legend, but stunned their fanbase when he departed for their mid Wales rivals Caersws. He then wound down his career with Aberystwyth, with whom he took his total number of top-flight appearances to a staggering 528, before hanging up his well-worn boots after a brief stint with Llanidloes Town in 2013.

His record has since been broken by two other Aberystwyth favourites, Welsh Premier League Hall of Fame inductee Wyn Thomas – who also served as the team's assistant manager – and more recently, Chris Venables, who stole the headlines in 2023 when he made his 537th top flight appearance while playing for Penybont. Although Venables holds the record for most appearances, there is a man who has featured in more *consecutive* matches in the division. That honour goes to former TNS goalkeeper Paul Harrison, who played more than 190 league games for The Saints on the trot, providing a reliable pair of hands between the sticks at the peak of their dominance.

At the other end of the pitch, Marc Lloyd Williams is the division's all-time leading goalscorer with 319 strikes from 419 starts and 49 substitute appearances. The prolific forward has banged them in all over Wales, notably for Bangor City across several stints, Aberystwyth, Porthmadog and a particularly fruitful stay at TNS between 2004 and 2006.

Although several of the other players on the Cymru Premier's all-time leading goalscorers' chart are still going strong - including Michael Wilde at Connah's Quay and Chris Venables of Penybont - Lloyd Williams' record looks set to remain. His closest rival for this accolade is Rhys Griffiths, currently player-manager at Penybont, and he is 50 strikes behind.

One of the Welsh national championship's greatest successes is the fact British, and even world records, have been set here. Notably, there was Bangor City's phenomenal spree of 15 consecutive league wins at the start of the 2010-11 season - a record for a UK team at the time - and, of course, TNS' world-record-breaking run of 27 straight victories in 2016.

The FAW and the league's founders can also take pride from the quality players the division has produced on occasion, some of whom have gone on to find success on bigger stages. A prime example of this is Mark Delaney, who cut his teeth at Carmarthen Town before working his way into the Welsh national team via Cardiff City and Aston Villa.

Later there was Lee Trundle - who caught the eye with Rhyl and went on to play at a high level in the English Football League - and recently, Christian Doidge, a hot prospect at Barry Town and Carmarthen, and later a fan-favourite at Hibernian of the Scottish Premiership.

The Cymru Premier has also made contributions to Wales' youth international teams over the years, producing prospects such as under-21 internationals James Coates (TNS) and Les Davies (Bangor), and no doubt this trend will continue as the league further improves.

On that subject, just how much has the Cymru Premier improved from the early days of the League of Wales? It's not easy to find an accurate barometer to measure where the standard of football is at right now, but there are signs it has developed somewhat.

Firstly, there have been times when the FAW can claim that European results have improved since the league's foundation, namely when Barry Town reached the first round proper of the old UEFA Cup in 1996 and won a Champions League qualifier several years later.

Granted, performances in Europe have been somewhat up and down since then, yet wins for the likes of Bangor City and Connah's Quay over Scandinavian and Scottish opposition have helped the Cymru Premier earn a modicum of respect on the continent.

For key figures in Welsh football and the fans of the country's biggest domestic clubs, however, this isn't quite enough. The goal, right now, is for a Cymru Premier team to reach the group stage of a European competition. Indeed, this is something former Welsh Premier League secretary John Deakin was vocal and passionate about towards the end of his tenure.

His ambition was to improve the division to such an extent that it stands alongside the League of Ireland. Two teams from there

- Dundalk and Shamrock Rovers - have qualified for group stage European football in recent years, and Deakin sought to emulate this: "My aim for us was to be on a par with the League of Ireland, where Shamrock Rovers reached the group stages of the Europa League, and to improve the perception of our league," he said in a statement published by *Wales on Sunday* in the summer of 2012.

This really *should* be an achievable goal now that European football's governing body has added the UEFA Conference League to its roster. In the 2022-23 Champions League qualifiers, TNS narrowly lost over two legs to Linfield of Northern Ireland. Their conquerors went on to miss out on the group stage of the Conference League by a whisker. Had The Saints progressed against Linfield and followed the same path as the Irish outfit from there, all that would have stood between them and the group stage of UEFA's youngest competition was a very winnable tie against Latvian side FK Rīgas Futbola Skola.

To date, no Welsh domestic side has made it this far, but that isn't for lack of trying. The New Saints are ambitious on this front and the team's owner Mike Harris has made no secret of their desire to become the first Cymru Premier side to achieve the feat.

Indeed, the club parted company with manager Anthony Limbrick when Iceland's Víkingur Reykjavík dumped them out of the 2022-23 Conference League qualifiers. Even though the Aussie coach was successful on the domestic front, European group stage football - or a distinct lack of it - was the yardstick his performance was ultimately measured against.

This paved the way for Craig Harrison's return to the Park Hall hotseat, and he believes European group stage football is achievable:

The next step for us is always to go that bit further in Europe, but you need the luck of the draw. I think group stage football is a realistic target for the top Welsh clubs now, since we've got the Europa Conference League. When you look at Southern and Northern Irish teams aiming for that, from a Welsh point of view, it should always be the goal too.

During my first spell at Park Hall, Mike Harris was talking about eventually getting the club into the group stage of the Champions League. People thought he was probably crazy when he came out with that, but to be fair to him, he's always setting new standards for where he wants the team to be and is proactive about driving everyone on towards them.

Former Bala Town star Will Evans in action for Wales C against England C. (© Nik Mesney/FAW)

> *I think a Welsh team getting into the Champions League group stage is further than ever, but for one to get into the Europa League or Conference League group stage is doable.*

Closer to home, there are indications that the Cymru Premier is heading in the right direction on the pitch. The New Saints and Connah's Quay Nomads have given good accounts of themselves against some of Scotland's lower league clubs in the Challenge Cup, but how does the standard of football measure up against the English system? More specifically, what level of the higher-profile pyramid across the border is it comparable to?

When the competition launched as the League of Wales in the early 1990s, it was widely agreed that the quality of football was below Conference level, but there is evidence to suggest that's changed for the better. For starters, some of the biggest European and FAW Premier Cup scalps that Welsh clubs have claimed suggest certain teams - such as Barry Town and TNS at their respective zeniths - have punched at a higher weight over the years.

Moreover, the Wales C national team has enjoyed positive results against their English counterparts of late. These internationals pit

Aeron Edwards celebrities Wales C's second goal with Kayne McLaggon in their 4-0 victory over England C. (© Nik Mesney/FAW)

the best Welsh players the Cymru Premier has to offer against an England team of largely full-time professionals from the National League.

They met in a friendly at The Oval in March 2022 and Wales C romped to a memorable 4-0 victory. Will Evans and Aeron Edwards - then of Bala Town, and Connah's Quay, respectively - both bagged braces as The Red Dragons defeated their Anglo equivalents for the first time. Granted, this was a friendly fixture and is merely one match to go on, but it's certainly encouraging for fans of Welsh domestic football to see a team representing the Cymru Premier win so convincingly against the best of the English National League.

Given that he has recent experience in the National League with Hartlepool United, TNS boss Craig Harrison is well placed to compare the two divisions. When asked what level on the English pyramid his team would be capable of playing at, his answer was surprising:

When I had that season in the National League with Hartlepool, I found it quite different. It was a lot more physical. The National League and League Two are very close together - there isn't much between them from the football I've seen and experienced - but there's a bit of a jump to League One and above. I'd probably say at our peak we were equivalent to the National

*League or League Two. We may have struggled with the physicality and
logistics of English football to start with, but once we'd acclimatised,
I think we'd be at the top end of the National League or bottom end of
League Two.*

Does all of this suggest that standards are on the way up? Perhaps;
but it's fair to say that the Welsh top flight has been more competitive
in the past. TNS have been largely dominant for over a decade and
several of their title-winning seasons have been one-horse races.

In the mid-to-late 2000s, there was more of a level playing field
between The New Saints and their fully-professional rivals Llanelli
and Neath, while other clubs such as Rhyl and Bangor City had large
enough budgets and ambitions to challenge this pack.

Former Rhyl boss Greg Strong played for The Lilywhites and
coached the team during this period and he believes that the top
flight may have reached its peak back then:

*I think this was the most competitive the league has been. TNS and Llanelli
were playing full time, there was ourselves and Bangor with decent budgets
and ambitions, and then Neath came along shortly after and they went
fully professional as well.*

*There were a lot of teams investing and a lot of good players coming to
Wales, whether that was to finish their careers there or kick-start them. I
think that standards during that period were reflected in the crowds at the
time. Take Bangor, for example. When we played home and away against
them the place was absolutely bouncing, and it was the same when we
played Prestatyn Town.*

Sadly, all of these teams, bar TNS, have run into financial trouble
and capitulated to one extent or another, which, on the one hand, is
testament to how well The New Saints are run - but it equally doesn't
bode well for the league that its top teams have been unsustainable.

All of these clubs have been a great loss to the division, particularly
Bangor and Rhyl, two teams with passionate fanbases and a raucous
atmosphere on matchday. On the flipside, however, all of these
stricken sides have returned from the abyss in some form, and this
is a credit to the strength of their legacies and the undying love their
supporters have for them.

Questions have been raised of the FAW and the way it has managed
the league at times, particularly in the aftermath of Bangor City's

collapse, with its absence of a fit and proper persons test for club owners cited as a contributing factor, but it's fair to say the governing body has, at times, been proactive about improving the league and exploring different formats for it.

Although UEFA-enforced, the 'Super 12' shake-up was a bold overhaul, and a successful one, for the most part. While critics may claim some clubs are now forced to play each other too many times under the conferences system - just ask Barry Town and Cardiff Met fans - and bemoan the scant publicity the competition gets, this format has prevented stagnation by giving the majority of teams something to play for until the season's bitter end.

Another bone of contention that has cropped up of late is the licensing and coaching criteria for the Cymru Premier, specifically the fact that they're often unattainable for grassroots clubs in the second tier, even those with serious promotion prospects. The Tier 1 licensing requirements are in place to protect the integrity of the league and ensure new teams who join it stand the best possible chance of sustainability. Sadly, for all involved, though, this means promotions and relegations have been decided off the pitch.

Ground improvements grants are available via the FAW and are a godsend for some teams, but for others, meeting the full criteria is still a flight of fancy, even with this support package. It's hard to be unsympathetic to a team that aces their league and tops the standings at the end of term, only to be denied a promotion earned on merit. One club who embodies this injustice is Llantwit Major AFC, the plucky Vale of Glamorgan outfit who won the 2021-22 Cymru South title, but had their application for a Tier 1 Licence rejected. The best season in their 60-year history ended with a trophy, followed by a crushing blow.

During a whirlwind seven-year period, Llantwit Major battled their way up from the amateur leagues to the second tier and won it convincingly not long after that. This was a fairytale to rival any Welsh domestic football has ever seen, though not one with a happy ending. Following an unsuccessful appeal against the Tier 1 verdict, FAW chief Noel Mooney took to *Twitter* to express sympathy for the club and clarify why the licensing requirements are necessary. He also vowed that the FA of Wales will "keep looking at [its] processes to see how they can improve to better support our clubs to reach their full potential."

Under Mooney's leadership, the governing body has made bold promises about taking the Cymru Premier forward but the league, as always, faces daunting challenges. Attracting the punters remains one of the biggest, with only four clubs managing average gates of more than 300 during the 2022-23 season - Haverfordwest County (364), Flint Town United (339), Aberystwyth (339) and Caernarfon (485) – and three of those clubs registering declining numbers compared to 2021-22: Flint Town United (405), Aberystwyth (409) and Caernarfon (585).

Expectations must be managed on this front since many of these teams are based in relatively small towns, some of which are located just a few hours away from the bright lights of the English Premier League's top clubs, as well as the likes of Cardiff City, Swansea City, and the recently reinvigorated Wrexham whose home games regularly attract 10,000 football fans from right across north Wales.

To add perspective, figures compiled by Toby Jones of the *North East Wales Football Fanpage* during the 2018-19 season shed light on the percentage of the local population each team in the league is attracting to its matches, and they make compelling reading.

Among the standout stats was Bala Town's average attendance and how it compares to the population of their local area. The Lakesiders were drawing 262 to Maes Tegid on a typical matchday, a figure that amounts to 13.2% of the population of Bala. Similarly impressive was Caernarfon Town, drawing in almost 10% of locals to their home games.

This compares favourably to the National League in England. Although there were a couple of teams way ahead - Leyton Orient (36.62%) and Barrow (29%) - none of the other clubs in the division could match Bala Town and Caernarfon's percentages that year. In fact, Wrexham were only pulling in 3.82% of the city's population each weekend in 2018-19.

Granted, there are mitigating circumstances behind the low attendance figures in the Cymru Premier and positive ways to frame these numbers, yet the harsh reality is that most football clubs in the world would struggle to stay afloat with only a few hundred fans passing through their turnstiles on matchday. S4C's broadcast coverage does a fantastic job exposing the competition to a wider audience, but more backsides on seats has to be the goal.

So how does the FAW and the league's member clubs address this? One possible solution that has been pitched on numerous occasions is repositioning the Cymru Premier as a summer league. It has been suggested that the biggest benefit of this would be the potential advantages it would give to Welsh clubs playing in European qualifiers.

Theoretically, they would enter these contests with a higher level of match fitness, having already played a portion of their domestic season. Clubs from the summer-spanning League of Ireland - who typically fare much better on the continent - are cited as an example of this.

Welsh football legend Neville Southall, who began and ended his playing career in the nation's domestic system, is firmly behind this proposal:

> *I think the Welsh top flight is on the up, but it needs more investment and they should change the season around. The calendar should be rejigged so the Welsh clubs are in the middle of their season when their European fixtures come around.*
>
> *This will mean the players are as sharp and match fit as possible. This would be a sensible move and it might even mean the matches would get better crowds. Better representation in Europe would likely come if we give the teams a greater chance to succeed.*

Better results in Europe would certainly help the Cymru Premier raise its profile, improve its standards and attract investment, but there's another benefit to summer football - at the beginning of a campaign, Welsh domestic teams would not be in direct competition for supporters with the Premier League or the Welsh teams playing in the English Football League. Whether this alone would have a major impact is unclear, though the FAW appears to be considering all options when it comes to the future direction of the competition.

S4C presenter Nicky John, meanwhile, believes that the division has seen key infrastructural improvements since she began covering it for *Sgorio*, and is adamant that the Cymru Premier is showing signs of evolving both on and off the pitch:

> *I think clubs are constantly having to try to find ways to bring fans through their gates - and that's often not because there's a lack of interest there, but it could be to do with some of the competition they face in the surrounding area at a higher level.*
>
> *However, I do think things are improving. There is certainly more interest, more coverage and a higher standard of football being played than ever*

before - when I began covering the league it would be common practice during the winter months to find numerous games being called off week after week due to waterlogged pitches, for example.

It would literally leave the fixture list all over the shop, then you'd have the issue of games having to be rearranged for midweek, which is far from ideal for players of a part-time league who have jobs to hold down away from the football pitch.

Installing 4G pitches has changed that entirely. Very rarely now would we experience a game being postponed - Covid aside - and fixture-wise it means that clubs usually know where they stand without having to standby at 10am for a phone call on the morning of a game to tell them that there's due to be a pitch inspection!

It has had its ups and downs over the years, but there are reasons to be upbeat about the Cymru Premier's future. Firstly, the governing body claims to be serious about improving the league and is working directly with its member clubs towards this. At the time of writing, the eagerly awaited plans are on the cusp of being unveiled.

The world's third-oldest football association has enjoyed great success engaging with supporters of the Welsh national team in the 21st Century. Just look at how effective the 'Together Stronger' campaign was in the run-up to Euro 2016. If the FAW can channel a drop of that fervour into its domestic league, who knows what the results could be?

Another reason to be positive is that there are some great clubs who have worked their way up to the top division, like Colwyn Bay and the recently-promoted Barry Town United. There are also several other clubs jostling to emerge from the second tier who could be a real credit to the top flight, like Prestatyn Town and Carmarthen, as well as Rhyl and Bangor City's respective phoenix clubs, if and when they fulfil their potential.

Then there's the diehard fans, the dedicated volunteers and the local communities that rally around these clubs, keep them alive and pick them up when they fall, as Nicky John notes:

I think there are communities in which the domestic game is thriving. As someone who has lived in Caernarfon for the last 15 years, I know from experience what an important role the football club plays in the lives of the people of this town.

A new all-seater stand was erected at Colwyn Bay's Llanelian Road ground to coincide with their promotion to the Cymru Premier. (© Colwyn Bay FC)

I see children and grandparents alike, kitted out in yellow and green as they walk down the street going about their daily lives. Where perhaps 10 years ago, all the kids would have been in Liverpool, United or Barça strips, now they wear their hometown colours with pride, a sense of identity and a chance to show the world who they are and where they belong.

I think the hope has to be that we see this continue to develop for all clubs. We know from post-Covid how important it is to get people through those gates to bring in revenue to each club - even if supporters are just coming in and buying a programme and a "panad", it goes a long way! There is also a great sense of community to be had inside these football clubs.

Let's remember that many of them survive on the time and good will of volunteers who do it purely for the love of their club. Without their commitment, these clubs just wouldn't survive.

One man who is uniquely placed to provide a summary of the Cymru Premier's journey over the last decade is the league's former general manager Gwyn Derfel. The ex-broadcaster began overseeing the competition in 2012, not long after the 'Super 12' reshuffle, and he genuinely believes that it has made progress both on and off the field during that time.

> *The main way that the league has improved is in the standard of play. It doesn't get the recognition it deserves. You look at former Welsh international players like Shaun MacDonald and Dave Edwards who have come into the league, and they have been genuinely surprised by the quality of the football in the Cymru Premier, the technical play and the physicality of it.*
>
> *The coaching standards have also increased as well as the quality of the infrastructure. I actually think the 3G surfaces are a good addition since they have enabled players to improve technically as well - I know that might be a contentious thing to say, but I firmly believe it's true.*
>
> *I also believe our partnership with S4C has taken the league forward. It isn't just a partnership on the screen. All of the footage they record from every game is uploaded to a central platform that the clubs can access. They can use this to analyse their own performances and also view footage of the opposition - this is something the public would not have been privy to.*
>
> *Then there's the little changes that have made a big difference, such as introducing names on the shirts. Not only does this look good, it helps broadcasters deliver better coverage too.*

The reasons a Welsh national football championship was launched in the early 1990s are well documented, but exactly where is the competition heading in the future? In order for it to improve, Derfel - who left the FAW in January 2023 - thinks that the league needs to focus on developing in two core areas: becoming more competitive and attracting larger crowds.

Echoing the comments of other leading figures in Welsh football, Derfel identified further progression for domestic clubs in Europe and greater engagement with their local communities as key to growing the league's audience. A more competitive division would go hand-in-hand with this, but Derfel admits that the member clubs need comprehensive support to reach the necessary levels. During his time at the helm, he championed a smaller division of 10 teams, claiming this would be more sustainable and help address the problem of resource limitations.

> *I was really proud when we introduced the new substitutes rule two years ago where teams can field a fourth and a fifth sub as long as they were*

produced by their academy. People are more likely to watch a local side if there's a local element of talent representing it.

But broadcasters and investors want competitiveness in the league as this is what generates revenue. I felt that the only way to make it more competitive was to reduce the number of teams in the division and properly resourcing them. Of course I'd rather see a league with a larger club count playing on grass surfaces, but because of where the Cymru Premier is currently situated, I think the 3G scheme has been a resounding success. I believe a smaller league would be more competitive due to the level of resources. I was trying to be a realist on that.

To progress upwards, I think each of the clubs needs a full-time administrator and commercial person to help make them more professional. At the moment, there is so much pressure on volunteers' time so it's difficult for them to run marketing campaigns to get punters through the gates. Many of the clubs need a helping hand to reach the required level of professionalism.

At the time of writing, the FA of Wales is on the cusp of unfurling its blueprint for a new version of the Cymru Premier, and several areas that Derfel earmarked for improvement, such as investment in marketing and outreach, will seemingly be addressed. His plans for a new league with a reduced club count, however, are unlikely to be revived by his successors.

Although the governing body is yet to fully flesh out its roadmap for a revitalised top flight, FAW CEO Noel Mooney offered a hint of things to come during half time of a Cymru Premier fixture between Colwyn Bay and Caernarfon on 13 August 2023. The Irishman gave a pitchside interview to *Sgorio* presenter Sioned Dafydd, during which he revealed that they are working on an eight-pillar plan for a new league that will "probably" host more teams than before.

Mooney also pledged that "a few million pounds" will be invested into the competition and outlined the areas where these funds can make a difference between now and 2030.

"There are eight pillars, we're going to have things like performance, facilities, marketing, and community engagement. The structure of the league [has been] discussed a lot," he told S4C. "People go straight to it, it's 12 teams, and it's not enough and all that kind of stuff. I think [after] discussions with the clubs, it's fair to say with people the general direction will be a bigger league, probably. I don't know if it'll be 14 or 16, that's not for me to say. They'll be a group set up among the clubs and the FAW, and then discussions will go on for a few more months. The general direction seems to be that you'll see a bigger league, I'd say, and that will be more investment for the FAW as well. I think it's time now. We're working closely with UEFA on what this league will look like."

While the new Welsh top flight is unlikely to be the streamlined competition Derfel once campaigned for, he believes that fans of the Cymru Premier should be optimistic about its future, pointing to the aforementioned success of the Wales C international team - which he introduced during his time at the FAW - as proof that the quality of football is on the rise.

Fans should be positive about the future of this league because it's fantastic value for money and is improving rapidly. If you look at the Cymru C results, the best of the National League in England versus the best of the Cymru Premier, the head-to-head record is only slightly in their favour because they beat us in Altrincham in March this year. Every year that fixture has been played, one player from the Cymru C team has gone on to play league football in England. The better players in our league are on par with the better players in the National League.

The Cymru Premier offers a good standard of football and fantastic value for money. You can move around the ground at matches, there's always a very friendly atmosphere and good banter going on. There's a friendly, community feel at games and that really tops it off.

The Cymru Premier is a weird and wonderful league of its own where brotherhoods have been forged, records have toppled and rivalries have been wrought in fire. It's easy to dismiss its significance when the division is juxtaposed to more glamorous top flights in Europe, but every one of the clubs in this league deserve their place in football history.

To a greater or lesser extent, they have had to overcome adversity to make it this far in a league where funding, publicity and big crowds are hard to come by. Many of them could teach the world a thing or two about resilience and the value of a never-say-die attitude.

From Bala Town and Connah's Quay Nomads up north to Penybont and Pontypridd United down south, these are your local football clubs, and they don't just need your support, they unequivocally deserve it.

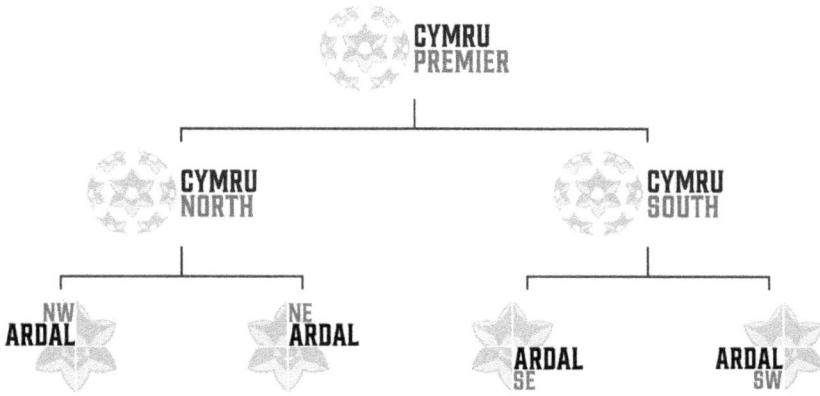

The Cymru Leagues pyramid. (© FAW)

Appendices

	(a) League Winners				
	Team	**Winners**	**Runners up**	**Third place**	**League Winning Seasons**
1	The New Saints	15	6	1	1999–2000, 2004–05, 2005–06, 2006–07, 2009–10, 2011–12, 2012–13, 2013–14, 2014–15, 2015–16, 2016–17, 2017–18, 2018–19, 2021–22, 2022-23
2	Barry Town	7	1	1	1995–96, 1996–97, 1997–98, 1998–99, 2000–01, 2001–02, 2002–03
3	Bangor City	3	2	4	1993–94, 1994–95, 2010–11
4	Connah's Quay Nomads	2	4		2019–20, 2020–21
5	Rhyl	2	2	2	2003–04, 2008–09
6	Llanelli	1	3	1	2007-08
7	Cwmbrân Town	1	1	2	1992-93
8	Inter Cardiff		4		
9	Bala Town		3		
10	Airbus UK Broughton		2	1	
	Newtown		2	1	
11	Afan Lido		1		
12	Ton Pentre			2	
	Ebbw Vale			2	
	Neath			2	
	Carmarthen Town			2	
13	Aberystwyth Town			1	
	Conwy United			1	
	Haverfordwest Cty			1	
	Penybont			1	
	Port Talbot			1	

(b) Top Goalscorers

Season	Top Scorer	# Goals
1992-93	Steve Woods (Ebbw Vale)	29
1993-94	Dave Taylor (Porthmadog)	43
1994-95	Frank Mottram (Bangor City)	31
1995-96	Ken McKenna (Conwy United)	38
1996-97	Tony Bird (Barry Town)	42
1997-98	Eifion Williams (Barry Town)	40
1998-99	Eifion Williams (Barry Town)	28
1999-2000	Chris Summers (Cwmbrân Town)	28
2000-01	Graham Evans (Caersws)	25
2001-02	Marc Lloyd Williams (Bangor City)	47
2002-03	Graham Evans (Caersws)	24
2003-04	Graham Evans (Caersws)*	24
2004-05	Marc Lloyd Williams (Bangor City)	34
2005-06	Rhys Griffiths (Port Talbot)	28
2006-07	Rhys Griffiths (Llanelli)	30
2007-08	Rhys Griffiths (Llanelli)	40
2008-09	Rhys Griffiths (Llanelli)	31
2009-10	Rhys Griffiths (Llanelli)	30
2010-11	Rhys Griffiths (Llanelli)	25
2011-12	Rhys Griffiths (Llanelli)	24
2012-13	Michael Wilde (TNS)	25
2013-14	Chris Venables (Aberystwyth Town)	24
2014-15	Chris Venables (Aberystwyth Town)	28
2015-16	Chris Venables (Aberystwyth Town)	20
2016-17	Jason Oswell (Newtown)	22
2017-18	Greg Draper (TNS)	22
2018-19	Greg Draper (TNS)	27
2019-20	Chris Venables (Bala Town)	20
2020-21	Chris Venables (Bala Town)	24
2021-22	Declan McManus (TNS)	24
2022-23	Declan McManus (TNS)	26

*Andy Moran of Rhyl scored 27 goals but was subsequently stripped of the leading goalscorer award after testing positive for the banned performance-enhancing drug nandrolone.

(c) Average Attendances			
1992-93	N/A*	2008-09	289
1993-94	N/A*	2009-10	276
1994-95	236	2010-11	343
1995-96	230	2011-12	329
1996-97	241	2012-13	279
1997-98	256	2013-14	325
1998-99	256	2014-15	329
1999-2000	262	2015-16	327
2000-01	252	2016-17	306
2001-02	276	2017-18	315
2002-03	284	2018-19	353
2003-04	300	2019-20	323
2004-05	273	2020-21	0**
2005-06	268	2021-22	352
2006-07	269	2022-23	309
2007-08	273		

*Attendance data unavailable

**All matches played behind closed doors due to Covid-19

(d) Welsh Club Representation in Europe

1992-93
Cardiff City (Cup Winners' Cup)

1993-94
Cwmbrân Town (Champions League)
Cardiff City (Cup Winners' Cup)

1994-95
Bangor City (UEFA Cup)
Inter Cardiff (UEFA Cup)
Barry Town (Cup Winners' Cup)

1995-96
Bangor City (UEFA Cup)
Afan Lido (UEFA Cup)
Ton Pentre (Intertoto Cup)
Wrexham (Cup Winners' Cup)

1996-97
Barry Town (UEFA Cup)
Newtown (UEFA Cup)
Conwy United (Intertoto Cup)
TNS (Cup Winners' Cup)

1997-98
Barry Town (Champions League)
Inter Cardiff (UEFA Cup)
Ebbw Vale (Intertoto Cup)
Cwmbrân Town (Cup Winners' Cup)

1998-99
Barry Town (Champions League)
Newtown (UEFA Cup)
Ebbw Vale (Intertoto Cup)
Bangor City (Cup Winners' Cup)

1999-2000
Barry Town (Champions League)
Inter Cardiff (UEFA Cup)
Cwmbrân Town (UEFA Cup)
Aberystwyth Town (Intertoto Cup)

2000-01
TNS (Champions League)
Barry Town (UEFA Cup)
Bangor City (UEFA Cup)
Cwmbrân Town (Intertoto Cup)

2001-02
Barry Town (Champions League)
Cwmbrân Town (UEFA Cup)
TNS (UEFA Cup)
Carmarthen Town (Intertoto Cup)

2002-03
Barry Town (Champions League)
Bangor City (UEFA Cup)
TNS (UEFA Cup)
Caersws (Intertoto Cup)

2003-04
Barry Town (Champions League)
Cwmbrân Town (UEFA Cup)
TNS (UEFA Cup)
Bangor City (Intertoto Cup)

2004-05
Rhyl (Champions League)
TNS (UEFA Cup)
Haverfordwest County (UEFA Cup)
Aberystwyth Town (Intertoto Cup)

2005-06
TNS (Champions League)
Rhyl (UEFA Cup)
Carmarthen Town (UEFA Cup)
Bangor City (Intertoto Cup)

2006-07
TNS (Champions League)
Llanelli (UEFA Cup)
Rhyl (UEFA Cup)
Carmarthen Town (Intertoto Cup)

2007-08
TNS (Champions League)
Rhyl (UEFA Cup)
Carmarthen Town (UEFA Cup)
Llanelli (Intertoto Cup)

259

(d) Welsh Club Representation in Europe

2008-09
Llanelli (Champions League)
TNS (UEFA Cup)
Bangor City (UEFA Cup)
Rhyl (Intertoto Cup)

2009-10
Rhyl (Champions League)
Llanelli (Europa League)
TNS (Europa League)
Bangor City (Europa League)

2010-11
TNS (Champions League)
Llanelli (Europa League)
Port Talbot Town (Europa League)
Bangor City (Europa League)

2011-12
Bangor City (Champions League)
TNS (Europa League)
Llanelli (Europa League)
Neath (Europa League)

2012-13
TNS (Champions League)
Bangor City (Europa League)
Llanelli (Europa League)

2013-14
TNS (Champions League)
Airbus UK Broughton (Europa League)
Prestatyn Town (Europa League)
Bala Town (Europa League)

2014-15
TNS (Champions League)
Airbus UK Broughton (Europa League)
Aberystwyth Town (Europa League)
Bangor City (Europa League)

2015-16
TNS (Champions League)
Bala Town (Europa League)
Airbus UK Broughton (Europa League)
Newtown (Europa League)

2016-17
TNS (Champions League)
Bala Town (Europa League)
Llandudno (Europa League)
Connah's Quay (Europa League)

2017-18
TNS (Champions League)
Connah's Quay (Europa League)
Bala Town (Europa League)
Bangor City (Europa League)

2018-19
TNS (Champions League)
Connah's Quay (Europa League)
Bala Town (Europa League)
Cefn Druids (Europa League)

2019-20
TNS (Champions League)
Connah's Quay (Europa League)
Barry Town United (Europa League)
Cardiff Met (Europa League)

2020-21
Connah's Quay (Champions League)
TNS (Europa League)
Bala Town (Europa League)
Barry Town United (Europa League)

2021-22
Connah's Quay (Champions League)
TNS (Europa Conference League)
Bala Town (Europa Conference League)
Newtown (Europa Conference League)

2022-23
TNS (Champions League)
Bala Town (Europa Conference League)
Newtown (Europa Conference League)

Index

Stockport County FC (England) 41, 63
Strong, Greg 119-27, 131, 246
Sturch, Gary 24
Summers, Chris 27, 56, 65, 256
'Super 12' 137, 139, 157, 247, 251
Super Eagles (see Nigeria)
Sutton, Shane 168
Swans, The (see Swansea City)
Swansea City 1-2, 5-7, 9, 11, 13, 15,
    37, 44, 56, 60, 74, 81, 83, 90,
    104, 107, 120, 131, 143, 160,
    223, 248; (Reserves) 3

T
Taff's Well FC 234
Taylor, Chris 91
Taylor, David 38-9, 256
Taylor-Fletcher, Gary 196-7
Team GB 11
Thomas, Leslie 62
Thomas, Wyn 110, 115, 241
Ton Pentre FC 3, 34, 37, 40, 43, 45,
    49, 54, 255, 258
Torquay United FC (England) 83-4
Torres, Rudi 106-7
Tórshavn, B36 (Faroe Islands) 172,
    218, 234
Total Network Solutions (also see New
    Saints, The) 54, 57, 60-5, 69-70,
    72-6, 78-9, 82-3, 86, 88-102
Total Network Solutions FC (also see
    New Saints, The) 62-3
Total Network Solutions Llansantffraid
    FC (also see New Saints, The) 62
Tranmere Rovers FC (England) 5, 33,
    35, 132
Tre Penne, SP (San Marino) 172
Trundle, Lee 83, 143, 242

U
UEFA 6, 11-2, 29-30, 37-8, 41, 62, 82,
    99, 129, 132, 137, 160-1, 194,
    196-7, 215, 218, 229
UEFA Cup 42-3, 47, 65-6, 71, 75, 88,
    94, 99, 109, 242

V
Vale of Glamorgan Council 181
Valletta FC (Malta) 218
Vardar, FK (North Macedonia) 80

Vasutas SK (Hungary) 51
Vaughan, Gary 24
Vaughan Sports Management (VSM)
    24
Vaughan, Stephen (Jnr) 195, 197,
    199-201
Vaughan, Stephen (Snr) 197, 204-5
Venables, Chris 142, 151, 165, 167,
    177, 216, 218, 241, 256
Vetch Field, The (Swansea) 1, 7, 9, 44
Víkingur Reykjavík FC (Iceland) 233,
    243
Viktoria Plzeň, FC (Czechia) 227

W
Wade, Ryan 192
Wales (national team) 7, 9, 57, 83,
    108, 110, 116, 170, 184, 196,
    207, 229, 233,
Wales C 191, 244-5, 254
WalesOnline 30, 89, 181
Walker, Josh 211
Wall, Luke 233
Walters, Steve 86-7
Ward, Nicky 100
Watford FC (England) 66, 123
Watkins, Chris 53
Watkins, Curtis 188
Weah, George 7
Webbe, Tyrell 179
Welsh Alliance League 4
Welsh Cup 5-10, 12, 14-5, 28-30, 37,
    43-4, 48, 52-3, 55-6, 59, 61, 63,
    65, 68, 72, 77, 83, 91, 96-8, 102,
    105, 109, 113-4, 116, 122, 130-1,
    139-42, 151-2, 159-60, 163-8,
    170-1, 176-8, 185, 190-1, 195,
    198, 201, 208, 210, 211, 216,
    224, 226-7, 236-7
Welsh Football League 2, 4, 6-11, 13-4,
    22, 27-8, 92
    Division One (National Division,
    1983-92) 6, 10, 13, 130
    Division Two 22
    Division Three 117
Welsh Government 131, 202-3, 219,
    222
Welsh Intermediate Cup 61, 207
Welsh League Cup 14, 22, 27, 34, 37,
    43, 47-8, 52-4, 58, 65, 69, 73, 77,

ST DAVID'S PRESS

SONS OF CAMBRIA
The Who's Who of Welsh International Football Players
VOLUME 1 - 1876–1946

Volume 1
286pp (inc. 400+ photos)

pbk • 978 1 902719 795 • £19.99
ebk • 978 1 902719 887 • £19.99

SONS OF CAMBRIA
The Who's Who of Welsh International Football Players
VOLUME 2 - 1947–1999

Volume 2 – 2024
300pp (inc. 450+ photos)

pbk • 978 1 904609 032 • £19.99
ebk • 978 1 904609 049• £19.99

SONS OF CAMBRIA
The Who's Who of Welsh International Football Players
VOLUME 3 - 2000–2023

Volume 3 - 2025

Sons of Cambria
The Who's Who of
Welsh International Football Players

Ian Garland & Gareth M Davies

"Indispensable. The primary source of information for anybody with an interest in Welsh football." **Phil Stead**

"A brilliant piece of research. Essential reading for anyone interested in the history of Welsh football." **Prof Martin Johnes**

On 25 March 1876, the Football Association of Wales played its inaugural match, against Scotland in Glasgow. On that day 11 intrepid footballers became the first of over 700 players to proudly represent the senior men's team of the world's third oldest football nation.

Sons of Cambria is a landmark three-part collection that will feature every footballer capped for Wales' senior men's team since 1876 and is the essential reference guide for all followers of Welsh international football.

Listed in the order in which they won their caps, every player has - for the first time - been assigned their unique player number, with Volume I containing biographical listings of the 374 players capped between 1876 and 1946 (as well as the 30 players who represented Wales in uncapped war-time matches) including photographs of almost all the players.

In addition to the players, each volume of **Sons of Cambria** will also list every international match (capped and uncapped), including all known team photographs:

Appendix 1: *Official International Matches*
Appendix 2: *Unofficial International Matches*
Appendix 3: *Managers*
Appendix 4: *Caps Awarded*
Appendix 5: *Goal Scorers*
Appendix 6: *Captains*
Appendix 7: *Clubs Represented*
Appendix 8: *Birthplaces of Welsh Internationals*
Player Index

Packed with incredible stories, fascinating facts and hundreds of photos, the three volumes of **Sons of Cambria** will be treasured by all Welsh football supporters.

Ian Garland is the author of *The History of the Welsh Cup*, is joint author of *The Canaries Sing Again – a history of Caernarfon Town FC*, and, with Prof. Martin Johnes, *'the new craze': Football and Society in north-east Wales c1870-1890*.

Gareth M Davies is the co-author of *Racecourse Robins: A Who's Who of Wrexham AFC 1929-1999*. In 1994 he also edited and compiled *A Coast of Soccer Memories 1894-1994*, the centenary book of the North Wales Coast Football Association.

ST DAVID'S PRESS

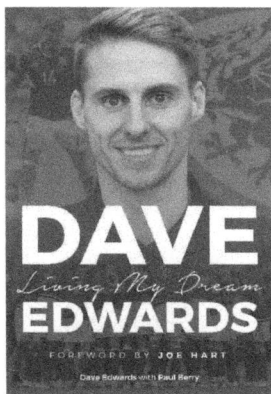

Living My Dream

Dave Edwards

with Paul Berry

'A fantastic behind-the-scenes insight of what it was like in the Welsh camp at Euro 2016. A special time and a great read.'

Gareth Bale

'Great to re-live the memories of a tournament which none of us will ever forget.' **Chris Coleman**

'A fascinating look at the journey made by all of us who set out as young kids with the dream of one day becoming a professional footballer.' **Joe Hart**

As a football-mad young boy growing up in rural Shropshire, Dave Edwards dreamt of playing the game professionally and perhaps, one day, of wearing the red shirt of his father's homeland - Wales.

269pp (inc. 32pp of photos)
pbk • 978 1 902719 641 • £13.99
ebk • 978 1 902719 658 • £9.99

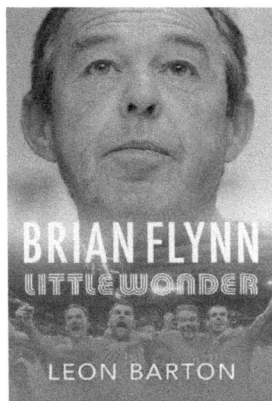

Brian Flynn
Little Wonder

Leon Barton

'One of the good guys of Welsh football.' **Chris Gunter**

'A national treasure, Welsh football owes him so much.'
Elis James

'His name is not only so well-known, but so immediately respected ... everyone should know the story of Brian Flynn.' **Chris Wathan**

'A wonderfully detailed study of the life and times of a Welsh working-class hero.' **John Nicholson, Football 365**

Brian Flynn may only stand at 5 foot and 4 inches, but this diminutive and modest man from Port Talbot has made a giant contribution to Welsh football: winning 66 caps for Wales; managing Wrexham and Swansea; and, as intermediate team manager under John Toshack, nurturing the national team's 'golden generation' that went on to qualify for Euro 2016. *Little Wonder* is his story.

240pp (inc. 16pp of photos)
pbk • 978 1 902719 696 • £13.99
ebk • 978 1 902719 913 • £9.99

Unbelievable Barry Town FC

Ian Johnson

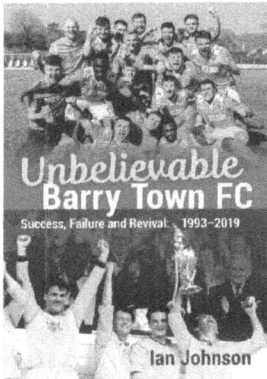

'This book captures the essence of the town's football club and the people and community who serve as its heartbeat'

Gavin Chesterfield

Few clubs have risen so high – facing Dynamo Kiev and FC Porto in the Champions League – and then sunk so low – going into administration, relegated and eventually withdrawn from football altogether – before being brought back to life by loyal fans who even had to take the Football Association of Wales to court in order to play.

Following the club over 25 years, starting with the 1993-94 season when the club beat Cardiff City to win the Welsh Cup, *Unbelievable Barry Town* covers the club's golden decade where they won the Welsh Premier League seven times, through the years of playing as an amateur team under controversial owner Stuart Lovering, until the fans were able to take over and turn the club around to once again play in Europe in 2019.

160pp (inc. 117 photos)
pbk • 978 1 902719 788 • £16.99

The Great Escape
Newport County 2016-17

Andrew Penman

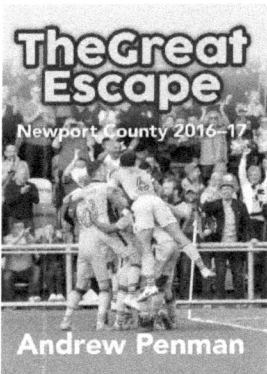

'Nothing compares to this – I will never forget this moment'

Mark O'Brien

'If you were making a film, this is the script you'd use'

Gavin Foxall

'I was trying to talk to the team after the match and I was getting emotional. I could feel tears coming because I knew what it meant.'

Michael Flynn

The Great Escape: Newport County 2016-17 tells the amazing story of how local boy Michael Flynn and his team beat the odds and confound their critics to secure their place in the English Football League. A remarkable seven wins in their final 12 games, and a spectacular 89th-minute volleyed winner from Mark O'Brien in the end-of-season finale, saw County's biggest crowd since 1983 pour onto the Rodney Parade pitch and celebrate an incredible end to an incredible story.

1128pp (inc. 45 photos)
pbk • 978 1 902719 689 • £14.99

ST DAVID'S PRESS

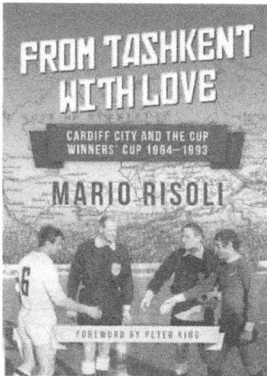

From Tashkent With Love
Cardiff City and the Cup Winners' Cup
1964-1993

Mario Risoli

"If this book evokes half the memories of those special times as it has for me, then you are about to begin an enjoyable and emotional read."
Peter King

"A great tribute to a glorious time."
Jeremy Bowen

From Tashkent With Love is a tale of courage, heartbreak and glory spanning four decades. It tells the remarkable story of Cardiff City's football adventures across Europe in the European Cup Winners' Cup.

From the thrilling 1.0 victory against the mighty Real Madrid at Ninian Park in 1971, to the heartbreak of a last minute 3.2 home defeat in the semi-final against FC Hamburg in 1968, Cardiff's 24 Cup Winner's Cup games are all recalled by the best-selling author Mario Risoli who interviewed over 70 former players in the writing of this comprehensive book.

424pp (inc. 63 photos)
pbk • 978 1 902719 412 • £16.99

Bluebirds Reunited
The Fall and Rise of Cardiff City

Aled Blake

"Aled Blake perfectly captures the astonishing tale of the fight for the heart of the football club and the unlikely messiah who delivered a dream and united a city."
David Owens

"How the manager transformed [Cardiff's] fortunes with a modest budget, when it felt like many people had given up on City's dream.'
Danny Gabbidon

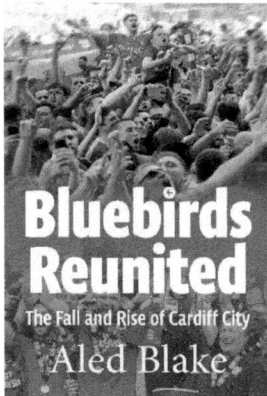

Bluebirds Reunited is the incredible story of the renaissance of Cardiff City: how a club in turmoil transformed its fortunes to win the unlikeliest of promotions, and how its loyal fans fell back in love with their beloved Bluebirds.

Featuring revealing fan insights and exclusive interviews with Neil Warnock, *Bluebirds Reunited* tells the story of Cardiff City's rebirth from the fans' perspective and explains how a club, its fans and a city were reunited in an euphoric promotion back to the Premier League.

192pp (inc. 32pp of photos)
pbk • 978 1 902719 757 • £13.99

St David's Press

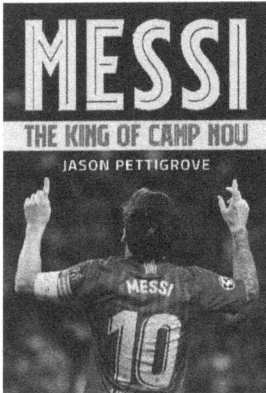

Messi
The King of Camp Nou

Jason Pettigrove

"He was born to play football and it's on the field where we see the happiest version of Lionel. It's what he does best and what gives him the most joy." **Lionel Scaloni**

"I guarantee this will be the best book on Leo Messi you haven't yet read." **Graham Hunter**

Widely regarded as the greatest footballer of all time, seven-time Ballon d'Or and six-time Golden Shoe winner, Lionel Messi, enjoyed a record-breaking 17-year career at FC Barcelona during which time he scored more goals, played more games, won more titles and provided more assists than any other player in the Catalan club's history.

Messi: The King of Camp Nou is the definitive story of Lionel Messi's entire Barça career, written by Jason Pettigrove, a football journalist who worked for FC Barcelona during Messi's final years in Catalonia.

276pp (inc. 50 photos)
pbk • 978 1 902719 849 • £16.99
ebk • 978 1 902719 993 • £12.99

Huddy
The Official Biography of
Alan Hudson

Jason Pettigrove

"A total one-off footballer. There's never been anyone quite like him, in his ability and what he was able to do with a football." **Malcolm McDonald**

"Alan was a top quality, gifted player." **Gordon Taylor**

Alan Hudson is still revered at Chelsea, Stoke City, Arsenal and Seattle Sounders, yet his professional success was dogged by injuries and enormous personal challenges. His love of the glitzy 'footballer lifestyle', dominated by hard-drinking and glamorous women, saw Alan descend into rampant alcoholism, depression, and frequent brushes with authority.

Huddy - his official biography - reveals for the first time, the full story of the real Alan Hudson, the man behind the lurid newspaper headlines and booze-fuelled anecdotes.

256pp (inc. 32pp of photos)
pbk • 978 1 902719 573 • £13.99
pbk • 978 1 902719 870 • £9.99

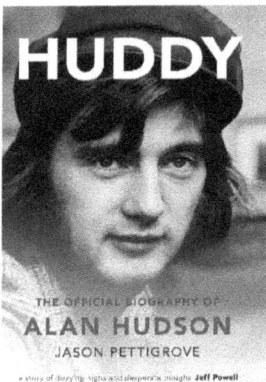

Milton Keynes UK
Ingram Content Group UK Ltd.
UKHW022301091123
432275UK00002B/4

9 781904 609100